George Bush

George Bush:

HIS WORLD WAR II YEARS

by ROBERT B. STINNETT

BRASSEY'S (US), Inc.
A Division of Maxwell Macmillan, Inc.

Washington • New York • London •

Brassey's (US), Inc.

Editorial Offices

Brassey's (US), Inc.
8000 Westpark Drive
First Floor
McLean, Virginia 22102

Order Department

Brassey's Book Orders
c/o Macmillan Publishing Co.
100 Front Street, Box 500
Riverside, New Jersey 08075

Brassey's (US), Inc., books are available at special discounts for bulk purchases, for sales promotions, premiums, fund-raising, or educational use through the Special Sales Director, Macmillan Publishing Company, 866 Third Avenue, New York, New York, 10022.

Library of Congress Cataloging-in-Publication Data

Stinnett, Robert B.
George Bush: his World War ll years/ Robert B. Stinnett.
   p. cm.
     Originally published: Missoula, Mont. : Pictorial Histories Pub.
     Co., c1991
   Includes bibliographical references and index.
   ISBN 0-02-881043-0 (pbk.)   ISBN 0-02-881048-1 (HC)
    1. Bush, George, 1924—Career in the military. 2. World War,
1939-1945—Military operations, American. 3. Air pilots, Military—
United States—Biography. 4. Presidents—United States—Biography.
I. Title.
[E882.2.S75   1992]
940.54' 4973' 092—dc20   92-10094
[B]   CIP

TABLE of CONTENTS

THE WHITE HOUSE

WASHINGTON

October 17, 1990

Dear Bob:

I was pleased to receive your letter and look
forward to seeing your book. Those of us who
served in Air Group Fifty-one will relive many
memories of those days because of your wonderful
efforts. My thanks.

Thanks again for writing. Warm regards.

Sincerely,

George Bush

PROLOGUE

In September 1988, presidential candidate George Bush startled an American Legion audience when he referred to September 7 as the anniversary date of the Japanese attack on Pearl Harbor. The perplexed veterans knew the vice president was a World War II bomber pilot who had performed with valor in the Central Pacific war theater. Certainly, he knew the "Day of Infamy" was December 7. [1]

The gaffe was puzzling but the explanation was logical — the first week of September 1944 would be long remembered by George Bush as his personal Pearl Harbor. Bush made his campaign gaffe during the week of the 44th anniversary of his narrow escape from death or capture near the Japanese island called Chichi Jima. Japan had designated the island as the last stronghold of defense against invasion of the homeland. As such, Chichi Jima figured decisively in the victory of American forces in the Pacific war theater. After the war, the United States discovered a secret "Hitler-style bunker" system on Chichi Jima leading American military authorities to hypothesize that the Japanese intended it as a command post for a last ditch defense.[2]

On September 2, 1944, Japanese anti-aircraft gunners riddled George Bush's three-man torpedo bomber as Bush and his crew, part of a navy carrier task force, were attacking the heavily fortified Chichi Jima. With his bomber's engine afire from the direct anti-aircraft hit and a split second away from exploding the aviation fuel in the wing tanks, Bush ordered his two crew members, William "Ted" White and John Delaney, to parachute from the doomed aircraft. The bomber was rapidly losing altitude. A successful exit by the crew required an altitude high enough, about 3,000 feet, to allow sufficient time to climb out and jump clear of the fuselage. Once clear of the bomber, the crew members would pull the rip cord releasing the chute for a billowing descent to the waters of the Pacific Ocean.

Bush managed to level the bomber and climb from the cockpit onto the horizontal wing. Then he jumped prematurely pulling the parachute ripcord. The chute began to billow out. The split second maneuver caused Bush to hit his head on the horizontal stabilizer at the rear of the airplane.

At nearly 2,500 feet and clear of the bomber, Bush could feel the parachute fully opening. Though groggy from his head injury, Bush evaluated his predicament as he floated downward. In the distance his smoking bomber was in a dive heading for a crash into the ocean. Looking around he thought he saw the white streak of another parachute trailing in the sky just below the stricken plane.

Below him was one of the deepest trenches of the Pacific Ocean. It was over 35,000 feet to the bottom of the Bonin Trench which with the Izu and Japan trench form seven mile depths. In the distance Chichi Jima's jagged volcanic land mass rose from the western horizon. To the west there were telltale wakes of small Japanese naval vessels. They were heading Bush's way, hoping to capture him as a prisoner of war and attempt to extract intelligence information during interrogation Nippon-style.

From his bird's eye view he could see the island was shaped roughly like an upside down comma. The head of the comma formed the south portion trailing off northeastward then west in crescent fashion to form an arc around a deep water anchorage. The distance, north to south, was about seven miles with varying widths of no more than three miles.

The island chain linking Chichi Jima and other islands in the group was the Nanpo Shoto (southern archipeligo). In 1944, together with the Mariana and western Caroline Islands, the Nanpo Shoto formed an 1,800-mile "home defense arc." This defense arc was considered by Japanese strategists to be the last protection of the Empire. If American and Allied offensive operations could break the arc then Japan was doomed to sustained direct air attacks and eventual invasion.

The arc of islands separated the Pacific Ocean from the Philippine Sea. The west shores of Chichi Jima were washed by the Philippine Sea, the east coast delved to the great deep of the Pacific Ocean. The Chichi Jima portion of the Nanpo Shoto is called the Ogasawara Islands by Japan but Bonin Islands by western cartographers.

This 1,800-mile arc was Ensign George Bush's tactical battleground from May to November 1944. During this period the strategic battle decisions were made by President Franklin D. Roosevelt and the Joint Chiefs of Staff and tactically carried out by the United States Pacific Fleet commanded by Admiral Chester W Nimitz. His tactical strength was concentrated in the

Fast Carrier Task Force of the Third and Fifth Fleets which alternated command under Admirals William F. Halsey and Raymond Spruance. Administratively this carrier armada was called Task Force 38 under Halsey and Task Force 58 under Spruance. However, the warships of the force essentially remained the same usually consisting of 16 carriers of the ESSEX and INDEPENDENCE class supported by battleships, cruisers and destroyers. Components of these forces included a vast supply train of oilers, ammunition and cargo vessels.

Bush was but one warrior in the huge U.S. Naval force fighting Japan. But the fortunes of war and time involved him in an historical scenario starring Emperor Hirohito of Japan who was the supreme ruler of the Empire. In his bombing attack on Chichi Jima Bush was facing the Imperial Palace anti-aircraft gunners of Hirohito's own brigade who had been dispatched to the island as part of Tokyo's defenders. [3]

Emperor Hirohito's palace gunners almost succeeded in burying George Bush that day. Ironically, as history played out, it was Bush who buried Hirohito when he attended the emperor's funeral in the winter of 1989 as the newly elected president of the United States.

Political cartoonists and pundits had a field day with George Bush's assertion that September 7, 1988 was the anniversary of the Pearl Harbor attack. *Feiffer, ©1988 by Jules Feiffer. Reprinted with permission of Universal Press Syndicate. All rights reserved.*

PART I

1941

The military importance of Chichi Jima was recognized as early as November 1941 when Commander Joseph Rochefort of the U.S. Navy's secret code-breaking group at Pearl Harbor intercepted coded Japanese naval communications. They revealed some startling information: Japanese warships, air units and supporting components were moving east and south from the Chichi Jima arc toward United States territory at Guam, Wake and Hawaii. On December 7, they would attack Pearl Harbor. The other units would be invading Wake and Guam. [1]

Navy officer Rochefort was commander of Station Hypo, the super secret U.S. Navy intercept center located at Pearl Harbor. Hypo was the headquarters of the most successful communications intelligence network ever operated by the American government. It furnished daily warnings of Japanese offensive moves to President Roosevelt and his Pacific Fleet commander Admiral Husband E. Kimmel. Hypo was President Roosevelt's primary intelligence source for information about Japanese naval movements throughout the Pacific conflict. [2]

A major source of Commander Rochefort's intelligence about Japan's fleet movements in the fall of 1941 was the huge military radio complex operated by the Imperial Japanese Navy on Chichi Jima. The complex included seven radio stations on Chichi Jima's east coast. From this point, 1,000 feet above sea level, Japan's naval command relayed war orders to its fleet and naval stations throughout the Central and South Pacific during the war years 1941–1945.

Only a handful of Americans knew of Chichi Jima's secrets in the last months of peace in 1941. Most certainly George Herbert Walker Bush was not one of the handful. He was in an age pool of potential civilian warriors who would be recruited by the American government to avenge the Lorelei calls emanating from the Chichi Jima offensive arc. [3]

In the fortnight prior to December 7, 1941, Bush was a 17-year-old student at Phillips Academy, a prep school for East Coast Ivy League colleges and universities. He participated in the school's activities serving as an elected deacon and working on a scholarship program to provide books for fellow students. Like many Americans, he listened to the CBS radio broadcasts of Edward R.

Lieutenant Commander Joseph J. Rochefort USN, was Franklin D. Roosevelt's principal intelligence source for Japanese fleet operations during opening months of the Pacific War in 1941 and 1942.

Source: Rochefort photo by Carl Mydans, LIFE Magazine ©1940. Used by permission.

Murrow and William L. Shirer for war reports from the European Theater. [4] For relaxation he and his secret fiancée, Barbara Pierce, [5] listened and danced to the music of Glenn Miller's radio broadcasts from Long Island's Glen Island Casino. From CBS news reports Bush knew that war was inevitable and he vowed to be involved.

COMMUNICATION INTELLIGENCE SUMMARY

8 November 1941

GENERAL -

Normal volume of intercepted traffic with no "dummies" appearing on the UTU. All UTU traffic was broadcast to the general call only. The Staff Communication Officer of the French Indo-China Force (So. Exp. For.) sent a despatch action to S.C.O. Combined INFO. S.C.O. Second Fleet, Combined Air Force, unidentified fleet unit, Radio stations at Tokyo, Palao and Takao. This may indicate a contemplated coordination of communications between the Indo-China-South China areas and the Palao Island-Taiwan area. Secret calls were used very little as compared to the past few days and only three circuits were heard using them, including the Combined Fleet Commanders circuit and Air Station Net. North Japan-Ominato circuits were quiet. All mandate circuits were active, with heavy interchange of traffic involving all classes of Mandate addressees in all areas, but with continued emphasis on the Palao area at one end and the Jaluit-Marshall area on the other. Chichijima Air Station was included in much of the traffic between Empire Offices and Saipan Air with Jaluit Base Force included for information. Inclusion of Chichijima usually presages an air movement between Mandates and Empire but the Units involved are unidentified. Commander of unidentified shore activity (NEO 66) previously associated with the Fifth Fleet, was addressed at Chichijima Air which tentatively identifies him as an air activity. Previous association of the Fifth Fleet traffic with Fourth Fleet and Yokosuka tends to confirm the belief that Fifth Fleet operations are, or will be, in the area adjacent to Chichijima-Marcus, supplementing the Fourth Fleet in the lower island areas.

FLEET -

Chief of staff First Fleet originated a despatch through Kure Radio. Batdiv Three of the First Fleet appears to be operating separately from the main force, possibly in connection with Cardivs Three and Four in the Taiwan-Naha area. An apparent movement report from Cardiv Four was addressed to CinC Combined Fleet, First Fleet, CarDiv Commander, Combined Air Force Commander and to movement offices at Tokyo, Yokosuka, Kure, Maizuru and Sasebo. Traffic from the Commander Indo-China Force is handled from the Japanese radio station at Saigon rather than from the KASHII, indicating that the staff is based ashore at present. No identifiable submarine activity was noted.

AIR -

Takao and Mandates continue to be the center of air activities. The area between Chichijima, Naha, Takao, Palao and Jaluit appears to be particularly concerned with movement of air forces and auxiliaries, while the formation of a force under Combined Air Commander in the Takao-Bako area appears to be nearly completed as indicated by reports addressed to CinC. Combined, Naval Minister, Commanders of Cardivs, Combined Air Force, First

With this Communication Intelligence Summary prepared at Station Hypo November 8, 1941, by Commander Rochefort and forwarded to President Franklin D. Roosevelt, Rochefort's staff began the initial tracking and identification of two major prongs of the Japanese offensive. The dispatch: *(1)* Identifies as Japanese objectives: South China to Palau an area encircling the Philippine Islands (then a U.S. possession); and Chichi Jima to eastern Marshall Islands (Jaluit) including Marcus Island, a Japanese naval air base north of Wake Island. *(2)* Predicts two separate Japanese air movements: one between Chichi Jima and Hawaii; and another in the area in South China region near Taiwan (Formosa-Takao) and The Pescadores Islands (Bako). *(3)* Warns the Japanese Fourth Fleet (based at Truk) and Fifth Fleet (associated with Chichi Jima) that the naval base at Yokosuka will be involved in operations eastward from Chichi Jima including lower island areas (Mandates, Wake). (Note: eastward from Chichi Jima is Wake, Midway and Hawaii). *(4)* Identifies Japanese carrier divisions Three and Four with the Formosa-Okinawa area (Taiwan-Naha), significantly separates these two carrier divisions from One, Two and Five (the eventual Pearl Harbor force). *Source: U.S. Naval Security Group Command.*

Station H,
26 November, 1941.

CHRONOLOGY
26 November

South China Area: No change in locations of CinC's China and South
China Fleets or Comdr. Indo-China Force was observed.

Takao was acting as radio guard for Comdr. Combined
Air Force and KORU∅∅ (Comdg. Officer Kanoya Air Station).

Sama, Hainan, was handling traffic for Crudiv Seven
showing that this unit had moved from Kure to South China or Indo-
China. Sama sent traffic to WISA8 (CinC S. China Fleet) addressed
to YAMU1 (NURA3), afloat call (Maru?), information RISUWA and
RIHITA (Army addresses ?). These messages were originated by NRU11
(Ship), EFU∅∅ (Flt. exp.), NUU66 (Ship), and RUH077 (Flt. exp.).

The Erimo (Tanker) is going from Sasebo to Takao.

Combined Fleet: CinC's Combined, First and Second Fleets, Comairron
7 and Comdesron One are at Kure. It is believed that the entire
First Fleet is in the Kure area. Indications point to the fact
that several Second Fleet units have departed from Kure for South
China.

The Takao (Former flagship 2nd Fleet) is still at
Yokosuka. KORE449 (Staff Comm. Officer 2nd Fleet) is aboard the
Atago - flagship Crudiv 4.

CinC Third Fleet and several of the Carriers are at
or near Sasebo. NERU8 (Cardiv 4) is at Sasebo.

The Carriers were heard using secret calls on 4963M
Kcs during the evening watch.

Submarines: Very little activity in the Subforce has been observed for the last few days. Chichijima acted as radio guard for
MUSA249 (Staff Comm. Officer Subforce), indicating Comsubforce and
possibly the entire Submarine Force are near that port.

Fourth Fleet: CinC Fourth Fleet and several other Fourth Fleet
units are in the Truk area. From study of traffic, routine operations are being carried out in the Mandates.

It is believed that CinC Fifth Fleet and several
Fifth Fleet units are in the Chichijima area.

69

Rochefort's staff had two bombshells for President Roosevelt in this Chronology dated November 26, 1941.
Here they distinguish between the Japanese carriers of the Third Fleet (CARDIVS 3 & 4) and "The Carriers"
(CARDIVS 1, 2 & 5). The date is most significant, for at this moment "The Carriers" sortied from Etorofu in the
Kurile Islands, and headed for Pearl Harbor. Supposedly on "radio silence" (according to post-war reports), the
carriers were heard and intercepted at Station "H" broadcasting on 4963 kilocycles. By adding letter "M" to the
frequency, Station "H" intercept operators indicated "The Carriers" were broadcasting over an extended period
of time, which permitted an electronic measurement of the kilocycles involved. (Note: These Japanese carrier
broadcasts by the Pearl Harbor force were also heard on the West Coast of the United States, according to
Robert Ogg, a special intelligence agent of the Twelfth Naval District.) The second bombshell in this dispatch,
prepared by Homer L. Kisner of Station H, tracks "possibly" the entire Japanese fleet submarine force, together
with its commander-in-chief, past Chichi Jima. (Note: Rochefort and Kisner were correct. These subs were
carrying the midget submarines used to attack Pearl Harbor. In later intercepts, Kisner tracks the sub force as it
turns eastward toward Hawaii. Kisner was Rochefort's radio traffic chief at Station H.)

Source: U.S. Naval Security Group Command.

This photo of Chichi Jima shows Japanese warships anchored in Futami Bay. The vessels appear to be the battleships Shikishima (left) and Mikasa. *Source: Cholmondeley, 1915.*

At Station Hypo in Pearl Harbor, Rochefort and his staff of cryptologists and radio intercept operators worked grueling 24 hour shifts monitoring Japanese naval communications. They believed that something major was in the works. On October 22, 1941, Rochefort warned the White House that Japan was planning a "large scale screening maneuver involving units of the Imperial Navy especially air operations." Rochefort predicted that this operation would involve a vast area of the Pacific, including the Kurile Islands and areas east of Chichi Jima — a sweep that would include Midway, Guam, Wake and the Hawaiian Islands. [6]

Rochefort thought the screening maneuver cloaked a covert Japanese offensive operation. From collateral communication intelligence, Rochefort learned this was not a training mission. He believed Japan was organizing its fleet for an aggressive expeditionary move in an unknown direction. To gain additional corroboration, Rochefort placed his entire organization on a "scoop watch" which called for every Japanese radio communication originating in the Pacific basin to be monitored and recorded by his staff of code-breaking experts.

In early November the Imperial Japanese Navy radio broadcasts provided Commander Rochefort with the needed corraboration. He forwarded the secret information obtained from these intercepted messages to the White House. His staff had detected the movement of the Japanese submarine fleet of about 26 U-boats, sub tenders and other auxiliary, heading away from the Em-

pire, led by its commander-in-chief. The Pearl Harbor Hypo staff, using radio direction finders, tracked the massive submarine movement through the Japanese Navy's Chichi Jima communication zone south and east toward American possessions. [7]

Toward the end of November, 1941, the continued eastern movement of Nippon war ships and invasion components through the zone prompted Commander Rochefort to issue a "War Alert" to Washington. The Roosevelt administration agreed with his startling assessment and on November 27, 1941, placed the entire U.S. armed forces on a war footing warning military commanders that Japan was expected to commit an agressive move within a few days.

At Rochefort's radio listening post at Heeia, Hawaii, Chief Radioman Homer Kisner coordinated the communication intercepts obtained from the Chichi Jima intelligence arc. All Japanese Navy radio facilities from Tokyo through Saipan and Palau verified the continued eastward movement of two-thirds of Japan's fleet submarines.

The secrets of Chichi Jima were out. On December 6, 1941, just hours before the Pearl Harbor attack, Radioman Kisner and staff obtained radio direction finder bearings indicating Japanese war ships were approaching Wake Island. In his daily intercept chronology on the last day of peace, Kisner warned that current communication procedures being used by the Japanese "were probably the first steps in placing the operations of the (Japanese) navy on a wartime basis." [8]

COMMUNICATION INTELLIGENCE SUMMARY
November 30, 1941.

GENERAL - Traffic volume less than for past few days. Todays traffic
consisted largely of despatches bearing old dates, some as far back
as 26 November. No reason can be given for the retransmission of
these messages unless the high volume of traffic for past few days
has prevented the repetition of despatches. The number of despatches
originated on the 30th is very small. The only tactical circuit
heard today was one with AKAGI and several MARUs. The TOKYO Intelligence activity originated two WIWI despatches to Major Fleet Commanders.
One urgent despatch was sent by NCS to Chiefs of Staff, Combined,
Second, Third, Fourth, and Fifth Fleets, Combined Air Force;
Submarine Force and China Fleets.

COMBINED FLEET - The Chiefs of Staff of the Combined Fleet and First
Fleet are in KURE. In the same message the Chief of Staff Second Fleet
was not at any location. Other traffic indications are that he is at
sea. Commander in Chief Second Fleet sent one to his usual addressees
of the Third Fleet and Combined Air Force but also included KONGO
and HIYEI, which places them as members of his Task Force. The
Commander in Chief Second Fleet is no longer adding PALAO activities
and has not for past two days. The RNO PALAO today addressed two
messages to TAIWAN GUNSIRSIBU (TAIWAN Army Headquarters).

THIRD FLEET - Commander in Chief Third Fleet addressed two messages to
COMDESRON Two, Four and Five; COMCRUDIV Five; First and Second Base
Forces and Defense Division One for information to Commander in Chief
Second Fleet. No information obtained as to the location of the
Commander in Chief Third Fleet, which gives the strong impression
that he is underway.

FOURTH FLEET - Believed to be still in TRUK area. D.F. activity in
Marshalls a little greater today than normal. JALUIT addressed
Commander Submarine Force and AIRRON 24 in one despatch. The
continued association of JALUIT and Commander Submarine Force plus
his known progress from the Empire to CHICHIJIMA to SAIPAN makes his
destination obviously the Marshalls. Since one of his large units
(SITI 4) arrived in the Marshalls some time ago this unit cannot
agree with Com 16 that there is not a submarine concentration in that
area. Every evidence points to a concentration of not only the small
Fourth Fleet submarines there but also a good portion of the Fleet
submarines of the Submarine Force. AIRRON 24 plus YOKOHAMA AIR CORPS
presence in that area points to intended air-submarine operations.
from the Marshalls. Also the presence of a unit of plane guard
destroyers indicates the presence of at least one carrier in the
Mandates although this has not been confirmed.

SOUTH CHINA - BAKO active with despatches to Second and Third Fleets,
Combined Air Force and SAMA. Commander in Chief China Fleet becoming
more and more active as an originator with despatches to the Task
Force. He made a movement report with the South China Fleet as an
information addressee. The Staff Communication Officer of the South
China Fleet was addressed at Shanghai today.   00228

171

SECRET

Warning that the Japanese navy plans air-submarine operations from the Marshall Islands, Rochefort continues tracking the sub force from the Empire, through Chichi Jima to Jaluit. Under "General," the AKAGI, flagship of the Pearl Harbor carrier task force was intercepted on tactical radio circuits. Both Japan and America assert the force was on radio silence during sortie to Pearl Harbor. The date was November 30, 1941. The attack was one week away. *Source: Naval Security Group Command.*

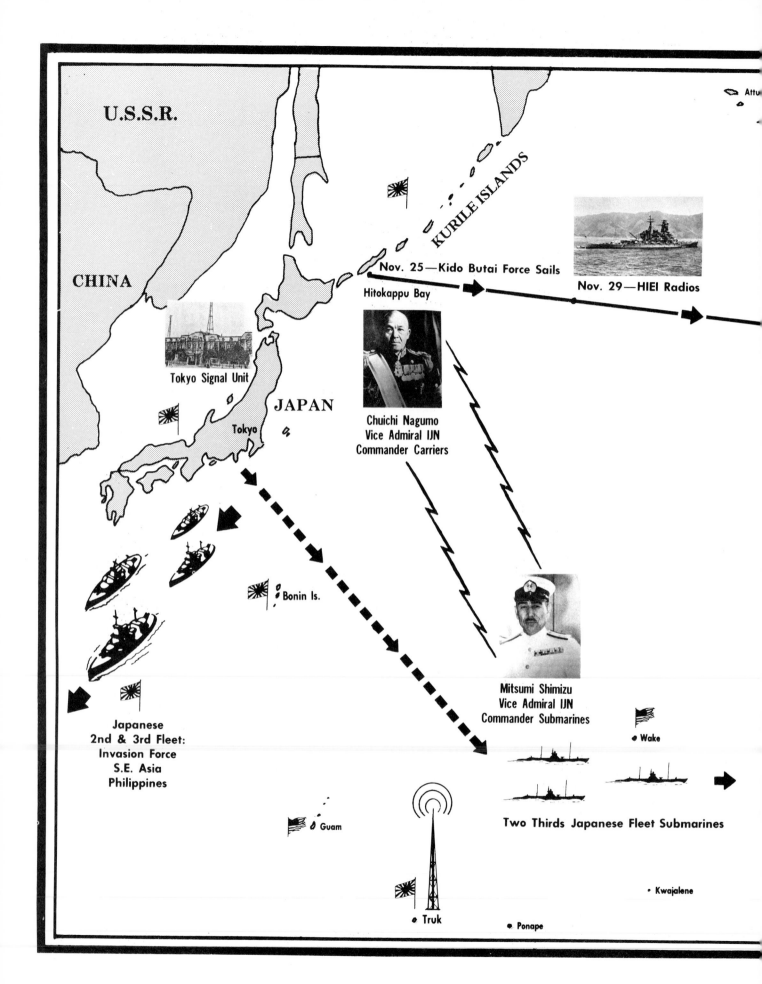

U.S.S.R.

CHINA

KURILE ISLANDS

Attu

Nov. 25—Kido Butai Force Sails

Nov. 29—HIEI Radios

Hitokappu Bay

Tokyo Signal Unit

JAPAN

Tokyo

Chuichi Nagumo
Vice Admiral IJN
Commander Carriers

Bonin Is.

Mitsumi Shimizu
Vice Admiral IJN
Commander Submarines

Japanese
2nd & 3rd Fleet:
Invasion Force
S.E. Asia
Philippines

Wake

Guam

Two Thirds Japanese Fleet Submarines

Kwajalene

Truk

Ponape

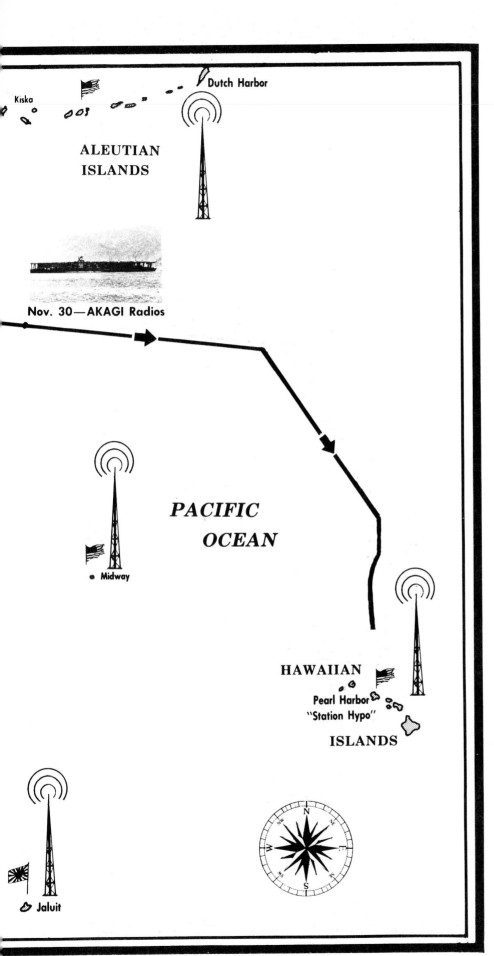

ALEUTIAN ISLANDS

Kiska

Dutch Harbor

Nov. 30—AKAGI Radios

PACIFIC OCEAN

Midway

HAWAIIAN

Pearl Harbor
"Station Hypo"

ISLANDS

Jaluit

Chichi Jima was scene of intelligence conference in winter of 1931-32 when Joseph Rochefort (left) met with Ethelbert Watts (center-rear) and H. Merrell Benninghoff (right). Japanese kempei (military policeman) is unidentified. On eve of Pearl Harbor attack, Watts was quartered at Station U.S. in Washington, D. C. and forwarded Rochefort's Station Hypo reports to FDR. Benninghoff in Tokyo on the night of December 6, 1941, drove U.S. Ambassador Joseph Grew to Emperor Hirohito carrying FDR's last minute message in an effort to avoid war.

Courtesy Janet Rochefort Elerding.

Days before the Pearl Harbor attack, Rochefort had identified the two-prong Japanese offensive. The main body of the Japanese fleet, together with expeditionary forces, was tracked to the Philippines–China region, while a screening force of submarines and air squadrons were electronically followed eastward toward Hawaii. In the north Pacific, Rochefort's listening points at Heeia and Dutch Harbor intercepted direct radio transmissions from the AKAGI, flagship of the Pearl Harbor force.

Map by Frank Pennock Jr., based on files from Naval Security Group Command.

On the eve of Pearl Harbor Japanese warships were located by radio direction finder (RDF) heading toward Wake Island by I. S. Benjamin (below), evening watch supervisor at Station H, Heeia, Hawaii whose intercept operators obtained the radio intelligence from Chichi Jima's naval radio station. The position reports came from the RDF housed in a small covering on the shore of Kaneohe Bay (below).

Source: Station H report from Naval Security Group Command; photos of the RDF and Benjamin courtesy Naval Cryptologic Veterans Association.

SECRET

H 6 DEC 41   EVE WATCH

NOTE PALAO'S WEATHER BROADCAST "KANATOKO" AT 1908 DID NOT SHOW.

SAIPAN'S BROADCAST ON 6030M WAS UP AT 1715 BUT VERY POOR DUE TO INTERFERENCE FROM A BROADCAST STATION. THIS WAS DROPPED IN FAVOR OF 8014M.

TOKYO(?) BROUGHT UP ANOTHER BROADCAST ON 6665A WHICH WENT "VA" AT 1918. AT SAME TIME THIS BROADCAST WAS RUNNING, TOKYO USING REGULAR CALL AS WORKING SAIPAN WITH HIS REGULAR TRANSMITTER RIGHT ALONG-SIDE THE BROADCAST. SAIPAN ANSWERING ON 7035 AS USUAL

NUA2   IS A GOOD GUESS FOR 1ST FLEET: MANY MESSAGES SHOW WITH THE HEADING READING TI COMB FLT, NUA2, 2ND FLT, 3RD FLT, 4TH FLT ETC.

FUKE3   BOTH IDENTIFIED AS 4TH FLEET. BOTH SHOW IN SAME HEADING
RIRO0   AS CINC 4TH FLEET, MAKING ONE OF THEM IN ERROR

YUHE4   BOTH IDENTIFIED AS 2ND FLEET, ONE IN ERROR   98327
YOA2

SOW16   IS IN ERROR AS "INDO CHI FOR" BUT MAY BE S.CHI.FLT.

                                                              98380

POSITION REPORTS/MOVEMENT REPORTS:

WAYU4	MARU	BAKO TO SAMA		79988
ROHA1	MARU	SASEBO	TO TAKAD	79991
RAR16	MARU	TAKAO	TO COMBAIRFOR	80013
HEN04	MARU	JAIUIT	TO TRUK	80047
			IN COMMN WITH	
SAA0	MARU	151.8E 25.7N	CHICHIJIMA	80006
ROH13	MARU	149.6E 27.1N	CHICHIJIMA	80012
KOM09	MARU	139.0E 07.3N		80070

                                          I.S.BENJAMIN

United States involvement in World War II was only hours away when Homer L. Kisner (right), Rochefort's radio intelligence traffic chief, warned that Japan's navy was nearly on a "war time basis." Kisner prepared his last peacetime chronology from radio intercepts gathered by his trained force of 64 radio operators. At 0755 the morning of December 7, 1941, the Japanese naval task forces which had been under radio surveillance by Rochefort for nearly a month, struck Pearl Harbor.

Source: Chronology, Naval Security Group Command; Kisner, courtesy Captain Kisner.

Station H
7 Dec. 1941.   CHRONOLOGY, Cont'd.

Fourth Fleet   : It has been definitely established by traffic study that CinC 4th Fleet is in the Truk area. Several times traffic routing indicated that part of the Staff of CinC 4th Fleet was at Jaluit. It is possible that this command has been split-up for better administration of all operations in the South Seas. The Kamoi (with Commanding Officer, Chitose Air Corps aboard) is in the Jaluit area.

Traffic continues to be exchanged between several 4th Fleet units and Commands in the Indo-China area.

Fifth Fleet   Ominato has been heard working the flagship and at least one other unit of the 5th Fleet for the last few days. This fleet has been based at Chichijima for some time. It is probable that part of this force has remained at Chichijima; it is known that KF06 (Airron attached to 5th Fleet) is there.

General   At 0430, Tokyo was heard using 32Kos, dual with 12330 Kos, for UTU broadcast of traffic. This broadcast was discontinued at 1800, but 7285 Kos (M) was immediately brought up and used until 1900, when it was secured. This broadcast was used in addition to Tokyo's regular UTU. Tokyo also broadcasted traffic on 6665 Kos (A) during the evening.

Saipan, Takao and Ominato were also heard broadcasting traffic to units in their vicinities. The use of this method of delivering messages tends to keep unknown the positions of vessels afloat, and is probably one of the first steps toward placing the operations of the Navy on a war-time basis.

SECRET

-9-

The devastating bombing and submarine attack on Pearl Harbor in the early morning hours of December 7 united an outraged America that had been divided by isolationist creeds. Like many young men, a grim and determined George Bush reacted immediately, wanting to join U.S. naval aviation to avenge the Day of Infamy. His father, Prescott Bush, and powerful family friend Secretary of War Henry L. Stimson wanted him to go onto college. But their persuasive arguments could not deter George from going to war. On his 18th birthday, June 12, 1942, Bush enlisted in the navy as a seaman second class.

The navy enrolled him in a 10-month "fly boy" program which included training at Chapel Hill, North Carolina, Minneapolis, Minnesota, and other USN aviation training units. On June 9, 1943, three days prior to his 19th birthday, Bush became a naval aviator receiving his ensign's commission and aviator wings from Rear Admiral Alfred E. Montgomery at Corpus Christi, Texas. In less than a year, Bush would encounter Montgomery again, this time when the Admiral would order Bush to his first combat role in the Pacific War.

George Bush was a 17-year old student at Phillips Academy, Andover, Mass., when he heard the news of the Pearl Harbor attack. In his senior year he was active in a scholarship program involving books for the student loan library. *Source: The White House.*

George Bush wanted to join the U.S. armed forces but was persuaded to remain at Phillips to finish his senior year. His first elected office was that of student deacon (above). He is shown with (front row left to right): Edward Foord, Bush, Kenneth W. Keuffel. Rear: Howard S. Weaver, Calvin Burrows and James P. Townsend. At left he is shown with the Phillips baseball coach, George L. "Flop" Follansbee. *Source: The White House.*

The Texas Connection

Early in 1942, President Roosevelt and his military advisors, desperate for aircraft carriers, decided to scrap plans for nine light cruisers. Instead the vessels were changed to light aircraft carriers of the INDEPENDENCE class. The USS SAN JACINTO, last of this class and named after a Texas battlefield, slides down the way of the New York Shipbuilding Corporation, Camden New Jersey. "The SAN JAC" became the carrier home of George Bush. *Source: USS SAN JACINTO photo file National Archives.*

LAUNCHING U. S. S. CVL
VESSEL LEAVING LAUNCHING WAYS
YORK SHIPBUILDING CORP. CAMDEN N. J.
SEPT. 26TH 194

Grumman Invents the Avenger

Like other pilots, Ensign Bush was offered a choice of either carrier or land-based naval aviation assignments. He chose aircraft carriers and began operational training at Fort Lauderdale, Florida, as a pilot of torpedo bombers. He selected the TBM Avenger bomber, largely because of its reputation as the biggest, best single-engine bomber in the Navy's carrier-based air arsenal.

The Avenger was designed by Leroy Grumman at his Bethpage, Long Island plant. Wartime production of the Avenger started in January 1942 as the TBF. In naval parlance, "TB" stood for torpedo bomber, "F" for Grumman. As wartime needs generated demand for larger production, Grumman licensed the manufacturer of the Avenger to General Motors which converted its east coast Chevrolet, Pontiac and Oldsmobile assembly plants to naval aircraft production. The GM-produced Avengers were known as "TBM's," the "M" being the designator for the Eastern Aircraft Division of General Motors. Almost all Avengers used by the Navy in the Pacific War from 1943 onward were built by General Motors. The Avenger became Bush's mobile combat home during his nearly three-year stint as a Navy bomber pilot. The aircraft required a three man crew—pilot, turret gunner and radio-radar man in the tail gunner position. The plane could carry a 2,000 pound bomb load, or equivalent, of depth charges or torpedoes for attacking Japanese targets.

Leroy Grumman.

Grumman Aircraft Company produced this first prototype torpedo-bomber for the U. S. Navy from its plant in Bethpage, Long Island, in late 1941 (opposite). In this photo a crewman climbs into the compartment behind the pilot. The USN used this space for radio gear during the Pacific War and assigned only two crewmembers for the pilot: a turret gunner in the ball-turret and a radar-radioman in the bomb bay compartment. Both crewmembers accessed their posts through the hatch shown on fuselage starboard rear (above). Called the Avenger, it was chosen by George Bush for his combat duty. Leroy Grunman, (opposite page) president of the firm, licensed production of the bomber to General Motors. All Avengers produced by Grumman are called TBF; General Motors, TBM. *Source: Grumman Corporation.*

Japanese Counterpart

The closest Japanese naval equivalent to Grumman's Avenger was this torpedo bomber called "Kate." The sleek lines of this carrier-based aircraft, which was built by Nakajima Company, contrast with the fat-belly-look of the Avenger.

Source: National Archives.

The submarine USS FINBACK (SS 230) being launched at the Portsmouth Navy Yard on August 25, 1941. George Bush was rescued by this sub off Chichi Jima on September 2, 1944. *Source: National Archives.*

George Bush spent nearly 30 days aboard the FINBACK in September 1944 awaiting return to the USS SAN JACINTO.

Source: National Archives.

This formal group of the pre-flight class at Chapel Hill shows George Bush seated in top row, fourth from left. Officially the USN regarded these men as aviation cadets.

Source: The White House.

Cadet George Bush.

Ensign George Bush.

President Franklin D. Roosevelt joins Rear Admiral Alfred E. Montgomery USN in post graduation luncheon at the Naval Air Station, Corpus Christi. Admiral Montgomery, who was commanding officer of the air station, presented George Bush and fellow pilot baseball star Ted Williams with their wings.

Source: National Archives.

George Bush requested flight training and was sent to pre-flight school at Chapel Hill, North Carolina. He is shown (rear) in this October 1942 photo with (from left) Blaine Hall, Bill Robinson and Dean Phinney.

Source: The White House.

1943 ....

Special training in Avenger flight techniques took 19-year-old Bush to the Naval Air Station, Fort Lauderdale, in June 1943. Fellow trainee Louis Grab recalled the instruction: "We were all teenagers or barely into our 20's, totally naive to the ways of the world. Our patriotic goal was to get even for Pearl Harbor. We all regarded the December 7 raid as an unprovoked sneak attack by Japan on a peaceful United States. We were determined to take revenge. We had no idea what awaited us. All 48 states were united. Aviators would be needed to defeat Japan. We were the fly boys. It was going to be an easy life. The dangers lurking in the combat areas of the Pacific were unfathomable to us. The glamour attached to the aviator wings pinned on our chest jackets opened every door imaginable. The glamour only lasted a few months. Japanese anti-aircraft fire turned us into survivors."

Nearly all World War II aviation training for the Avenger torpedo-bomber was conducted at the NAS Fort Lauderdale, Florida. The air station's newspaper was entitled THE AVENGER. *Courtesy, Lou Grab.*

George Bush chose to get even for the Day of Infamy. The US Navy's Avenger torpedo-bomber was Bush's choice and he received indoctrination at the Naval Air Station Fort Lauderdale, Florida. Bush is shown in back row (hatless) second from right. Ensign Lou Grab (standing on Bush's left), along with Bush, was assigned to Torpedo Squadron 51 and the USS SAN JACINTO. Others are: (kneeling left to right): Mike Goldsmith, Leslie Mokry, Bill Shawcross, Tom Campanion, Tex Ellison. (back row left to right): Bill Donovan, Ralph Cole, Mort Landsburg, Bush and Grab. *Photo courtesy, The White House.*

Chincoteague Naval Air Station was still under construction when George Bush reported to his newly formed combat squadron, VT-51, in September 1943. TBF's (folded wings) dot the service apron along with some SNJ's. *Source: National Archives.*

This 1943 photo shows the Naval Air Station, Chincoteague, Virginia.
Source: National Archives.

Bush's only operational mishap with an Avenger in World War II took place when the "wheels collapsed on landing," during a practice bombing flight at the NAS, Chincoteague, Virginia. This accident took place, November 1, 1943 in Tare Two, unofficially known as "The Barbara", after his fiancée, Barbara Pierce.
Source: The White House.

Bush Joins VT-51

In September that year, Bush and Grab along with 11 other pilots were assigned to their combat posts in newly created Naval Air Group 51 assembling at Norfolk, Virginia. By November 8, 1943, the air group formed into two squadrons for its future combat role: Fighter Squadron Fifty-One (VF-51) of 24 Hellcat fighters and Torpedo Squadron Fifty-One (VT-51) of nine Avenger bombers. [9]

George Bush's immediate superior in charge of the torpedo bombers was Lieutenant Commander Donald Melvin, a 32-year-old seasoned naval aviator educated in aerodynamic engineering at private schools. Commander Melvin, like most pilots of VT-51, did not have operational experience on aircraft carriers. In its combat mission the squadron was issued nine of the new torpedo bombers direct from the former General Motors auto assembly plants.

Beginning in late September 1943, Bush and his fellow aviators trained in aerial combat techniques involving bombing and torpedo targets. Instruction, mostly all land-based, was rushed and corners cut as the navy pushed the newly formed air groups to meet forthcoming fleet deadlines for the Japanese island hopping strategy devised for the Pacific War theater by the Joint Chiefs of Staff.

Air Group 51 eventually became a model of competence but had a less than auspicious beginning. At the Chincoteague Naval Air Station on Virginia's east shore near the Maryland border, 19-year-old George Bush was practicing "carrier landings" on the air station's runway. [10] Whooooomp! He belly-landed his Avenger on the tarmac, noting in his flight log that the wheels collapsed on landing. Scratch one TBM and $96,159.00. One piece of luck, however. He was unhurt. [11]

Barbara Pierce and George Bush had become engaged—secretly during the summer of 1943. In September Barbara went off to study at Smith College in Northampton, Massachusetts. Late that fall, the squadron was moved to Hyannis, Massachusetts, and Charlestown, Rhode Island, for torpedo training. There was little free time for George Bush to visit Barbara, even though Smith College was only a short distance from the air operations. To keep Bush on flight training regimen, New Year's Eve 1943, Commander Melvin assigned him to nearly four hours of gunnery and torpedo flying. The training days were about over. Soon Bush and his squadron would join the carrier USS SAN JACINTO.

George Bush makes practice landings in "The Barbara" on the Chincoteague runway, November 1943.
Source: Jacqueline Forshay.

An Avenger torpedo-bomber and a Hellcat fighter were spotted on the bow of the USS SAN JACINTO in January 1944 when the warship was at anchor in lower Delaware Bay.

Cake Celebration

Festive occasions in the US Navy are celebrated with frosted cakes. The British navy's colorful custom of "splicing the main brace" with rum is prohibited on American warships. At the commissioning of the USS SAN JACINTO on December 15, 1943, Captain Harold "Beauty" Martin USN cut the ceremonial cake. George Bush and his fellow aviators of Air Group 51 participated in the festivities.

One of the 1944 camouflage patterns of Atlantic Fleet warships in shown (lower) as the SAN JACINTO prepares to leave for her shakedown cruise near Trinidad in the British West Indies.

Source: USS SAN JACINTO photos from National Archives.

PART II

1944

On January 23, 1944, Captain Harold "Beauty" Martin (called so because of his good looks) had his 1,600-man crew of the USS SAN JACINTO ready for the first airplane qualification landings. [1] The initial air operations would be conducted in the lower regions of Delaware and Chesapeake Bays. The navy wasn't about to imperil the greenhorns of the SAN JACINTO and Air Group 51 with the prowling Nazi submarines in the Atlantic Ocean waters.

For these carrier landings George Bush [2] and fellow aviators had to wait their turn. Air Group commander Thomas Bradbury [3] pulled rank to become the first pilot to land. He made a perfect landing, his tail hook catching cable number three. Any landing on a carrier was ranked as a big success but perfection was getting cable number three. The carrier's landing area was 70 feet wide by about 350 feet long. Nine cables extended across the width of the flight deck; it was up to the pilot to "squat" his tail and catch the cable.

At the end of the landing area, three elevated cables formed a net to catch any aircraft failing to engage the deck cables. Hitting this barrier safety net could cause extensive damage to the aircraft and possible injury to the pilot and aircrewmen.

Carrier landing procedures called for a counter clockwise circle of the SAN JACINTO by all planes. The first leg of the circle would start parallel to the starboard side of the flattop, followed by a turn left when well forward of the bow, then a turn left to proceed down leg parallel to the port side, then another turn left in a wide circle to line up with the stern of the bobbing flight deck. A landing signal officer guided the pilot in the final 500 feet. The pilot could not see the flight deck at this point and had to trust the hand signals of the landing signal officer. Total pilot concentration was imperative. A split second of thought digression could result in crashing into the

Original commissioned officers of Torpedo Squadron Fifty-One (VT-51) pose at Norfolk Naval Air Station in January 1944. Front row (left to right): Ensign Francis M. Waters, aviator; Lieutenant Forrest H. Daniels, personnel officer; Lieutenant Richard R. Houle, aviator; Lieutenant Ross G. Allen, intelligence officer; Lieutenant Commander Donald Melvin, commanding officer; Lieutenant Legare R. Hole, executive officer and aviator; Lieutenant (j.g.) Milan S. Nemsak, aviator; Lieutenant Richard B. Plaisted, aviator; (back row) Ensign James J. Wykes, aviator; Ensign, Stanley P. Butchart, aviator; Ensign Jack O. Guy, aviator; Ensign Lou J. Grab, aviator; Lieutenant (j.g.) William G. White, ordnance officer; Ensign George H. W. Bush, aviator; Ensign Howard G. Boren, aviator; Ensign Douglas H. West, aviator. By October 1944, 25 percent of these men had been killed in combat operations: Wykes, White, Daniels and Houle. Nemsak was detached from the squadron in April 1944 at San Diego. *Source: U.S. Navy photo, National Archives.*

sea, the stern or catwalks of the carrier.

Captain Martin had guided the SAN JACINTO south on the Delaware River from Camden, New Jersey, to Delaware Bay. The warship had been commissioned on December 15, 1943, at the New York Shipbuilding Corporation in Camden. Of the ship's complement of officers and men, eighty percent had never been to sea before. Most were in their late teens or early twenties and had been recruited from all over the United States. Now with the arrival of the Air Group they were prepared to test their skills in wartime carrier operations. For this test the navy set aside ten weeks for a shakedown cruise which took the Air Group and the vessel from the Chesapeake to Trinidad's Gulf of Paria in the West Indies.

The SAN JACINTO would be the floating airport home of Air Group 51, supplying all needs from barber shop to bomb supply. In turn, the two squadrons of the group would carry the war to Japan, protecting the SAN JACINTO and crew from hostilities. In 15 months of combat the Japanese tried but never touched the SAN JACINTO.

Captain Martin was himself a pioneer USN aviator. He received his wings at Pensacola in 1921, three years after graduating from Annapolis. At the Naval Academy, Martin was a star athlete in varsity football and basketball. Prior to his assignment on the SAN JACINTO, he was commanding officer of the Kaneohe Naval Air Station on Oahu's windward side. The first aerial bombs of the Pacific War, on December 7, 1941, struck Kaneohe, when planes from the Japanese strike force hit Martin's command. [4]

He viewed the arrival of the Air Group aboard his ship as an aviation calamity. Expecting reasonably trained carrier pilots, the captain was gravely disappointed. The skills of the aviators during the shakedown period were "below average in fundamental carrier operations," Captain Martin complained. Evidence abounded. He saw the Air Group's bombers and fighters crash into his ship causing severe damage to the carrier never matched by the Japanese.

During the shakedown period from mid-January to mid-March 1944, more than half of the Air Group's planes were involved in flight crashes either on deck or in the sea. The human toll was heavy. Two men were killed, nine were injured, and there was moderate damage to the ship's flight deck areas. The normally mild mannered Martin was appalled. He would later write Admiral Nimitz: "When they came aboard, Air Group 51 was below average in training and fundamentals of carrier operations. Operational casualties would have been less if the pilots had been given an

intensive shore syllabus". Martin was not privy to the Air Group's training and was not acquainted with the squadron's east coast instruction and discipline.

That evaluation fell to the Navy's "Lindbergh," the appellation assigned to Rear Admiral Albert Read, Commander Air Force of the Atlantic Fleet. Admiral Read was responsible for all carrier aviation of the fleet. At the time, both the USS SAN JACINTO and the Air Group were attached to the Atlantic Fleet. Read had become a celebrity as the first aviator to cross the Atlantic Ocean. His 1919 flight differed from Lindbergh's 1927 non-stop solo crossing because he carried a crew and made several stops. To Martin, Admiral Read was a model aviator. Esteem and respect for Admiral Read was almost boundless. Unless he gave approval, no pilot of the Atlantic Fleet could fly and no carrier could operate. Read took his responsibility seriously, personally conducting rigorous inspections of both carrier and squadron operational qualifications.

Ensign George Bush was one of the bomber pilots certified by Admiral Read to land on the SAN JACINTO and he did not disappoint him. Between January 24, 1944 , and November 29, 1944, Bush made 116 successful landings on the carrier's flight deck. His aviation skills were quickly recognized by the ship's photographers who recorded every landing and take off by the air group. Navy policy called for the photography to be used for crash analysis should accidents occur. Bush never appeared in the SAN JACINTO's flight deck crash file.

As a USN torpedo bomber pilot, Bush was responsible for the safety of his two-man crew. As pilot, he was captain of the Avenger. All operational judgments including navigation, radio communication, bombing and torpedo ordinance were the pilot's exclusive responsibility. Military tactical and strategical orders came down to Bush through Commander Melvin. Bush carried them out.

Photo reconnaissance was another of Bush's duties as pilot of the torpedo bomber. In late summer of 1943, Admiral Nimitz' planning staff sent out orders to newly forming air groups to be prepared for aerial photography, an innovation at the time. After receiving these orders, Commander Melvin named Bush as the squadron's photographic officer and sent him to learn basics of aerial photography at the Navy's Photo Squadron Two (VD-2) at Norfolk, Virginia. Bush spent nearly a month at Norfolk learning the complexities and value of aerial photo intelligence. At Norfolk, Bush learned basic aerial photography including film processing and chemistry and how to operate the

No aviator could fly, no carrier could operate in the USN Atlantic Fleet in 1944, without the approval of the Navy's "Lindbergh," Rear Admiral Albert C. "Putty" Read. In photo at right, the Admiral is inspecting the USS SAN JACINTO's interior quarters followed by Captain Harold Martin and Commander Clifford S. Cooper, executive officer. In 1919, Read's feat rated an eight column headline in the NEW YORK TIMES when he became the first aviator to cross the Atlantic Ocean.

Source: USS SAN JACINTO photo by Robert Stinnett.

The New York Times, 28 May 1919

John T. McCutcheon Cartoon
The Chicago Daily Tribune, 17 May 1919

First carrier landing aboard the USS SAN JACINTO was made by Lieutenant Commander Thomas B. Bradbury in a F6F Hellcat on Sunday, January 23, 1944, in the south portion of Chesapeake Bay. Bradbury made a perfect landing, attesting to Admiral Read's certification. The SAN JACINTO's hull number, "30," is painted fore and aft on the flight deck for pilot identification pur- poses. *Official US Navy photo by NAS Weeksville, N. C.*

The first landing cake is cut by Tom Bradbury as fighter pilots George F. Dailey (left) and Ed Boddington look on. In background, bomber pilots Stan Butchart, Lou Grab and Dick Plaisted and landing signal officer Ralph Bagwell (behind Boddington). *USS SAN JACINTO photo National Archives.*

Several ammunition boxes serve as a temporary cake table as Commander Bradbury poses with his fighter, Fox 1. *USS SAN JACINTO photo, National Archives.*

The entire crew of the USS SAN JACINTO turned out to celebrate the first carrier landing. Captain Harold Martin (right center) watches as two U.S. Marine honor guards present the cake to Tom Bradbury (center). *USS SAN JACINTO photo, National Archives.*

Tare Three forms backdrop for both officers and enlisted men of Torpedo Squadron 51 in this official portrait taken aboard USS SAN JACINTO during the shakedown cruise to Gulf of Paria. George Bush is in back row to right of engine. *USS SAN JACINTO photo, National Archives.*

Navy's aerial cameras for reconnaisance under combat conditions.

As squadron photo officer, Bush was committed to obtain photo intelligence on the Japanese navy and forward the documentation to the navy's intelligence center at Pearl Harbor. All military intelligence obtained by the U.S. Army, Navy, Marines and Coast Guard was evaluated at the Joint Intelligence Center for the Pacific Ocean Areas. The center was known by the acronym, JICPOA. Heading the navy portion of JICPOA was Captain Wilfred J. Holmes, one of Rochefort's original code breakers at Station Hypo. [5]

Bush enlisted the help of other squadron pilots and convinced aircrewmen to use the hand-held K-20 aerial camera during combat flight. John Delaney, Bush's first radioman, was one of the best of the squadron's air crew photographers. He manned the 30

caliber tail machine gun, released bombs and torpedos on Japan fleet units, and took photographs to document Bush's combat hits. As if that were not a one-man band, he also operated the radar to identify Japanese targets.

Radioman Delaney was one of the Bush crew of three. The other was turret gunner Leo "Lee" Nadeau whose machine gun could rotate on a 360 degree axis to drive off any enemy aircraft. During flight each Avenger crew member was restricted to his own cramped space. Bush could not see his crew and they could not see him. Intraplane communication was via the aircraft's intercom. Two-way radio transmitting from the Avenger was controlled by the pilot. Dictates of radio silence kept navy radio broadcasts to a minimum.

Air Group 51's bombers and fighters line aft end of flight deck and are part of the formal Captain's inspection in February 1944 at Trinidad, British West Indies. *USS SAN JACINTO photo by Robert Stinnett.*

Aerologists O. B. Munro and Tom Cernak prepare to take early morning weather reading. Silhouetted at right is a TBM Avenger. *USS SAN JACINTO photo by Robert Stinnett.*

The SAN JACINTO's skipper, Captain Harold "Beauty" Martin conducts inspection of the crew.
USS SAN JACINTO photo by Robert Stinnett.

Flight Deck Terror

One man was killed and six injured when Fox 2 jumped the safety barrier wires and crashed into the SAN JACINTO's island structure on February 13, 1944. The Hellcat went over the starboard side and into the waters of the Gulf of Paria. Ensign Thomas Lindsey, though injured, escaped from the sinking plane and was rescued by a Coast Guard cutter. The official report said the accident was caused by an arresting hook failure. Flight deck crew members (lower), always on the alert to such danger, seek escape into the catwalks.

USS SAN JACINTO photos, National Archives.

Because of carrier operation procedures no one plane of the squadron was assigned exclusively to an individual pilot and crew, but Bush, Nadeau and Delaney managed a partial exemption to the exclusive plane rule. Their bomber, Tare Two, had been equipped with special aerial camera mounts and was the squadron's photo plane. Three aerial cameras could be mounted in the bomb bay area allowing for vertical plus port and starboard oblique coverage of enemy targets. This mount was devised early in 1944 to provide U.S. Marine Corps needs for invasion beach photo intelligence coverage. The photography was deemed critical because at Tarawa in November 1943, the Japanese defenders, using gunfire from undetected gun emplacements, bombarded U.S. Marines as they landed on the invasion beach. In the 1944 planning for future amphibious operations, Marine Corps strategists wanted complete photo intelligence of all invasion objectives. Skilled photo interpreters were assigned the task of locating enemy battlements both on-shore and off-shore.

Informally, Bush called Tare Two "The Barbara" for his fiancée. But the nickname could only be verbalized. Commander Melvin was a stickler for adhering to naval regulations and prohibited any "romantic scribbling" or unofficial decor on the Avengers' fuselage. It was a rule made to conceal the identity of squadrons and vessels from Japanese intelligence in case an aircraft was seized. Only the "X" and number could be marked on the aircraft.

By early April 1944, the SAN JACINTO and Bush's air group had arrived in the Pacific combat zone. The Atlantic Fleet was left behind when the carrier traversed the Panama Canal and came under the direct command of Admiral Nimitz. [6]

A native Texan, Admiral Nimitz was pleased that the flagship of the Texas Navy was now a part of his command. He directed that the Lone Star Flag of the Republic be flown under the U. S. ensign. Many crew members of the SAN JACINTO privately regarded the Lone Star Flag flying from the yardarm as a "Big Texas" novelty but they were not about to question openly the direct orders of Admiral Nimitz. Others, like squadron photo pilot Dixie Mays, heartily applauded flying the Texas flag as a patriotic symbol. Besides, the people of Texas had contributed huge sums in war bonds to help build the SAN JACINTO, which was named after a 1836 bloody battle that won Texas its independence from Mexico.

George Bush's adoption of Texas as home base did not take place until after World War II, but he like other members of the SAN JACINTO were declared citizens

Using "body language", landing signal officer Ralph M. Bagwell brings in a Hellcat. Pilot has full flaps to slow approach to the flight deck. Two Avengers can be seen off the fighter's port wing-tip approaching the landing pattern. Bagwell lowered the wind deflector screen (bottom) so photo could be taken.

USS SAN JACINTO photo by Robert Stinnett.

of Texas by unanimous vote of the Texas legislature during the war years. SAN JACINTO photographs of 1944 show "The Barbara" moving up the flight deck while the Lone Star flag whips in the wind.

The addition of the SAN JACINTO to the Pacific Fleet carrier force provided Admiral Nimitz and his staff with extra muscle as they prepared to launch the first major naval battle of the island hopping strategy.

In mid-March 1944 the battle plans that pulled George Bush and his squadron mates into combat action were drawn up by the Joint Chief of Staff at Washington, D.C. The strategy called for a direct assault by Allied Forces on Japan's inner defenses which were protected by the 1,800-mile Chichi Jima-Palau barrier. Capture of key islands in the barrier would open up the Philippine Sea to American military strength and permit direct penetration of the Japanese home islands by the United States.

Lou Grab and George Bush

The first battle of the strategy was called "Operation Forager," and its goal was the capture and occupation of the Japanese-held Mariana Islands of Saipan, Tinian, Rota and recapture of Guam, the American possession seized by Japan during the opening weeks of the war. D-Day for Operation Forager was set for June 15, 1944.

Breaking through Japan's outer defenses came in two stages. In late summer 1942 at Guadacanal U.S. Marines and army ground forces had stopped the Japanese advance. This allowed time for defense plants at home to produce the fast carrier task forces needed to fight the enemy. In November 1943 the navy's island hopping campaign began at Tarawa when the first of the new ESSEX and INDEPENDENCE class carriers joined the Pacific Fleet and provided air cover for the ground troops.

Bush and the SAN JACINTO joined this critical mass of Pacific Fleet vessels at Majuro Atoll in the Marsall Islands on May 8, 1944. Majuro Atoll had been seized from Japan earlier that year and was converted to the Pacific Fleet's advance base and anchorage. The atoll served as the initial staging area for the offensive that would break the Japanese inner defenses.

From the deck of the SAN JACINTO, Bush could survey a virtual armada in the vast Majuro lagoon. In addition to his own carrier, there were 15 flattops, plus supporting units of battleships, cruisers, destroyers, a supply train of oilers, ammunition and cargo vessels. The carriers were formed into four task groups built around two of the large ESSEX Class carriers plus two of the light INDEPENDENCE class which included the SAN JACINTO and was manned by over 200,000 sailors. This mighty force, the greatest the world had ever known to assemble in one place, was called Task Force Fifty Eight (TF-58).

Lucky Lou Escapes Injury

The SAN JACINTO's bouncing flight deck separated the arresting hook of Tare 8 from engaging the deck cables and alerted photographers to start clicking.

The safety barrier catches wheel assembly of Tare 8 nosing over the bomber near forward elevator. Pilot Lou Grab throws up his hands to protect his face.

This angle shows Tare 8 at the instant of nose–over. Barrier prevented the bomber from crashing into fighters on bow. Fire rescue man is at far right.

Smoke pours from the engine as pilot Lou Grab exits the cockpit. Crewmen of the bomber are preparing to leave from the fuselage hatch.

Fire crews of the USS SAN JACINTO quickly extinguish engine fire. There were no injuries but Tare 8 was severely damaged.

Flight deck crews survey damage to Tare 8 as they prepare to lower the bomber to the hangar deck. Author is shown upper left on island.

USS SAN JACINTO photos by Robert Stinnett and J. E. Haythorn, National Archives.

Land Any Way You Can

The safety barrier upended Fox 22 piloted by Lieutenant Howard Isherwood Jr. Luckily, Isherwood was not injured but the plane was severely damaged. *USS SAN JACINTO photo, National Archives.*

Flight deck emergency crews rush to rescue Ensign Robert Wilson as his Hellcat is shown wheels up in the SAN JACINTO's safety barrier wires. Wilson was unhurt. *USS SAN JACINTO photo, National Archives.*

Some Found the Ocean

Attempting a deck-launch from the SAN JACINTO, Legare Hole, executive officer of VT-51, had to ditch when Tare 4, his torpedo-bomber, failed to gain air speed. Hole can be seen on starboard wing inflating his life raft while crew members, E. V. Lanier and J. H. Richards swim in the Atlantic waters (top center). All members of the crew got into the life raft, cleared Tare 4 before depth charges exploded and were rescued unhurt by the USS ENDICOTT.

Seconds after Tare 4 hit the water, gunner J. H. Richards can be seen climbing from the gun turret. The bomber sank in two minutes according to the SAN JACINTO's deck log.

Crew members Richards and Lanier swim aft of the tail section as they await pilot Hole and the life raft. They escaped through the circular turret hatch seen hanging on the port side of the Avenger.

USS SAN JACINTO photos by Robert Stinnett.

Some Walked Away

Fighter pilot Leo A. Bird has unstrapped his parachute harness as he climbs from Fox 6 after his tail hook failed to catch the deck cables and the Hellcat crashed into the safety barriers. *USS SAN JACINTO photo, National Archives.*

...Others Were Carried

Unconscious Ensign Herbert Fichman is carried from Fox 9 (upper left) after Fox 21 piloted by Lieutenant (j.g.) Rufus Henderson missed arresting gear and plowed into the SAN JACINTO's forward elevator shaft which was lowering Fichman and his Hellcat to the hangar deck. Both aircraft were heavily damaged. *USS SAN JACINTO photo, National Archives.*

The U. S. Pacific Fleet's Majuro Anchorage sheltered the carriers of Task Force 58, May 1944, as it organized for Operation Forager, the invasion of Saipan and recapture of Guam. George Bush and the SAN JACINTO's crew could count 12 carriers (including the SAN JAC) silhouetted by the sunset: six ESSEX class and five INDEPENDENCE class. An Avenger sits on carrier catapult at far left. *USS SAN JACINTO photo by Robert Stinnett.*

The Captain Was Peeved
"This Air Group Is Below Average..."

As the SAN JACINTO completed the shakedown cruise, "Beauty" Martin (left) had a problem: Air Group 51. Since arriving on board, January 23, 1944, pilots had been involved in two deaths and nine injuries. More than half of all aircraft were involved in crashes either onto the SAN JACINTO or in the ocean waters. Martin had to cancel planned night carrier operations. "The pilots are too green" he wrote. Complaining to Admiral Chester Nimitz, Martin indirectly took a pot shot at Admiral Read who had certified the Air Group as fully trained: "The training status of the air group, when it first joined the ship, appeared to be below average."

USS SAN JACINTO photo by Richard P. Names.

The entire crew of the USS SAN JACINTO mourns those killed and injured in the series of flight deck mishaps. Chaplain Deitrich B. Cordes conducts memorial services from pulpit on the carrier's island.

USS SAN JACINTO photo by Robert Stinnett.

PART III

A significant element of the Saipan invasion's Operation Forager assault strategy called for disguising the true target of Task Force 58 by ordering Allied military feints over a vast area of the western Pacific. The ruse was intended to dilute the military strength of the Japanese by forcing them to cover all possible targets. [1]

One of these planned deceptions was a USN carrier raid on Japanese-held Wake and Marcus Islands and attacks on the "Doolittle picket boats" which were stationed by Japan in the North Pacific about 600 miles east of Tokyo. Admiral Nimitz believed the "Hail Mary" ploy would confuse Japanese defensive strategy. By penetrating into the picket boat area with a portion of his carrier fleet, Nimitz contemplated Japan might anticipate another Tokyo raid and pull naval forces back to the empire as was done on April 16, 1942, when General Jimmy Doolittle's B-25 bombers encountered the picket line during the famed Tokyo raid launched from the carrier, USS HORNET.

The ploy mission would also serve as combat indoctrination for the untested air groups of the carriers. The SAN JACINTO, ESSEX and WASP were detailed to carry out this decoy tactic which was actually the opening salvo of Forager.

In another feint north of Japan the U.S. Army Air Force flying from bases in Alaska mounted bombing attacks on the Kurile Islands site of Japan's sortie for the Pearl Harbor attack. Radio intercepts by Station Hypo during the operation confirmed the Japanese Navy had detected the various decoy forces unleashed by Nimitz and dispatched radio alerts to Nippon forces in the North Pacific region.

George Bush's first enemy encounter was set for a one-week period, May 17-23, 1944, about three weeks in advance of the Saipan invasion. Rear Admiral Alfred E. Montgomery, who had awarded Bush his naval aviation wings at Corpus Christi a year before, was commander of the task group and in charge of Forager's initial combat phase. Montgomery's flagship was the ESSEX where he presided as Commander of Task Group 58.6. (In naval parlance of the time 58.6 meant unit #6 of Task Force 58.) Air Group 51's air intelligence officers Ross Allen and Edward Brewster obtained the target maps and intelligence monographs of Wake and Marcus Islands. They also drew up bombing and strafing plans in coordination with the ESSEX and WASP. In addition, all pilots were briefed on the "Doolittle picket boat" chain which operated in the area northwest of Marcus in the area 31 north latitude and 155 east

longitude. As intelligence officer, Lieutenant Ross Allen's job was to brief the Avenger aviators and crewmen on target objectives using the latest information forwarded by Captain Wilfred "Jasper" Holmes from his Pearl Harbor data gathering center. [2] The briefing took place in the ready room just below the flight deck.

The ready room was the exclusive retreat of the aviators, definitely off-limits to outsiders. This place was like a Hollywood star's dressing room held in awe by the carrier's sailors. Certain areas had an almost funeral like aura. Blackboards and bulletin boards reminded the airmen of the dangers inherent of war with recognition posters of Japanese aircraft and warships. Indirect ceiling lighting created the pall of a mortician's viewing room. The airmen spent their waking hours camped in overstuffed black leather lounge chairs. In the sanctity of the ready room military punctilio between the officer pilots and the enlisted aircrewmen was minimal. Card games, chess, and gossip took up most of the leisure time. The pilots were mostly to themselves in the front portions of the room; the gunners and radiomen who made up the aircrew usually gathered in the rear lounge chairs. [3]

In this private sanctuary, aviators sometimes harbored superstitions regarding the regimen of U.S. naval aviation operations. Each bomber pilot was allocated a permanent air crew. Nadeau in the turret, Delaney in the bomb bay, Bush in the plane's cockpit formed "The Barbara's" team. Occasionally, due to illness or squadron necessities, substitutes sat in as crew members. Nadeau, Bush's turret gunner, objected vociferously to interlopers assigned to fly in "The Barbara." Substitutes, in his thinking, were a bad omen, an airplane jinx. Whenever a substitute came aboard trouble, either directly or indirectly, soon followed, he observed. Nadeau and other squadron flyers could easily prove their jinx theories by pointing to a series of mishaps involving crew substitutes.

The substitute jinx sensed by Nadeau first hit the Bush crew in mid-May, 1944, as the squadron was heading for the diversionary strike on Wake Island. The setup for the jinx occurred earlier on May 1, 1944, when Bush bumped Nadeau and Delaney from "The Barbara" to substitute two flight deck workers of the SAN JACINTO. Both were aircraft handlers of "The Barbara" and had asked Bush for a ride. Appreciative of the handlers' work he obliged with a routine three hour anti-submarine patrol flight. Nadeau's jinx theories, deeply rooted in his Massachusetts background, were

Prepared for Combat

Readying for his first combat mission, Ensign George H. W. Bush checks out his TBM Avenger torpedo-bomber, Tare Two. Bush had been issued this plane at Chincoteague NAS on November 11, 1943, after his previous Tare Two had belly-landed on the runway. The USN's official "Bureau Number" for this aircraft was #25123 and listed as a TBM-1C.

Bush unofficially called Tare Two "The Barbara" after his fiancée, Barbara Pierce (right). Though some reports say Bush wrote his fiancée's name on the fuselage. He did not, as this photo shows. Bush's skipper, Don Melvin, prohibited any writings on the fuselage of the Avengers fearing a intelligence breakthrough if the plane should fall into Japanese custody.

USS SAN JACINTO photo by Robert Stinnett. Barbara Pierce, courtesy The White House.

scoffed at by Bush. In the eerie environs of the ready room Nadeau worried where and when the jinx would strike sure that it would. And it did.

On the afternoon of May 15, 1944, Bush's roommate Ensign James J. Wykes and his two crewmen, Robert E. Whalen and Charles L. Haggard were flying an Avenger on anti-submarine patrol as the task group was en route to the area north of Marcus. Suddenly, they disappeared from the SAN JACINTO's radar screen. In a brief moment they were gone without apparent reason. None of the other pilots or ships of the Task Group saw the disappearance. There were no radio transmissions from Wykes' plane. A detailed search of the area by destroyers and aircraft of the task group failed to find any debris or survivors. So far as they knew there were no Japanese units in the area. To this day, there has been no explanation for their disappearance. Japanese radio intercept operators in the Central Pacific heard the USN search effort for the missing Wykes' Avenger and reported the action to Tokyo.

Admiral Nimitz' plans called for the diversionary raids on Marcus and Wake Island to take place between May 17–23, 1944. The raids were in two phases. Phase One called for a special surface-air task unit to be "seen" by the Japanese "Doolittle picket line." Carrying out the decoy orders of Nimitz on May 18, 1944, the SAN JACINTO and its air group, along with the cruiser SAN DIEGO and four destroyers departed from the ESSEX and WASP and headed to an area off Japan's northern coast where no other USN surface warship had ventured since the start of the Pacific War.

George Bush was part of this feint. For three days, May 19–21, 1944, Bush and "The Barbara" crew scouted the supposed picket boat area but found nothing. Bush's section leader, however, had better luck. Lieutenant Richard "Rich" Houle found a 75-100 foot armed trawler and, along with Ensign Edward Boddington of the fighter squadron, bombed and strafed the vessel leaving it in a sinking condition.

Though Houle and Boddington reported no sign of a radio antenna on the stricken warship the Japanese airwaves were soon reporting a U.S. Navy task force in the North Pacific Ocean.

The Japanese military were alerted but not the way Admiral Nimitz and his staff had hoped. The Pacific Fleet commander wanted Japan to think the carriers were headed for attacks on the northern islands of Japan. Some Japanese admirals may have snapped at the decoy bait. One radio dispatch directed the destroyer NOKAZE to transmit "meaningless messages to the Northern Force." But most likely Japan was playing Nimitz' game by creating phantom fleet locations for the USN intelligence to ponder. [4]

An intercept of Japanese naval communications by Station Hypo shortly after Houle's and Boddington's May 20th attack on the trawler clearly indicated Japan was checkmating Nimitz' communications decoy chess game. On Saipan, Admiral Chuichi Nagumo warned all his units on Saipan, Guam and Tinian to be on the alert: "Two carriers and four battleships [sic] were located 140 miles from Marcus Island." Nagumo's dispatch ordered urgent unloading of vessels in port and to disperse cargo to storage areas. In an earlier dispatch of May 12, 1944, Nagumo must have sensed Nimitz' true plans for he predicted: "Great likelihood of an attack on the Marianas." [5]

Phase Two of the Nimitz decoy strategy called for bombing Wake Island on May 23, 1944. The SAN JACINTO, Bush and his fellow pilots departed the picket boat area and rejoined the ESSEX and WASP for a scheduled full day of bombing missions. The three previous days of continuous daylight patrol far off Japan's eastern coastline rendered "The Barbara" out of commission for the Wake assault. For his first scheduled bombing mission George Bush and crew were substituted into Tare 8.

Pilots of Air Group 51 were well acquainted with Wake Island. Americans knew the island as a refueling stop on the Pan American China Clipper route from Alameda, California, to Hong Kong. Wake was captured on December 23, 1941, by Japanese naval forces which had been electronically tracked from the island of Chichi Jima by listening devices at Station Hypo, Pearl Harbor. The SAN JACINTO crew remembered the heroic but failed defense of the island led by U.S. Marines under Major James P.S. Devereux and the U.S. naval garrison commanded by Commander Winfield S. Cunningham. [6]

Wake Island consists of three islets formed by a submerged volcano. The islets of Peale, Wilkes and Wake are grouped horseshoe-like around a central lagoon. A fringe reef encircles all three. During the Pan American clipper flights, which started in 1935, the lagoon was the scene of landings and takeoffs by the clippers. In 1941 the main Pan American facilities were on Peale Island while the U.S. Marine corps operated an air station on Wake Island.

As conquerer of Wake Island in December 1941, Japan took all United States military personnel and the War Department civilian workers on the island as prisoners of war. The military troops were sent to POW camps in Japan and mainland China. Most of the civilian defense workers were kept on Wake and forced to assist the Japanese in building fortifications.

Bush's Chain of Command

(Source: USN photos, National Archives)

President Franklin D. Roosevelt,
Commander-in-Chief

Admiral Ernest J. King,
Chief of Naval Operations

Admiral Chester Nimitz,
Commander of Pacific Fleet

Admiral Raymond Spruance,
Commander Fifth Fleet

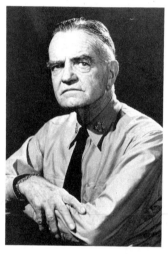

Admiral William F. Halsey,
Commander Third Fleet

Admiral Marc Mitscher,
Task Force Fifty-Eight.

Admiral John McCain,
Task Force Thirty-Eight.

Captain Harold Martin,
Commanding Officer,
USS SAN JACINTO

Lieut. Cmdr. Donald Melvin,
Commanding Officer, Torpedo
Squadron 51.

Ensign George H. W. Bush,
USN aviator and Photographic
Officer, VT-51

Bush's 1944 Adversaries

Emperor Hirohito of Japan

General Hideki Tojo,
Prime Minister of Japan

Lieutenant General Yoshio
Tachibana, Japanese Army
Forces, Chichi Jima.

Vice Admiral Kunizo Mori,
Commander, Japanese Naval
forces, Chichi Jima.

Admiral Soemu Toyoda,
Commander-in-Chief,
Imperial Japanese Navy.

Rear Admiral Shigematsu Sakaibara,
Commander Japanese forces,
Wake.

Vice Admiral Chuichi
Nagumo, Commander,
Central Pacific Fleet IJN.

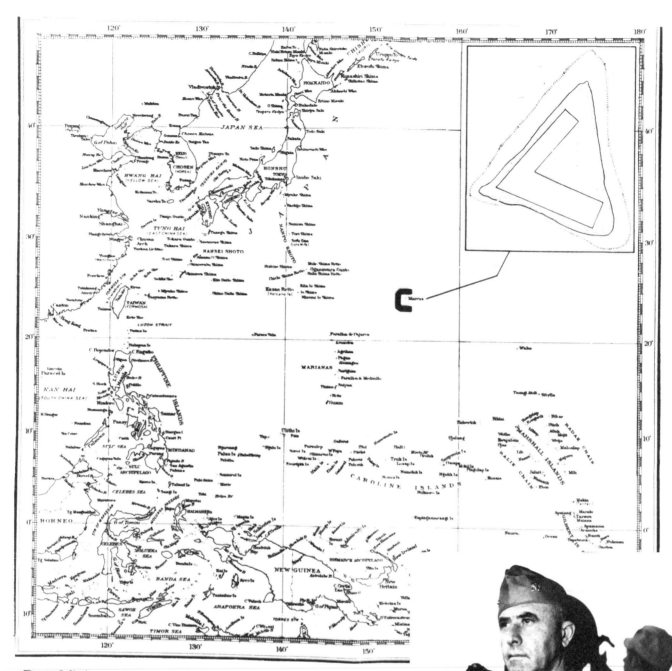

Decoy Mission

Will It Work?

This map (above) in the JICPOA "8 × 8 series," so familiar to George Bush and his fellow pilots, shows the strategic location of Marcus. Inset is diagram of the aircraft runways. *Source: JICPOA Bulletin #75-44.*

Few crew members of the SAN JACINTO, including George Bush, had ever seen the Pacific Ocean. Almost none had ever heard of Marcus Island, the tiny Japanese Central Pacific island of the Chichi Jima defensive arc. Its scouting aircraft and radio direction finder facilities were part of Japan's early warning air raid network.

As commander of the Marcus-Wake Task Group, Rear Admiral Alfred E. Montgomery (right) was George Bush's tactical boss. Just a year earlier, at Corpus Christi, Montgomery had commissioned Bush as a naval aviator. *USS ESSEX photo, National Archives.*

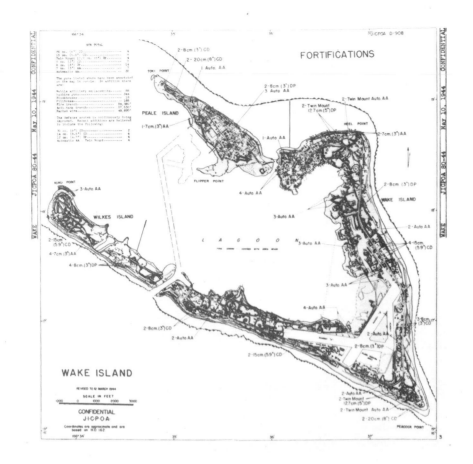

WAKE ISLAND

REVISED TO 12 MARCH 1944

SCALE IN FEET

CONFIDENTIAL
J.I.C.P.O.A.

Coordinates are approximate and are based on H.O. 162

Intelligence briefings for the Wake raid were based on these 8 × 8 maps which fit in a special pocket strapped to each pilot's thigh. For reference co-ordinates, pilots used latitude and longitude points which proved cumbersome in the heat of combat. In later operations, detailed grid maps were prepared by JICPOA. This map is based on photo sortie of October 5-6, 1943. The photo planes triggered a panic reaction by the Japanese commander, Rear Admiral Sakaibara, who believed it presaged an American invasion. The Admiral led a massacre of 98 American prisoners of war on Peale Island (upper left).

Source: JICPOA Bulletin #23A-44.

JICPOA D-633

HEEL POINT   RESTRICTED

N

WAKE ISLAND

LEGEND
- COASTAL DEFENSE GUN
- DUAL PURPOSE GUN
- HEAVY AA
- MEDIUM AA
- MACHINE GUN
- BLOCKHOUSE
- COMMAND POST
- SEARCHLIGHT
- RADAR
- FUEL STORAGE
- WATER STORAGE
- AIRCRAFT REVETMENT
- ANTI-TANK TRENCH

SCALE IN FEET

J·I·C·P·O·A

George Bush's first bombing target was assigned as the Heel Point area of Wake Island. His bombs were intended for area E-2 (upper left) which contained the headquarters of Admiral Sakaibara as well as the radio direction finding unit.

Source JICPOA Bulletin #23-A, issued February 23, 1944.

TARGET AREA WA-2

01. Two bridges connecting WAKE ISLAND to PEALE ISLAND. One of these is of U.S. Construction and the other was added by the enemy, apparently as a precaution.
02. 1300' diameter circle enclosing the Navy bivouac area consisting of a great many small frame buildings averaging about 18' by 40', most of which are deeply dug into the ground and disruptively painted.
03. Radio station, 70' by 90', of heavy concrete construction with roof probably 40' thick and earth cover, perhaps 24' thick. Five masts are in the vicinity.
04. Blockhouse of very heavy concrete construction with medium AA beside it.
05. Two buildings, one of which is a hospital 35' by 160' and the other probably a medical storehouse 27' by 160'. These buildings are not revetted.
06. Mound of earth 100' by 135', near the destroyed U.S. machine shop. This is probably an underground machine shop of undetermined construction.
07. This 1500' diameter circle includes at least 40 buildings most of which are for Navy storage and repair purposes. The majority of the buildings are deeply dug in or revetted and appear to be of frame construction.
08. Reported garage and motor repair shop 50' by 150'.
09. Reported carpenter shop 30' by 80'.
10. Two 5" DP and very heavy command post with roof and walls 40' thick.
11. 40' by 160' barracks-type building, partially damaged and perhaps not in use.
12. Two heavy A.A. with many associated small buildings.
13. Grid type radar, undamaged, high above ground on west wing of largely destroyed U.S. BOQ.
14. Long wave R.D.F. installation in usual circular pattern. To the west is the R.D.F. operational building group including a probable power plant and four other buildings averaging 25' by 40' and all revetted.
15. Three small R.D.F. buildings of frame construction.
16. Concrete blockhouse. To the west are at least six small buildings two of which are revetted.
17. Included in this 1400' diameter circle is fairly extensive fuel and ammunition storage in underground and deeply dug-in buildings. Photographic coverage is such that a detailed description is not possible.
18. Underground magazine, probably with concrete roof 40" thick.
19. Two 8cm(3") DP with command post, ready ammunition storage and three small barracks buildings.
20. Buried stores, possibly ammunition and fuel, approximately 60' by 120'.
21. Concrete blockhouse.
22. Two medium AA.
23. Battery of four CD and two concrete command posts partially buried in sand.
24. 30' by 60' revetted building.
25. Bomber dispersal area including approximately 3000' of coral surfaced taxiway in the easterly lane and 1800' in the westerly lane. Twenty-three semi-octagonal bomber revetments 90' by 70' are present. Twelve, of concrete banked with coral and with a "Z" shaped shelter built into the wall of each, are complete and the remainder are in various stages of construction.
26. Three medium AA.
27. Group of two large concrete and several small buildings comprising a water distillation or power plant and a covered water tank.
28. Three revetted buildings, each 12' by 80', for gasoline storage.
29. Three medium AA with command post and associated buildings.
30. Three probable fuel storage buildings 25' by 40' each. Loose stores are piled in the vicinity.
31. Group of three revetted buildings, the largest of which is 30' by 60', probably comprising the quarters of the gun crews for Target 32.
32. Three medium AA.
33. This 800' diameter circle includes a storage area for navy supplies. Some of the storage is underground and is not piled in trenches.

34. Group of several large buildings and two circular tanks comprising a water distillation plant. The two circular tanks have been damaged and are useless. Both of the larger buildings are reported to be of concrete construction.
35. Four medium AA, a command post and a blockhouse are in this position strategically sited for defending the bridges to PEALE ISLAND.
36. Probable headquarters for the Navy area. This is a concrete building, walls at least 24" thick and roof probably 60" thick buried in a pile of sand.

TARGET ANALYSIS SUGGESTED PRIORITY: 2

This is the HEEL POINT area of WAKE ISLAND and includes a bomber dispersal area, gasoline and ammunition storage, an RDF station, Navy bivouac and workshop areas, two water distillation plants, an underground radio station and an underground headquarters. Two strategic bridges at the north end of the area connect it with PEALE ISLAND.

Regarding the selection of priority targets: Greater than usual consideration has been given here to the size and vulnerability of individual installations, due to the fact that practically every remaining target is either small, or protected by revetments, or both.

All defenses of the area are shown on the accompanying map but nothing smaller than medium AA is numbered in the target listing. The beaches are probably mined and have been so reported.

JICPOA D-904

Bush Assigned Task

George Bush participated in the strike aimed at target "WA-2" on Wake Island. His specific objectives were items one through five and 34, 35 and 36. Before December 1941, this area was part of the U.S. Marine headquarters on Wake. The Japanese hospital area is listed under target #5 usually out-of-bounds for USN bombing. *Source: JICPOA Bulletin #75-44 issued May 10, 1944.*

CONFIDENTIAL

Joint Intelligence Center

Pacific Ocean Areas

INFORMATION BULLETIN
AND
TARGET SURVEY

MARCUS

JICPOA Bulletin No. 75-44
May 10, 1944

Information Bulletin and Target Survey for Marcus Island of May 10, 1944. George Bush not only benefited from the information but provided the photo intelligence for bulletins. *Source: JICPOA Bulletin #75-44 of May 10, 1944.*

Japanese strategy was to use Wake as a screening base to locate American naval forces that might approach the Chichi Jima defensive arc or the home islands of the Empire. Along with Marcus Island, 800 miles north-west, Wake served as an airbase for scouting aircraft and was part of Japan's far flung radio direction finder network eavesdropping on American communications.

Since December 1942, command of Japan's Wake Island garrison was under Rear Admiral Shigematsu Sakaibara who is shown in photos as a lean naval officer sporting a clipped mustache. In October 1943, Admiral Sakaibara notified Tokyo his command had executed the 98 Americans on Wake for "riotous conduct." After the war, he was charged with war crimes, tried and convicted by a US Naval military court convened by the International War Crimes Tribunal of the Far East. He was hung on the gallows at Guam on June 18, 1947. Sakaibara told the tribunal he personally had used his sword to decapitate an American prisoner of war. The 98 victims of the atrocity were buried in a mass grave on Peale Island. A similar POW butchery at Malmedy, Belgium, on December 17, 1944, by German Panzers killed 71 unarmed POWs, a well-known brutality. But the Wake massacre has been largely ignored by historians.

Admiral Sakaibara had extensive anti-aircraft batteries manned by expert gunners. At Heel Point, the site of the former US Marine barracks, medium and heavy anti-aircraft batteries were strategically sited to take aim at US aircraft attacking targets on Peale or Wake. Admiral Sakaibara's forces were George Bush's first Japanese war adversary.

Intelligence officer Ross Allen and Commander Don Melvin provided an early morning briefing to the crews participating in the Wake strikes. The unexplained loss of Wykes, Whalen and Haggard eight days earlier cast a pall throughout the ready room. The tragedy had hit home.

As pilot Lou Grab had observed months earlier, "We were the fly boys, we were invincible. Tragedy always struck the other guy."

The Bush crew was assigned target area WA-2 on Wake Island's Heel Point which included Admiral Sakaibara's underground command post, his radio transmitting and receiving station and the radio direction finder facilities. Fighters of the squadron would hit the target first, strafing the WA-2 area to keep down the anti-aircraft fire. Since "The Barbara" with its fixed camera mounts for oblique aerial photography was out of commission, Bush was unable to wear his hat as squadron photo officer. Photos taken during the Wake raid were by Ensign Dixie Mays from his Hellcat.

Lieutenant Ross Allen had the latest intelligence based on a target survey issued two weeks earlier on May 10, 1944. Allen warned: "The Wake Island complex was the most heavily fortified area per square foot in the world." Pointing to the fortification targets identified on the joint intelligence map, Allen confirmed 55 heavy and medium dual purpose and automatic anti-aircraft defense positions.

Another eight guns were unconfirmed. The bomber squadron which included Bush, would face 3″ and 5″ anti-aircraft fire from at least 55 and possibly 63 enemy guns concentrated in a four-square-mile land mass. Admiral Montgomery assigned four bombing strikes to the SAN JACINTO's Air Group starting at 0730 and ending at 1740 (7:30 a.m. to 5:40 p.m).

Gunner Nadeau did not like the May 23 plane assignment as posted on the ready room blackboard. Instead of flying from Tare Two, otherwise known as "The Barbara," the team's first combat action would be conducted from substitute Tare 8 because "The Barbara" was temporarily out of service for maintenance repairs. Expressing his "substitute" superstitions to Bush, Nadeau attempted to get Tare Two reinstated for combat flight. Surely the plane handlers who bumped him earlier in the month could work fast and get "The Barbara" ready for flight. Nadeau's plea fell on deaf ears. Bush wouldn't buy Nadeau's "bad omen" theory, insisting that Tare 8 would do the job and bring them safely back to the SAN JACINTO carrier.

Tare 8 and the Bush crew were assigned to Strike "D" with a launch time of 0730 hours. In the bomb bay, Delaney checked the 2,000 pound bomb load. There were four 500 pound general purpose bombs, two set with instant hit fuses and the other two set with a one-quarter-second delay to allow penetration of Admiral Sakaibara's underground facilities at Heel Point. Visibility was 12-15 miles with a scattering of cumulus clouds rising to 9,000 feet. From the ready room briefing Bush and the pilots knew a navy rescue submarine was in surface position south of Wake. If their bombers or fighters were seriously damaged they were instructed to head for the rescue sub, the USS STURGEON, and either parachute or try a forced water landing in the ocean. During the approach flight to Wake the fighter cover from VF-51 headed by executive officer Lieutenant Robert Jarvis broke radio silence to remind all SAN JACINTO pilots that the submarine's radio code call was "Lovely Louise" in case emergency contact was required. [7]

Commander Melvin led the division during the 44-mile flight to Wake from the SAN JACINTO. One pilot was on his left wing, the other flying right wing. Bush was

Leo "Lee" Nadeau, Bush's turret gunner, sensed an aircraft jinx based on "substitute" superstitions.
USS SAN JACINTO photo by Robert Stinnett.

assigned to what he called the "sniffer position" at Melvin's rear below the tail section.

The four torpedo bombers were escorted by eight Hellcats. They rendezvoused with the main attack group of 70 aircraft furnished by the ESSEX and WASP. The raid plan called for the bombers to climb to 9,000 feet. Then the dive bombing would begin from the northeast.

Commander Melvin ordered his Avenger bombers to push over into a 50-degree dive, eventually gaining a speed of 300 knots. Upon reaching 2,000 feet, Bush could clearly see his Heel Point target in the bomb sight and released all four 500 pound bombs. In his official report, skipper Melvin said the bombs were observed to hit in the assigned target areas, but dust and smoke and the low altitude of retirement prevented observation of bomb damage. None of the Avengers were hit by what Melvin called "meager" AA fire. The entire bombing run, which plunged from 9,000 feet to nearly 1,000 feet, took about 28 seconds. After regrouping, George Bush piloted Tare 8 back to the SAN JACINTO and turned the bomber over to Ensign Doug West for the afternoon strike on Wake. Tare 8 was West's regularly assigned aircraft.

Upon exiting from the substitute craft, Nadeau wondered what jinxes had been conjured up by the switching of crews. The answer soon came. It was West and his crewmembers, Joseph Foshee and H.F. McHugh, who would get the scare of their lives from the jinx.

During the afternoon strike Admiral Sakaibara's AA guns hit Tare 8, knocking out the electrical controls to the bomb bay and turret gun. The hit, fortunately, was not fatal. West had no need for "Lovely Louise," the rescue sub, and piloted the bomber back to the SAN JACINTO where, it was discovered, a piece of shrapnel had severed the main electrical conduit. The piece of shrapnel was embedded into the fuselage and upon examination was found to be a product of the U.S. Army ordnance factory. Tare 8 had been hit by U.S. Army shells confiscated on Wake by the Japanese conquerors.

Japanese casualties as reported by Sakaibara were 5 killed and up to 50 wounded during air raids on the island which took place between May 18–26, 1944. The tally included bombings from B-24's as well as the carrier task group. The Marcus raid drained Japanese ordnance. On May 25, Yokosuka Naval Base advised the commander on Marcus that 328,000 rounds of anti-aircraft shells were being sent by four picket boats and a small cargo vessel, Unkai Maru #7. Station Hypo intercepted the message which revealed

Date	Type of Machine	Number of Machine	Duration of Flight	Character of Flight	Pilot	PASSENGERS	REMARKS
2	TBM-1C	25123	1.7	G	Ens. Bush	Self + Delaney	Kaneohe Bay field, Hawaii
3	"	"	5.0	N A/S	"	" "	1c1 —Kaneohe Bay field to ship
5	"	16935	3.8	H-K	"	" "	1cat 1c1 San Jacinto
6	"	25124	3.7	A/S	"	" "	" " San Jacinto
8	"	25123	3.1	GHK	"	" "	" " Arrived at Majuro (MARSHALL Is.)
17	"	16931	3.4	A/S	"	" "	" " San Jacinto
19	"	25123	3.8	ferry	"	" "	" " San Jacinto
20	"	"	4.0	J	"	" "	" " San Jacinto
21	"	"	3.7	J	"	" "	" " San Jacinto
★23	"	16955	3.2	G	"	" "	STRIKE ON WAKE IS.
29	"	25123	2.6	G	"	" "	1cat 1c1 San Jacinto MAJURO AREA
30	"	"	1.4	H-K	"	" "	San Jacinto MAJURO AREA PRE DAWN

May, 1944

TORPEDO SQUADRON - 51
Brought Forward 13.4.4
This Month.... Pilot.... Pass 58.4 Total 39.9
Total to Date 173.8
I certify that the foregoing flight record is correct.
L. H. Nadeau
Signature
Approved:
George H. W. Bush
Lt. Comdr., USN, Comdg.

Total time to date.

Jinx fears jumped out at Lee Nadeau when he viewed his May 1944 flight log. The Bush crew used substitutes 33% of the time, a sure sign something terrible was in the offing, according to Nadeau. "The Barbara" (Tare Two) is listed in the log as TBM-1C, number 25123. The log is attested to by George H. W. Bush USN. *Courtesy Lee Nadeau. Copy by Robert Stinnett.*

the route of the Unkai Maru and the picket boats was via Chichi Jima. On August 4, 1944, the Unkai Maru and the boats were sunk by U.S. forces as they staged through Chichi Jima. [8]

In his post-attack report, Admiral Montgomery was critical of the pilots of the SAN JACINTO, ESSEX and WASP for missing what he said was 95% of their assigned Wake targets. He dismissed the failure of hitting the combat targets to "inexperienced pilots." The Admiral was more concerned with the pilots breaking radio silence. He said said he heard the broadcast "There's Lovely Louise" over the flagship's radio and was concerned that the "thoughtless transmission" may have provided Admiral Sakaibari's radio direction finder crews with location of the rescue submarine and endangered the STURGEON and its crew. [9]

Japanese military strategists were not fooled by the Wake-Marcus Island diversion raid nor the American deceptive communications engineered by Admiral Nimitz. A small portion of a land-based Japanese air arm was diverted north to the Kuriles and a warning went out to naval units in the North Pacific, but the main force of the Japanese navy including all its operating carriers, never moved from protected anchorages south of the Philippines where they had a

source for bunker oil and aviation gasoline. This force lay waiting for Admiral Nimitz and Admiral Mitscher to reveal their strategy.

Early in 1944, Japan's military leaders were unanimous that a Mariana Island invasion would precipitate a struggle that would decide the fate of the Empire. The staff of General Hideki Tojo, Japan's Prime Minister and war architect, expected an Allied offensive on the Chichi Jima defensive arc.

Two areas were possible targets of an American attack: the Mariana Islands midway in the arc or the Palau group at the south end. General Tojo believed the Marianas would be the next U.S. objective because Admiral Nimitz could build long-range bomber bases at Saipan and Tinian islands. From these bases the B-29's "Superfortress" could reach the home islands of the Empire with a full bomb load. Tojo had received intelligence reports of the new American bomber whose huge bomb capacity could wreak havoc on Japan's countryside. The first B-29 raid on Japan took place June 15, 1944, bombing the island of Kyushu but did little damage. These Superfortresses of the U.S. Army Air Force were based in Chengtu, China.

Beginning in late January 1944 seasoned Japanese army troops were transferred from Manchuria to bolster Nipponese defense capabilities along the Chichi Jima arc. The water journey by Japanese transport vessels took the troops across the Philippine Sea, an area heavily patrolled by American submarines. Other re-enforcements were dispatched by ship convoy from the home islands.

The movement of these Japanese army units from Manchuria was known in advance to the United States through the communication intercepts obtained by Station Hypo at Pearl Harbor. Pacific Fleet submarines, alerted by Hypo, pounced on the Manchurian troop movements sinking one out of three transports and damaging others. [10]

American military folklore, bolstered by the 1937 Amelia Earhart legend, pictured an efficient Japanese military bastion lurking in the Central Pacific islands prior to 1941. Earhart, America's most famous woman pilot, was on an around the world flight in July 1937 when she and her aircraft disappeared in the Central Pacific. Reports later suggested she was making a surreptitious photographic fly-over of the Japanese Central Pacific islands for American intelligence. [11]

Her purpose, the reports speculated, was to obtain reconnaissance of military bases including the Truk Naval Anchorage which was supposed to rival Pearl Harbor. These reports proved to be inaccurate. With the exception of Chichi Jima, Japan did not begin construction of major military facilities in the Pacific islands until summer of 1940. Improvements to the Mariana defenses began in early 1944. The late awakening by Japan's militarists to lack of Central Pacific offensive bases had a simple explanation. Their plans envisioned winning the Pacific war in six months and did not provide for an extended defensive conflict. When the six month's strategy failed, some proponents, in retribution, were dumped on Saipan. A notable one was Admiral Chuichi Nagumo. As the successful commander of the Pearl Harbor raid but the loser at Midway, Nagumo was demoted to Saipan in 1944 to lead a ragtag Central Pacific force of minor war ships. Nagumo died on Saipan during the battle. [12]

Scene inside the SAN JACINTO's fighter pilot ready room, May 23, 1944, as intelligence officer, Edward C. Brewster (standing) provides the latest data on Japanese defenses of Wake. Pilot plane assignments listed on the blackboard indicate the radio call sign that day was "Panzer." At right, on bulkhead, are intelligence photos of Japanese aircraft and warships. Seat-type parachutes rest on backs of the ready room lounge chairs.

USS SAN JACINTO photo, National Archives.

Bombs explode on the Japanese airfield, Wake Island, May 23, 1944. The Heel Point target area of George Bush is at right center. *USS SAN JACINTO photo by Dixie Mays.*

The "airdales" of the SAN JACINTO's flight deck crew ready Fox 18 for its May 23, 1944 mission on Wake Island, while others relax on the port catwalks. Identification numbers for the fighters were painted on the strut plates, not on cowling as was done with the Avengers. Harold Matthews was assigned to Fox 18 for this mission; Ray J. Swanson piloted Fox 19.
USS SAN JACINTO photo, National Archives.

Ultra Intercepts:
Japanese React to the Bush Raid

Pacific Fleet planners hoped the Marcus-Wake decoy raids would cause Japan to shift its forces to the North Pacific before the coming Saipan invasion, Operation Forager. Station Hypo intercepted a Japanese naval dispatch (opposite) to all ships making the distinction of "shipboard" planes attacking Marcus Island on May 20, 1944. The Naval headquarters from Tokyo, speculated that a "striking force" might be in the vicinity." The Base Force 5 commander (NO MO 2) on Saipan was not fooled, as the bottom dispatch indicates. He was correct about two carriers attacking Marcus (ESSEX and WASP) but there were no battleships. He ordered Guam (Omiyajima), Saipan and Tenian [sic] to expedite defense construction and to disperse newly arrived materials. This dispatch, which refers to USN bombings at 1100 hours (11am), was intercepted at 1340 hours (1:30 pm), May 20, 1944 at Station Hypo.

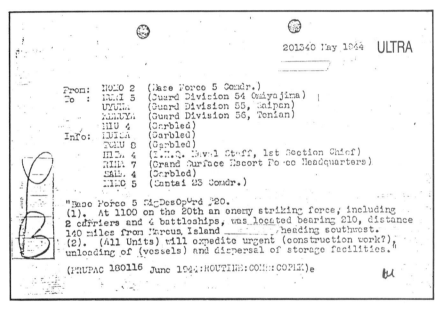

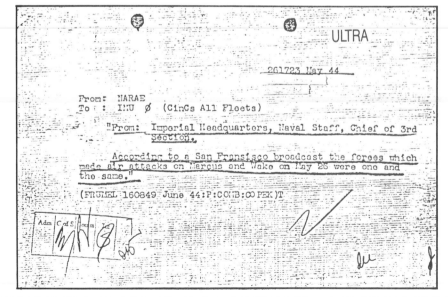

Japan's naval intelligence used regular commercial broadcasts from San Francisco as source material for the Marcus-Wake raid. The notation at lower left indicates Nimitz' chief of staff Charles McMorris saw this report, but not the Admiral.

Source: All intercepts in SRN series, National Archives.

PART IV

June 6, 1944, was a momentous day on both war fronts for the United States. It was D-Day on the beaches of Normandy. Landing craft spilled out allied troops on the European continent as the land march on Germany's Nazis began. Half a world away, the massive Task Force 58 together with other units of the Pacific Fleet sortied from Majuro Atoll. The force included more than 600 vessels, 2,000 aircraft and 300,000 Navy, Marine and Army men. Heading for Operation Forager and the direct assault on the Chichi Jima arc they intended to capture Saipan, Guam and Tinian. Fourteen months into the future, Tinian would be the launch base for the atomic bombing of Hiroshima and Nagasaki.

The SAN JACINTO, was part of a task group commanded by Rear Admiral J. W. Reeves Jr., and included three other carriers, the USS ENTERPRISE, USS LEXINGTON and the USS PRINCETON. Rounding out the warships in this impressive task group were five cruisers, seven battleships, 16 destroyers and the USS INDIANAPOLIS, flag ship of Admiral Raymond Spruance, commander of the Fifth Fleet. Rear Admiral Reeves was based on the ENTERPRISE. Vice Admiral Marc Mitscher, heading Task Force 58, had his flag flying from the LEXINGTON. The presence of the top admirals in the Task Group was regarded as "heavy duty" by the sailors of the SAN JACINTO. In the adjoining sea lanes and spreading out over a 50-75 mile area were the other three Task Groups.

On the bridge of his flagship, Admiral Spruance reviewed his plan for Operation Forager. He read intercepted Japanese communications indicating the strong possibility of a major Japanese response to the Saipan invasion. In Pearl Harbor radio intercepts and radio direction finder fixes placed the enemy fleet carrier forces south of the Philippines. Contingency plans were drawn up to engage the carrier fleet should it become a threat to the Saipan invasion forces.

Aboard the SAN JACINTO a future president of the United States reviewed the flight plans for his missions in Operation Forager. Bush and all other aviators of Task Force 58 would support the landings by U.S. Marine and Army units that would invade Saipan on June 15, 1944.

In his operations order Admiral Reeves defined the mission of the carrier Task Group: "DESTROY ENEMY AIRCRAFT AND AIRCRAFT FACILITIES AT SAIPAN AND TINIAN BY REPEATED AIR STRIKES AND SHIP BOMBARDMENT AND PROVIDE AIR SUPPORT FOR THE ATTACK FORCES IN ORDER TO ASSIST IN THE CAPTURE AND OCCUPATION OF SAIPAN, TINIAN AND GUAM." Pre-invasion air strikes began on the afternoon of June 11, catching the Japanese by surprise. The attack destroyed 150 aircraft on the ground and in the air.

Bush and Squadron VT-51 were not assigned to these opening strikes. Much to their dislike they were on anti-submarine patrol in the waters off the Marianas. They considered these three-and-four hour flights boring. At first the squadron was not "ring wise" to their humdrum assignment of peering down at the water looking for Japanese subs. They complained that the big ESSEX class carriers and their air groups were given the more exciting bombing and strafing attacks on the Marianas.

In these pre-invasion strikes aerial photo intelligence conducted by Task Force 58 played a crucial role in keeping the commanders of Operation Forager informed of Japanese counter tactics on the ground. As photo officer of the squadron Bush had the responsibility of coordinating aerial photographic coverage of Japanese targets. Strategic orders for aerial photo coverage were issued by the task group commander, Admiral Reeves, to the SAN JACINTO. Then Captain Martin passed them to his photo team which included Bush, Lieutenant (j.g.) Jerome Pasto, the ship's photo interpretation officer and Ensign Richard Names, the ship's photo officer in charge of the photo lab and equipment.

Two types of large format aerial cameras were available to Bush for photo reconnaissance: hand-held by pilots and aircrewmen and fixed installations mounted in the belly or fuselage of both the Avenger and Hellcat. Lens shutter control of the fixed cameras was electronically controlled from the cockpit by the pilot. In addition, gun cameras using 16mm black and white motion picture film were synchronized with the machine guns of all squadron aircraft. When the pilot or aircrewman fired the guns, the camera was triggered automatically.

Aerial photography duty was voluntary in Air Group 51. John Delaney, Bush's radioman, tail gunner and bombadier wanted to operate the hand-held K-20 aerial camera from his position in the belly of the Avenger. Delaney, in effect, was Bush's in-air "truth squad" because he brought back photographic proof of damage inflicted on the enemy for evaluation. The photos were first reviewed by the SAN JACINTO's

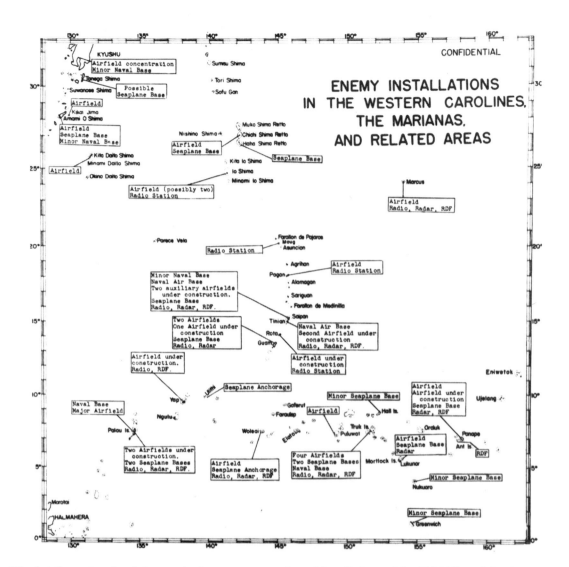

Pilot briefings pinpointed the massive Japanese army and naval installations of the Chichi Jima defensive arc. The JICPOA map of enemy installations pictured a vast array of Japanese air and naval bases poised to stop Task Force 58. Japanese officials shuttled replacement aircraft from the empire through Chichi Jima and Iwo Jima to Saipan and points beyond. *Source: JICPOA Bulletin #73-44 of May 10, 1944.*

041044 June 44

Japan's code breakers had difficulty penetrating U.S. Naval communications and relied, in part, on United States commercial radio broadcasts for intelligence. In this intercepted dispatch sent to Admiral Nimitz, Station Hypo's cryptologists suggest, tongue in cheek, that CBS radio news has been compromised.

Source: SRN series, National Archives.

From: TORORO Ø (Communication Unit Tokyo)
To : SANOHO 2 (Southeast Fleet and 8th Fleet CinC's)

"Reenoipherment of SMS 0221(10?).
Gist of U.S. Radio broadcasts up to 1st June.
1. Kwajalein is being equipped as a fleet air base.
2. Blanks
   Landing craft Infantry /LCI/ with armament already installed found very effective in raids in submarines engaged in transportation.
   Land fighters very effectively employed in landings
3. The Indo-(Burma?) campaign blanks.
4. The Army blank(jungle?) war school on Oahu has turned out 100,000 men.
5. Converted carriers and the light cruiser Milwaukee blanks with regard to the Anglo-American dividing of the Italian Fleet."

-(FRUPAC 150416 June 44:P:COMB:COPEK)T
LOCAL COMMENT: Reference not on file.

COLUMBIA BROADCASTING SYSTEM IS APPARENTLY COMPROMISED

Bush Targets On Saipan

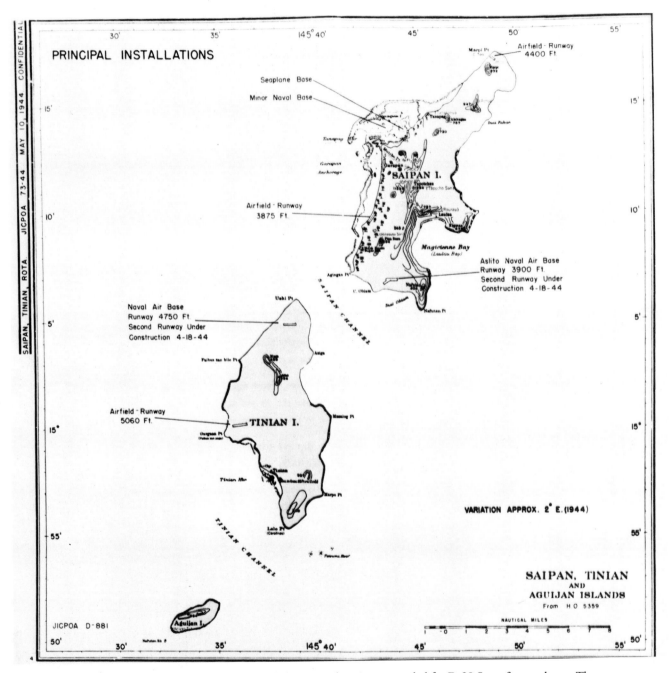

The airfields and level plateaus of Saipan and Tinian (above) were needed for B-29 Superfortress bases. These islands and Guam would also serve as a planned launch base for the invasion of Japan. The Aslito Naval Air Base on Saipan was one of the largest in Japan's Central Pacific installations. *Source: JICPOA Bulletin #73-44 of May 10, 1944.*

The USS SAN JACINTO leads Task Force 58 toward the Saipan invasion in this photo taken June 9, 1944. An Avenger is poised on the catapult ready to be launched. In left background is the USS LEXINGTON, flagship of the Task Force and a destroyer of the screen. *USS SAN JACINTO photo by Robert Stinnett from TBM flown by Ensign George H. W. Bush.*

Japanese communications operators at work at the radio headquarters, Saipan. This unit was one of Bush's bombing targets.

Captured photo from JICPOA Bulletin #71-44.

The underground radio communications center on Saipan, a Bush target, escaped bomb damage. Banks of receivers line wall at left.

Photo by JICPOA in Bulletin #71-44.

Tropical landscaping decorates the Administration building at the Aslito Air Base prior to bombings by Task Force 58.

Captured photo published in JICPOA bulletin #71-44.

```
SA M  MO (#5 Comm. Unit, SAIPAN)
DE:
FU A  HI (TOKYO Comm. Unit)
- I RA  W39   NR 589                        12    2 00
- - - - - - - - - - - - -

From:      MO  TO  HI  NA      (?)
Action:    A   MAMG  AF        (Japanese Ships in Inner So. Seas)

06/111728/I   1944            (TOI 06/112040/I on --- kcs)


# 99?


        At 1150, sighted an enemy striking force
including carriers in position 13-20 North, 147-40 East.

        At about 1300  SAIPAN, TINIAN, GUAM and ROTA
were attacked.
```

Japan Sights Task Force 58

An unknown Japanese unit spotted Task Force 58 at 1150 hours June 11 as the huge armada approached the Mariana islands of Saipan, Tinian, Guam and Rota. This warning (left) from Radio Tokyo apparently was ignored by Admiral Chuichi Nagumo as aircraft of TF-58 caught Japanese defense forces by surprise in the 1300 hour (1pm) attack. The SAN JACINTO (below) was assigned anti-submarine patrols and did not participate in the June 11 bombings.

Source: Intercept, SRN series, National Archives.
Photo of SAN JACINTO by USS LEXINGTON, National Archives.

At least eleven carriers of Task Force 58 can be seen in this photo as the war ships turn into the wind for launching of aircraft. *Source: U.S. Navy photo, National Archives.*

SAIPAN ISLAND TARGET AREA S-II

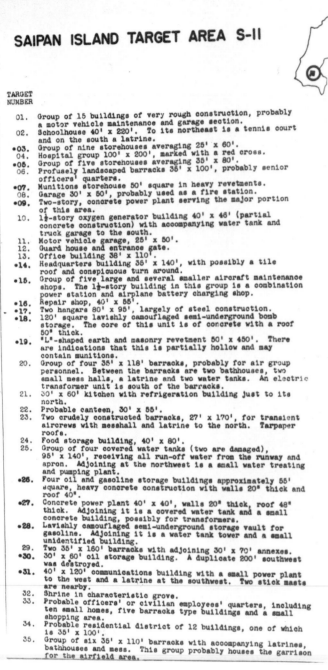

TARGET NUMBER

01. Group of 15 buildings of very rough construction, probably a motor vehicle maintenance and garage section.
02. Schoolhouse 40' x 220'. To its northeast is a tennis court and on the south a latrine.
•03. Group of nine storehouses averaging 25' x 60'.
04. Hospital group 100' x 200', marked with a red cross.
•05. Group of five storehouses averaging 35' x 80'.
06. Profusely landscaped barracks 35' x 100', probably senior officers' quarters.
•07. Munitions storehouse 50' square in heavy revetments.
08. Garage 30' x 50', probably used as a fire station.
•09. Two-story, concrete power plant serving the major portion of this area.
10. 1½-story oxygen generator building 40' x 46' (partial concrete construction) with accompanying water tank and truck garage to the south.
11. Motor vehicle garage, 25' x 50'.
12. Guard house and entrance gate.
13. Office building 38' x 110'.
•14. Headquarters building 35' x 140', with possibly a tile roof and conspicuous turn around.
•15. Group of five large and several smaller aircraft maintenance shops. The 1½-story building in this group is a combination power station and airplane battery charging shop.
•16. Repair shop, 40' x 55'.
•17. Two hangars 80' x 95', largely of steel construction.
•18. 120' square lavishly camouflaged semi-underground bomb storage. The core of this unit is of concrete with a roof 50" thick.
•19. "L"-shaped earth and masonry revetment 50' x 450'. There are indications that this is partially hollow and may contain munitions.
20. Group of four 35' x 118' barracks, probably for air group personnel. Between the barracks are two bathhouses, two small mess halls, a latrine and two water tanks. An electric transformer unit is south of the barracks.
21. 30' x 60' kitchen with refrigeration building just to its north.
22. Probable canteen, 30' x 55'.
23. Two crudely constructed barracks, 27' x 170', for transient aircrews with messhall and latrine to the north. Tarpaper roofs.
24. Food storage building, 40' x 80'.
25. Group of four covered water tanks (two are damaged), 95' x 140', receiving all run-off water from the runway and apron. Adjoining at the northwest is a small water treating and pumping plant.
•26. Four oil and gasoline storage buildings approximately 55' square, heavy concrete construction with walls 20" thick and roof 40".
•27. Concrete power plant 40' x 40', walls 20" thick, roof 48" thick. Adjoining it is a covered water tank and a small concrete building, possibly for transformers.
•28. Lavishly camouflaged semi-underground storage vault for gasoline. Adjoining it is a water tank tower and a small unidentified building.
29. Two 35' x 160' barracks with adjoining 30' x 70' annexes.
•30. 30' x 60' oil storage building. A duplicate 200' southwest was destroyed.
•31. 40' x 120' communications building with a small power plant to the west and a latrine at the southwest. Two stick masts are nearby.
32. Shrine in characteristic grove.
33. Probable officers' or civilian employees' quarters, including ten small homes, five barracks type buildings and a small shopping area.
34. Probable residential district of 12 buildings, one of which is 35' x 100'.
35. Group of six 35' x 110' barracks with accompanying latrines, bathhouses and mess. This group probably houses the garrison for the airfield area.

Scale in Feet
500   0   500'   1000'

TARGET ANALYSIS SUGGESTED PRIORITY: 6

This area includes most of the service buildings and other installations associated with ASLITO airfield, including at least 15 motor vehicle earth revetments, 28 cylindrical concrete water collecting tanks and 22 earth or concrete air raid shelters. Buildings are of wooden construction with galvanized iron or tarpaper roofs and are one story high unless otherwise stated.

There is an excellent network of roads, mostly of new hard-surfaced construction.

Storage, administrative and power facilities are extensive and dispersal is not pronounced. The dimensions of this area are slightly over one-half mile in each direction. However, prevailing winds are usually insufficient to suggest extensive use of incendiaries.

TARGET	%wt.	BOMBS	NOSE FUZE	TAIL FUZE
14 thru 17	60%	100-250-500# GP / 350# DB	Inst. Inst.	Non-delay None
	40%	100-250-500# GP	.1	.01
09,10,18,19 26,28	100%	500-1000# SAP	.1	.025
01,03,05, 20,29,35	100%	100-250-500# GP / 350# DB	Inst. Inst.	Non-delay None

SUGGESTED BOMBS AND FUZINGS BASED UPON ANALYSIS OF CONSTRUCTION AND ARRANGEMENT OF TARGETS

SELECT BOMB SIZES GIVING MAXIMUM LOAD FOR EACH PLANE, SMALLER SIZES IF THE SAME TOTAL WEIGHT IS POSSIBLE.

STRAFE: All building groups except target 04.

Bush 20 Years Old
Birthday Bombing of Saipan

On his 20th birthday Ensign Bush was sent on a bombing mission. He was assigned target area #S-11 on the northern edge of Aslito Airfield, Saipan. Almost all buildings shown in the inset were hit including the communications unit circled as item #31. Robert McIlwaine, Bush's fighter escort, was killed in action after a direct hit on the underground fuel storage (item #28). His Hellcat was hit by the anti-aircraft guns located just south of item #25. Aviators were ordered not to attack the hospital located in circle #4.

Source for S-11: JICPOA Bulletin #66-44.

George Bush and his fellow pilots bombed the Aslito Airfield installations shown in center right foreground. Dark areas are caused by cloud shadow. *Source: US Navy photo by USS ENTERPRISE.*

photo interpretation officer, then forwarded to the intelligence center at Pearl Harbor for dissemination to the entire fleet. Bush also arranged for K-20 cameras to be issued to other VT pilots and aircrewmen.

"The Barbara" had been equipped at Norfolk, Va., for vertical and oblique mapping missions using fixed installation cameras called F-56. However, aerial photo tactics involving mapping and large format photography were changed by the time of Operation Forager. The aerial photo missions of the Task Force were switched to the more maneuverable Hellcats of the fighter squadrons. To accomplish this switch-over, fighter pilots, Ensigns Dixie Mays and Thomas Hollowell, joined the Bush photo team in Air Group 51. Hand-held photography was still continued from the SAN JACINTO's Avengers, however.

Photographs taken during aerial strikes produced valuable tactical intelligence by confirming damage claims and revealing details of Japanese military facilities. Pre-attack photos of the targets were used for strategic planning in selecting suitable invasion beaches and estimating enemy military strength.

Pre-invasion photo intelligence for Operation Forager began in February 1944. Orders for the photography came from Major General Holland M. Smith who headed the Marine Corps amphibious force. Because of the high losses at Tarawa in November 1943, General Smith vowed to minimize future casualty lists with better evaluation of targeted invasion beaches and off shore reefs. With this strategy in mind, he asked Admiral Nimitz to supply detailed aerial reconnaissance of Saipan, Tinian and Guam. These three islands were the major targets of Operation Forager. In his specifications to Admiral Nimitz, General Smith wanted high priority photo reconnaissance flights flown on D minus 90, D minus 60,

D minus 30 and D minus 15, then continuous photo coverage during the actual invasion process. To translate the "D minus" military jargon, begin with June 15, 1944, as "D" day or invasion day. "D minus 90" meant three months prior or March 15, 1944; "D minus 60" is April 15, 1944, and so on. [1]

In compliance with the general's request, Task Force 58 was dispatched by Admiral Nimitz on D minus 113 day, February 22-23, 1944, to conduct raids and photo intelligence sorties on the Southern Marianas including Guam, Saipan, Tinian and other smaller isles. The remaining photo dates requested by General Smith were not attempted by Task Force 58 because of other military commitments. However, Admiral Nimitz arranged for land-based aerial photography during the D-60 and D-30 time frame. Subsequently, the Marine Corps said the lack of aerial photography from Task Force 58 hampered planning of the Saipan attack and, in their post-attack report, issued a five-point criticism of U. S. Naval photo intelligence operations. Major Carl Hoffman of Marine headquarters staff cited five points as handicapping the Marine Corps planning of Forager: (1) Inadequate photo coverage; (2) Lack of timely intelligence information ; (3) Faulty land contour maps based on incomplete photo coverage; (4) Misleading of Marine Corps planners; (5) Scarcity of detailed information on enemy strength. [2]

Admitting that the alleged "inadequate" February intelligence photography was received, then augmented by land-based photo flights on April 18 and May 28, 1944, Major Hoffman dismissed the later photo sorties as "too little and too late." "The initial assault troops which hit Saipan's beaches never received the photo intelligence," according to Major Hoffman. The Marine Corps also said they had received eye-level views of Saipan taken offshore from the U.S. submarine, USS GREENLING. Unfortunately the GREENLING apparently had photographed the wrong invasion beach, according to the Marines.

Records of the intelligence center at Admiral Nimitz' headquarters refute the Marine Corps indictment of Navy reconnaissance photography at Saipan. Some of the Marine generals in charge of the island-hopping campaigns adopted a position of "blaming Navy aerial photography" to explain high battle losses. This stance was also used at Peleliu and Iwo Jima.

Five comprehensive intelligence bulletins were issued between May 1-15, 1944 to all American forces participating in Operation Forager. In the target analysis contained in these bulletins, photo interpreters pointed out 35 different Japanese positions and added detailed descriptions. Bush's briefing was based on

The Lone Star flag of Texas flew from the yardarm of the USS SAN JACINTO when the flattop was engaged in battle. *Source: USS SAN JACINTO photo, National Archives.*

these bulletins and included examination of the targets. In fact, Bush's Saipan briefing materials show that the joint intelligence center at Pearl Harbor warned General Smith of extensive Japanese beach defenses and inland fortifications. [3]

The SAN JACINTO and the combat neophytes of the Bush aerial photo team, once on the scene, continually expanded the reconnaissance file with added photo warnings. They went about their combat missions unaware of the Marine Corps-Navy photo intelligence dispute regarding Saipan. On the orders of Admiral Reeves, the SAN JACINTO's Task Group commander, pre-invasion photo sorties of the Saipan landing areas were flown by Ensign Mays. From Bush's Avenger, John Delaney took low level obliques for damage assessment evaluation. In one flight, Bush flew through smoke and debris as Delaney snapped pictures of undamaged Japanese defenses along the Charan Kanoa invasion beach. One photo shows a tall

Sniffer Position for Bush

George Bush joked about being assigned the "sniffer position" during combat flight. He defined "sniffer" as being below and to the rear of skipper Melvin's Tare 1. Tare Two, Bush's plane, is in lower right corner, the "sniffer position."

Source: USS SAN JACINTO photo, National Archives.

George Bush used this JICPOA grid map to locate his targets on Aslito Airfield. With fellow pilots he bombed the areas in #130 and #121. Robert McIlwaine hit Japanese aviation fuel dumps at #130-U x #121-A. The military importance of communication-command centers was never lost on George Bush. During the Persian Gulf War in 1991 he authorized the bombing of similar facilities operated by Iraq. *Source: JICPOA Bulletin ATF-77-A.*

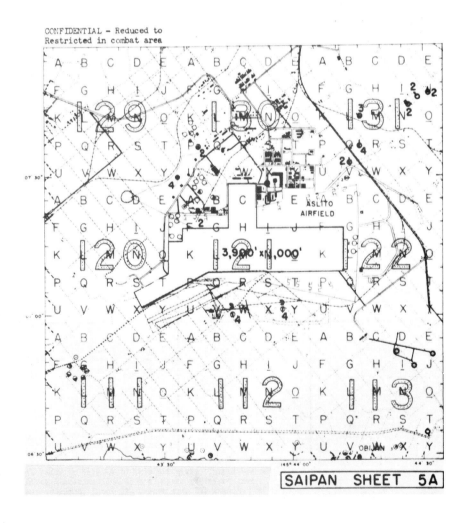

CONFIDENTIAL - Reduced to Restricted in combat area

SAIPAN SHEET 5A

tower used by the Japanese defenders to report on movements of U. S. Marine troops. Although the photos were rushed to the Marine Corps they took no action to destroy the tower for several days.

June 12, 1944, was the first full day of attacks by Task Force 58. Aerial combat and photo missions of Saipan were coetaneous. These bombing and strafing missions were designed to soften up the defenses for the scheduled invasion set for June 15, 1944. Photographs taken during the missions would allow the admirals and generals to evaluate the reported damage. June 12 was "D-minus 3 day" and George Bush's 20th birthday. In the squadron ready room air intelligence officer Lieutenant Martin E. Kilpatrick laid out Bush's combat role: a bombing mission on the big Aslito Airbase and surrounding facilities on the southern coast of Saipan. [4]

Bush made mental notes of the briefing. He would be catapulted from the SAN JACINTO carrying a load of 500 lb. bombs. The plan was to fly 75 miles with seven other Avengers led by squadron skipper Donald Melvin. Twelve Hellcats of the fighter squadron would escort the eight bombers and precede the bombing attack with a strafing run on targets at the north edge of Aslito. Strafing by the fighters would knock out Japanese anti-aircraft gun emplacements or at least scatter the gunners from their posts, enabling the Avengers to make a fast bombing run and elude the anti-aircraft fire.

As usual the Bush team included Nadeau in the gunner's position and Delaney at the bombadier's post in the belly. That was the good news. The bad news for Nadeau was they were not flying in "The Barbara." It had been grounded by engine trouble. The jinx omens were nearly overwhelming Nadeau. On June 9, Captain Martin had ordered Bush to fly two of the SAN JACINTO's ship's photographers, Howard Rowe and Robert Stinnett, the author, on a special photo mission. These two June 9 substitutions were considered by Nadeau as a double whammy.

Then June 12 brought more ill omens. Because "The Barbara" was grounded for repairs Bush, Nadeau and Delaney were substituted into pilot Lou Grab's bomber. Grab had flown the craft earlier on a predawn raid over Saipan. As they climbed into Grab's bomber for its second flight of the day, Nadeau noticed the Navy's assigned plane number was 16928. A terrible number, Nadeau thought as he entered the figures in his flight log book, because the sum of $1 + 6 + 9 + 2 + 8$ equaled 26 and the second flight of the day, in Nadeau's conjure, meant a divisor of two. This resulted in the unlucky number 13. Nadeau decided

this was a third bad omen on Bush's birthday.

As for Bush, he paid no heed to the soothsayers' fears as he guided his bomber from the SAN JACINTO to Saipan.

The bombing of Saipan began at 0845 (8:45 a.m.) after a 30-minute flight from the SAN JACINTO. The eight Avengers of the flight were in two divisions of four bombers each escorted by 12 squadron Hellcats. After launching, the bombers and fighters climbed to 10,000 feet. Aslito Airbase, one of Japan's major air installations, came into view as they neared the southern coast of Saipan. The flight attack plan called for the fighter escort to attack the fuel facilities of Aslito which were protected by Japanese anti-aircraft emplacements. Bush's group was assigned target "S-11," an area on the northern fringe of the airbase which contained major aero services such as fuel dump and the radio command post.

As he was beginning his dive from 6000 feet Bush could see the machine guns of the preceding fighters spraying the target area on the north side of the air field. Each of the 12 fighter escorts had six machine guns mounted on the wings bringing a total of 72 guns to bear on the Japanese manning the anti-aircraft positions.

When it reached pullout altitude of about 2,000 feet Fox 22 piloted by Ensign Robert D. Mc Ilwaine, one of Bush's escorts, was hit by the intense and accurate Japanese anti-aircraft barrage. The fighter plane disentegrated in mid-air and Bush saw the plane crash and burn on the ground. Ensign Mc Ilwaine was unable to bail out and the disastrous crash produced a large explosion followed by furious burning of gasoline.

Bush pressed home his attack on the radio command post, releasing all four bombs at the target. He eluded the heavy anti-aircraft fire then guided the bomber to the safety of the Saipan coastal waters. Here he rendezvoused with the air group's fighters and bombers and returned to the SAN JACINTO, landing aboard at 1050 (10:50 a.m.). In the safety of the ready room, Nadeau wondered: "Why Mc Ilwaine?" All the jinx signs pointed to trouble during the Bush flight but Nadeau expected the hex signs to affect his bomber. What did the future have in store for them? He was certain other hexes were waiting.

Bush's dive bombing attack on Aslito Airbase did not directly hit the Japanese radio command post but did sever the radio control lines, temporarily knocking out radio communications to the Saipan and Chichi Jima network radio stations. The radio log of the command post was captured several weeks later on Saipan and the translation provides the Japanese account of the bombing raid. The anonymous author said the raid began at 0820 hours, forcing the radio station off the air as operators retreated to prepared underground shelters. In the dive bombing attack radio control wires to several transmitters were severed, cutting off communication with other Japanese radio stations of the Chichi Jima defensive arc network including Palau, Woleai, Truk, Manila and Okinawa.

Radio service to Tokyo was not affected. None of the buildings of the command post or crucial radio towers was hit. By 2300 hours (11pm that night) the control wires were repaired and radio service to the network was restored according to the Japanese radio log. [6]

Other than receiving the birthday afternoon off there were no festivities for Bush and his crew. The next day was June 13 and the superstitious Nadeau was not pleased with the flight omens. "The Barbara" was still in repair status and Nadeau noted that he, Bush and Delaney were scheduled for a pre-dawn strike on the principal invasion beach on Saipan's west coast. Their targets were the coastal defense guns, machine gun emplacements and other beach fortifications erected by Japan to stifle landing by the U.S. Marines. [7]

Bush, Delaney and Nadeau were part of an eight-bomber force launched at 0515 hours (5:15 a.m.). Almost immediately after Bush had been catapulted from the SAN JACINTO's deck his substitute plane developed a hydraulic failure. Bush declared an emergency and successfully landed back aboard the SAN JACINTO at 0535 (5:35am). The emergency came as no surprise to the uneasy Nadeau. The omens of the past few days converging on June 13 seemed to foretell that bad luck was going to befall them.

Then war operations took a turn for the better in the afternoon of the 13th. Aviation mechanics pronounced "The Barbara" back in service and ready to fly. The Bush team was launched on an anti-submarine patrol mission to search the waters off the east coast of Saipan and Tinian. As "The Barbara" reached the northern leg of a patrol off Tinian Bush spotted six small vessels he identified as armed Japanese trawlers. Flying closer Bush and Nadeau saw the crew of one of the trawlers waving the U. S. flag. The ruse did not fool Bush and he dropped depth charges on the vessels. Other pilots of the division joined in with their depth charges. Both Nadeau and Delaney strafed the ships with machine gun fire. After the initial attack, Bush moved "The Barbara" in closer to obtain excellent damage photos that clearly showed the trawlers sinking. In the action report to the Task Group, Air Group 51 claimed four of the trawlers sunk and two damaged.

The Bush team in "The Barbara," with seven other Avengers, returned to bombing action on June 14 with an early morning mission on Rota Island between Saipan and Guam. The Japanese were using Rota's air fields as a staging point in the re-supply of aircraft to Aslito and air bases on Guam.

On the bombing raid Bush performed his duty as squadron photographic officer. He and fighter pilots Ensigns Dixie Mays and Thomas Hollowell combined efforts to supply General Smith with latest photo intelligence pertaining to the Saipan invasion set for the next morning. Photographs of the Rota strike and an afternoon bombing raid on the Saipan invasion beaches produced valuable last minute photo intelligence of Japanese defense positions. The film and prints were developed on the SAN JACINTO then flown five miles away to task group commander Admiral J. W. Reeves Jr. aboard the ENTERPRISE. Reeves sent a "well done" commendation to Captain Martin and in succeeding days assigned additional photo missions to the Bush aerial photo group. Their reputation for aerial photography was building within the high command of the Task Force.

The operational plans of Forager called for invasion and capture of Guam soon after the June 15 Saipan landings. Performing both bomber and photo duty, Bush participated in afternoon raids on Guam, June 16. Bush's targets included the Japanese radio station and the former Pan American Airways base which Japan had converted into a military sea plane base. [8]

This bomb damage assessment (BDA) photo taken after the June 12th raid pinpoints areas hit by Air Group 51: "A"=fuel storage tanks; "B" communications center and "C" underground fuel storage hit by McIlwaine.

Source: USS SAN JACINTO photo by Dixie Mays.

Ensign Robert McIlwaine

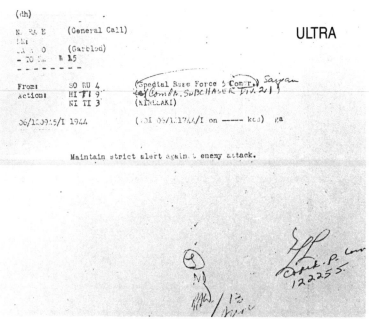

Prior to George Bush's bombing of Aslito Airfield, the Japanese Base Force Five commander on Saipan (SO RU 4) sent out an air raid warning.

Source: SRN series, National Archives.

George Bush flew through smoke and debris to obtain this photo of the sugar mill at Charan Kanoa. SAN JACINTO photo interpretation officer Jerome Pasto said smoke stacks of the mill could be used as a Japanese observation post and should be destroyed. A Japanese "spy" was later discovered using the height advantage to report US troop movements. The Marine Corps ultimately destroyed the tower (below). [9]

Aerial photo by Ensign George H. W. Bush from TBM Avenger, National Archives; Ground photos by U. S. Marine Corps, National Archives.

Station Hypo's intercept summary indicates Chichi Jima radio has taken over Saipan's damaged local broadcast circuits and indirectly confirms loss of Aslito's communications facilities by air attack.

Source: SRN series, National Archives.

ULTRA

At 0600/16 Subchaser 51 (IYORI) originated an operational type despatch to commands in the YOKOSUKA area but no flurry of operational resulted.

SAIPAN, TENIAN, ROTA and GUAM remained unheard throughout day on regular circuits. CinC FIRST AIR FLEET was heard on 8137J, however, and both GUAM and TENIAN air bases were active on 9035 kcs. Charlie call for SAIPAN Air Base (7HAYO) was heard three times on same circuit. CHICHIJIMA appears to have taken over 5375J kcs, SAIPANs local circuit, several broadcasts being intercepted.

GUAM has apparently burned some of its codes. A despatch at 0700/16 from GUARD DIV 54 (TAFUTA) has appearance of report to this effect in being sent for action to Navy Minister (YOWITI) and A GOO Force (YOTIWA) info to Chief Bureau Military Preparations (RINUMI). Only three kana calls thereafter were used by the Guard Div but the air base has continued use of OTSU7 calls.

(FRUPAC 162048 JUNE:44:P:COMB:CETYH)
(Part 5 of 8)

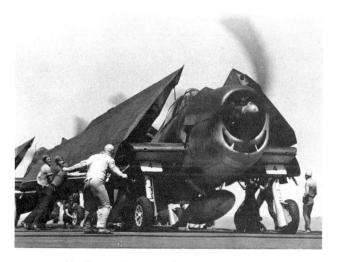 

Air Group 51 gave daily aerial support to U. S. troops in the Saipan invasion. At left, the SAN JACINTO's flight deck officer signals Fox 4 to unfold wings in preparation for takeoff. At right an Avenger bomber returns from a Saipan bombing mission. *Source: USS SAN JACINTO photos, National Archives.*

While patroling off Tinian Island, VT-51 bombers sighted a group of six Japanese trawlers attempting to reinforce the Mariana garrisons. Bombing and strafing attacks left the vessels sinking. George Bush took this photo from "The Barbara" using his remote control F-56 camera.

USS SAN JACINTO photo by Ensign George H. W. Bush.

Japanese Resistance Slows Marines

American casualties are evacuated to hospital ships waiting in the offshore waters of Saipan.

U. S. Marine Corps photo, National Archives.

U.S Marine Corps invasion troops are pinned down by Japanese fire as they land on Saipan's western landing beaches, June 15, 1944. Due to the tenacious Japanese defense, United States commanders postponed the recapture of Guam.

U. S. Marine Corps photo, National Archives.

Small landing craft were used by the Japanese Mariana garrison in attempt to reinforce their ground troops.

U. S. Marine Corps photo, National Archives.

"Lousy Photos" Says General Smith

U. S. Marine Corps commanders at Saipan blamed U. S. Navy photography, in part, for failure to locate the dug in pockets of Japanese resistance on Saipan. Asserting they were handicapped in planning for the invasion by "inadequate photographic coverage" Marine Corps generals complained to the top commanders of the USN.

Marine Corps generals, H. M. Smith (second from left) and Roy Geiger (far right) told the Navy's top brass that Saipan photo coverage was "inadequate." The admirals are (at left) Richmond K. Turner, Raymond Spruance, and Marc Mitscher. *Source: US Navy photo, National Archives.*

General H. M. "Howlin' Mad" Smith, U.S. Marine Corps commander.

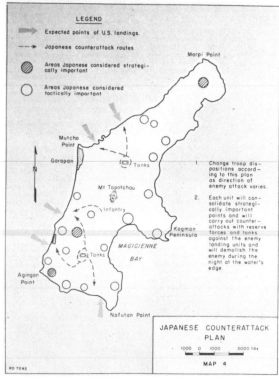

Despite Admiral Nimitz' decoy plans, Japan's military leaders correctly anticipated American invasion plans (right). The actual plans are at left. *Source: U.S. Marine Corps monograph Saipan/Hoffman.*

PART V

The American landing on Saipan triggered instant reaction in Tokyo. Determined to oust the Americans from the Marianas, the Japanese general staff activated its main fleet forces for what would be the greatest carrier air battle in history, the Battle of The Philippine Sea on June 19-20, 1944. [1]

As for the American high command, in his Operation Forager order to Task Force 58, Admiral Nimitz warned there could be a major fleet engagement. Intercepts available to him from Station Hypo had tracked the Japanese carrier fleet to anchorages south of the Philippines. Shortly after the U. S. Marines landed on Saipan, Japanese navy communications ordered the carrier units to sortie from their Borneo anchorages and "annihilate the American forces on Saipan." These intercepts were forwarded to Admiral Spruance who prepared to engage the formidable Japanese carrier fleet of nine carriers, battleships, cruisers, destroyers and the fleet train of oilers.

By early morning of June 18 confirmation of the Station Hypo reports reached Admiral Spruance. Sightings by U. S. submarines counted 54 Japanese warships and six oilers. Further confirmation came from radio direction finder bearings obtained by Station Hypo. Admiral Spruance ordered Admiral Mitscher to move the 137 warships of Task Force 58 west of Saipan from the Pacific Ocean into the Philippine Sea. The Americans had a nearly three-to-one advantage over the Japanese navy units.

When rumors of the Japanese sortie reached the SAN JACINTO on June 17, George Bush and the squadron prepared to engage the main body of the Japanese carrier fleet. Captain Martin announced a major engagement involving all or most of Japan's carrier strength was probably about to take place. After that morning's flight operations, all USN air operations were cancelled. The entire Task Force 58 was regrouped in anticipation of the imminent battle. First, however, the elusive Japanese carrier fleet had to be located.

On June 18 the flight operations of the SAN JACINTO and the huge Task Force 58 were dedicated to scout searches west of Saipan/Guam. The Bush team was part of the effort, but not "The Barbara." The plane was again out of service because of engine trouble. Gunner Nadeau got the superstition jitters and for good reason. Bush was flying his 13th combat flight of the month in a substitution aircraft, not his usual plane. Since the June flight operations began there had been six plane substitutions due to problems with "The Barbara's" engine. Nadeau was convinced the hex signs were there. Something ominous was about to happen to the Bush team, but what?

These were some of Nadeau's worries as he peered out at the water of the Philippine Sea looking for the nine Japanese carriers and escorts. Over their radio earphones they heard a radioed "tally ho" as their escorting fighters shot down several Japanese carrier-based scout planes. However, June 18, 1944, ended without sighting of the Japanese fleet and Bush was recalled to the SAN JACINTO, landing safely during late afternoon recovery operations.

Although the three hour flight had been smooth and uneventful, Nadeau was still uneasy. The omens were overwhelming. Something terrible must be in store for the Bush team, he thought.

The morning of June 19, 1944, dawned bright and clear. On the Philippine Sea visibility was over 20 miles. In the ready room the availability section of the blackboard had good news for Nadeau. "The Barbara" was restored to duty and available for attacking the still elusive Japanese carrier fleet. Task Force 58 launched early morning searches but despite several hours of scouting, the enemy was not located. At mid-morning the SAN JACINTO was instructed to prepare its fighters for combat air patrol and to equip two bombers with depth charges for anti-submarine patrol. Admiral Spruance anticipated the enemy would assign U-boats as the vanguard for the approaching fleet battle. The Bush team and "The Barbara" received the combat assignment and a full load of depth charges intended for the submarine patrol.

At 1000 hours (10 am), SAN JACINTO radar indicated enemy aircraft approaching, distance about 130 miles to the west. Bong! Bong! Bong! The SAN JACINTO's general alarm sounded throughout the warship as the crew scrambled to general quarters. All pilots and aircrewmen were ordered: "Man your planes."

At 1016 hours a signal was sent to the SAN JACINTO: "Scramble all fighters!" Over 400 Japanese carrier planes were swarming in on Task Force 58 like a cloud of hornets. Radar scopes on the SAN JACINTO showed at least four raids approaching at an altitude of 20,000 feet. The Bush team in "The Barbara" baked in the tropical sun on the SAN JACINTO's crowded flight deck as they anxiously awaited launching orders. Between 1021 and 1147 hours the plane handling

Anatomy of Radio Intelligence

Homer Kisner, Station Hypo Traffic Chief.

These are some of the dispatches based on the ULTRA intelligence received by Spruance that forecast the major fleet encounter between Japanese and American Carrier Task Forces in what turned out to be the greatest carrier air battle in history.

Source for intercepts: SRN series, National Archives.

Top: Time clocked: 10:44 am, June 14, 1944 . . . Japanese Navy places "A-Go" operation into effect.

Middle: Time clocked: 2:36 am, June 15, 1944 . . . Links the Japanese Strike Force to Central Pacific.

Bottom: Time clocked: 2:40 am, June 15, 1944 . . . Places units of Strike Force at sea with Japanese reporting intercepting of a USN (Blue) submarine which had reported sighting the force.

ULTRA

141044 June 1944

From: No originator
To : AHO 1

THIS IS MORE COMPLETE THAN NEGATS EARLIER VERSION —

(Part 1 only of Nip 2 parter-part 2 intercepted and being worked).

"From Chief of Staff Combined Fleet. The gist of important messages which have not been reported to you because of the code situation and the summary of the recent war situation is as follows:.
(1). An enemy striking force composed of many large and medium carriers has been attacking the Marianas area since the afternoon of 11 June. This force has launched air attacks daily until the afternoon of 13 June and since 13 has been shelling Saipan and Tenian.
(2). Although an occupation force has not yet been sighted, since there is a strong possibility that an occupation is planned, "A" (Kane) operations which are to be decisive, were

ULTRA

Additional evidence linking the STRIKING FORCE with the Central Pacific is as follows:

(1) Concealed originator "H" Intelligence despatches 1947/14, 2152/14 and 2215/14 were addressed to CinC FIRST MOBILE FLEET (NEE5), CinC COMBINED, CinC FIRST AIR FLEET (MEME2), Commander CHICHIJIMA Base Force (KOHO1), MARCUS Guard Division (HAYOO) and Headquarters Grand SurEsco Force (SASE3). The appearance of MARCUS and CHICHIJIMA in each despatch suggests that Nip intelligence may have deduced that a threat to CHICHIJIMA and MARCUS exists. This is also significant in that CinC FIRST MOBILE FLEET is addressed.

(FRUPAC : 150236:JUNE'44QPE:COMB:CETYH)
(PART 1 of 3)   PRIORITY

ULTRA

(2) PELELIU Air Base (HANO5) probably covering for ComAirFlot 61, addressed despatch at 2123/14 to 41st Western Air Attack Force (RIRA5) info CinC FIRST MOBILE (MUKE4), CinC COMBINED (HAKE9), and F/S 5th Base Air Force (KIE4). This is first noted association of the 41st Western Air Attack Force and CinC FIRST MOBILE FLEET. Special searches or air coverage for MOBILE FLEET units could be the subject matter.
That units of the STRIKING FORCE are at sea is indicated by SOERABAYA's 0105/15 to STRIKING FORCE (YCYA7). By collateral, this is DF fix on Blue sub in position 5-30 N 127-40 at 2331/14. To effect delivery to the STRIKING FORCE this message received following treatment: SOERABAYA, SINGAPORE and TOKYO placed it on their broadcast. Handling to effect delivery is further indication that STRIKING FORCE units are at sea.

(FRUPAC :150240: JUNE'44:QPE:COMB:CETYH)
(PART 2 of 3)   PRIORITY

-70-

(Continued from part 1)
This may be a directive to the escorts and tankers to join
the three Replenishment units. KANJU, MIYAKE, YUUKO MARU,
EIHOO MARU, and MANEI MARU probably recently returned to
the PHILIPPINES from BALIKPAPAN as collateral on June 3rd
pointed to a BALIKPAPAN movement. That all of the action
addressees were in the DAVAO-TAWI TAWI vicinity late on
6/14 is suggested by the BASE FORCE 32 association and by
the fact that SUBCHASER 39 originated a contact at 0425/14
in position 06:30N 121:58E.

(FRUPAC: 150056 :JUNE:44:XOPERATIONAL P(IORITY:COMB:CETYH)

(Part 2 of 2)

Time clocked: 3:56 am, June 15, 1944 . . . Tankers and
replenishment vessels of Japanese fleet associated with
Strike Force. Strike Force is at sea, requiring refueling
on the high seas.

152310 JUNE 44

From: MIHI 9   (31st Comm Unit)
To : 19JJ.1   (Addressees Sub Reports Inner South Seas Area)
       HLOTU
       IHI 2   (South Expeditionary Fleet #3 CinC)
       HINI 3 (Escort Force #5 Southwest Force)
       HJS1 0 (Base Force 32 Comdr)
       TIRO 4 (1st Fleet Mobile)
"At 2200 May 15, Sub by D/F 12-30 North, 134-30 East,
(Grade A), originated an urgent despatch addressed to Honolulu."
                                        ⌐ SAN BERNADINO STR
(FRUPAC 152128 JUNE 44 OP COMB COPEK)m

FLYING FISH REPORTING JAP TASK FORCE
1ST STRIKING FLEET MUST KNOW IT WAS
SIGHTED!

Time clocked: 2128 hours, June 15, 1944 . . . Japan
radio interceptors pick up the US submarine, FLYING
FISH, reporting a sortie by a Japanese Strike Force
through San Bernadino Straits.

The day's traffic presented an unusual picture. The
great bulk of traffic consisted of operational despatches
from the Marianas which were broadcast again and again
on all major circuits, routine traffic obviously had
been sidetracked for this purpose. Almost all reports
went to the "A" Force, either singly or with compara-
tively minor mid-Pacific commands.

Exchange of messages between high commands practically
disappeared. Presumably prearranged plans are now
proceeding or the major commands are at sea and
maintaining radio silence. CinC FIRST MOBILE FLEET
was seldom seen and CinC SECOND FLEET not at all, and
no messages which might have been originated by them
were detected. Presumably, the major fleet commands
are embodied in the "A" Force and are advised and
directed individually by addressing the force. The
Replenishment Units were not seen.

(FRUPAC 161000 JUNE 44:P:COMB:CETYH)
(PAGE 1 of 7)

Time clocked: 1900 hours June 16, 1944 . . . Associates
the Japanese Strike Force with the Marianas. Notes major Japanese fleet commanders are "hidden" within the
regular radio messages.

CinC FIRST MOBILE FLEET was increasingly associated with
the Central Pacific theater. On 14th and 15th, "H" Intel-
igence reports pertaining to the MARIANAS-BONINS were addressed to CinC FIRST MOBILE FLEET. CinC COMBINED FLEET informed him of the air countermeasures resulting from the
IWOJIMA strike. Several urgent despatches from CinC FIRST AIR
FLEET went to CinC FIRST MOBILE FLEET or Commander Striking
Force for information. An excellent example of this associa-
ion was blank originator 1254/15, first intercepted on the
TOKYO broadcast hence from CinC COMBINED FLEET, it was add-
ressed for action to CinC FIRST MOBILE FLEET (MAHI3), CinC
FIRST AIR FLEET (SAKA0) and CinC CENTRAL PACIFIC, (SOII5).
It appears well established, therefore, that the Striking
Force is at present destined for action in the CENTRAL
PACIFIC.

FRUPAC: 151940   JUNE 44 P COMB CETYH
(PART 1 of /C)

Time clocked: 1940 hours (7:40 pm), June 15, 1944 . . .
Predicts the Japanese Strike Force is headed for the
Central Pacific.

171605 June 1944

From: MEIO 7   (Soerabaya Comm. Unit)
       TABA 1   (Striking Force)
       YOKO 9   (CinC Combined Fleet)

"From 3rd Blank. Although believed to have got blank by
means of blank of a total of 4 enemy submarines which
appeared to the east of the Philippine Islands on 16, an
enemy submarine which showed up at 1106, 17 (bearing 45
degrees from Soerabaya) sent a 66 group. "Urgent" message
which immediately was broadcast by Honolulu. It is guessed
that this message was a report of the sighting of Japanese
forces.

1. (FRUJIL 171039 June 1944: OP:COMB:COPEK)e

Time clocked: 1839 hours, June 17, 1944 . . . Further
proof the Japanese Strike Force is aware they have been
sighted by USN forces.

Continued from part 9. At 1620 and 1630 GUAM Air Base #1
addressed short most urgents in aircraft code to Striking
Force less Training Force (FUPU5). At 1815 the 4th Weather
Unit sent an urgent weather report to CinC FIRST MOBILE
FLEET. All of this correspondence probably deals with
flights of carrier aircraft into the Marianas and carries
further indication that Nips intend to use existing fields
in SAIPAN area.

An especially significant message was blank originator 1021
on 18th. It was addressed to CinC FIRST AIR FLEET (MUGARU),
GUAM Air Base #2 (RASLA), unident air base info CinC COMBINED,
ComCarDiv 2 (REHE8), ComCarDiv 3(SGFU4), ROTA Air Base and
a garble. Of urgent precedence, this reveals a definite
carrier-Marianas association and suggests that Marianas air
bases were ordered to prepare to receive carrier aircraft.

(FRUPAC 192052 JUNE:44:P:COMB:CETYH)

(Part 10 of 15)

Time clocked: 2052 hours, June 19, 1944 [sic, must
mean June 18] . . . Definitely associates the Japanese
Strike Force with the Marianas and says the aircraft
from the Strike Force carriers will use Mariana air
bases. *Source: All intercepts from SRN series, National Archives.*

Turkey Shoot Begins

At mid-morning, June 19, 1944, vapor trails at 24,000 feet signaled the start of the greatest carrier air battle in history as Japanese and American fighters engaged in battle. George Bush saw this scene as he sat in the cockpit of "The Barbara" awaiting launch orders. The USS LEXINGTON is shown on horizon.

USS SAN JACINTO photo by Robert Stinnett, National Archives.

A Hellcat of Air Group 51 frames the "sky-writing" of the Marianas Turkey Shoot as American and Japanese aviators fight it out at 24,000 feet.

USS SAN JACINTO photo by Robert Stinnett, National Archives.

crews maneuvered the fighters around the bombers to obtain launch position. The scramble order gave priority to fighters who were ordered to climb to 24,000 feet and form an umbrella over Task Force 58. From this umbrella position a navy fighter director would coordinate the attack on the approaching Japanese carrier craft.

At the 24,000 foot elevation, atmospheric conditions produced a contrail, a white vapor of condensed water that formed in an aircraft's wake. Bush could see the contrails from his cockpit position. Soon what earlier had been a cloudless sky looked like an aerial smoke writers' convention as the American fighters began engaging the Japanese raiders.

Gunner Lee Nadeau recalled the next moments. "At 1155 we were told, 'Get ready to launch.' Captain Martin wanted all bombers off the flight deck for easier recovery and launching of fighters. There wasn't time to lower us to the hangar deck. We were catapulted at 1157 hours with no destination and no specific orders, just clear the decks of the SAN JACINTO."

As Bush put "The Barbara" into a climb the anti-aircraft guns of the SAN JACINTO and the task group started firing at attacking Japanese planes. The time was 1158 am. Bush was in a dangerous situation as hundreds of anti-aircraft guns of the task group fired at the diving Japanese aircraft. In the chaos of an aerial attack American airplanes were sometimes mistaken for the enemy.

Bush was at 1,000 feet when he saw a Japanese "Judy" (the American intelligence name given this particular Japanese dive bomber) shot down by the SAN JACINTO gunners. He poured the fuel to "The Barbara" in effort to distance his plane from the range of the anti-aircraft fire and headed away from the task group at the highest possible speed. Nadeau and Delaney were alert for Japanese aircraft, their machine guns charged and ready to go. But "The Barbara"—now flying at about 1500 feet—was below the fighter plane aerial battle going on in the higher atmosphere. Except for an occasional Japanese dive bomber that slipped through American defenses, the fierce exchange took place at the 20,000 foot level.

Suddenly a black cloud enveloped "The Barbara." Nadeau thought the bomber had been hit by shrapnel from the intense anti-aircraft fire aimed at the Japanese dive bombers. In the cockpit, Bush looked at his instruments and saw the oil pressure gauge heading for zero. A black mist was spewing forth from the engine's cowling ring. On the plane's intercom Bush told Nadeau and Delaney, "We are losing oil pressure. I think the oil lines have sucked up shrapnel."

Without proper oil flowing through the engine parts, extreme heat would develop causing a fusing of the metal and shut off the power. There wasn't time for a landing on the SAN JACINTO. His life and that of his crew depended upon a controlled water landing where he could touch down with least damage. He wanted to limit damage and allow enough time for the crew to exit the bomber before it sank. Bush also wanted time for them to enter the emergency life raft and clear away from the bomber because the depth charges were sensitized to blow up when they reached 50 feet below the water surface. [2]

Warning Nadeau and Delaney to prepare for a water landing Bush set "The Barbara" down tail first on the waves. The resulting splash surrounded Nadeau with a wall of water. Momentarily he thought the plane was sinking. In fact, Bush had made a perfect water landing. The air ballast within the plane would keep it afloat for about two minutes. Nadeau looked down into the bomb bay and saw Delaney had hit his head on the radio transmitter and seemed to be dazed. Nadeau popped the circular escape hatch on the port side of his gun turret to allow access to the port wing. Then he reached down and guided the groggy Delaney up into the turret and out onto the port wing. "The Barbara" was still afloat and bobbing on the choppy ocean waves. Glancing over on the starboard side Nadeau saw Bush standing on the wing pulling the three-man life raft from the stowage area just aft of the cockpit. The two crewmen scrambled over the fuselage top and helped Bush get the raft into the sea. All three aviators climbed into the raft and Bush began rowing. As he maneuvered the raft away from "The Barbara" the lanyards attached to the raft and securing emergency rations became entangled in the plane's tail section. At that moment "The Barbara" perilously began a slow descent nose first into the water causing the tail section to rise into the air.

Nadeau grabbed his hunting knife and slashed through the lanyards. Since the raft's emergency rations were attached to the lanyard Nadeau was cutting off their emergency rations. "It was either us or the rations," Nadeau recalled.

He needn't have worried about spending too much time in the raft without rations on the waters of the Philippine Sea, however. The U.S.S. CLARENCE K. BRONSON, a plane guard destroyer for the Task Group, saw "The Barbara" hit the drink. Lieutenant Richard Patterson, the C.K. BRONSON's officer of the deck, recorded the crash time as 1309 (1:09pm) in the ship's log. One minute later, Patterson stationed the BRONSON's special rescue detail and by 1317 hours

(1:17pm) had pulled the three men from the raft to the safety of the destroyer. Bush, Nadeau or Delaney did not even get their feet wet during the eight minutes it took to exit "The Barbara," enter the raft and climb to safety aboard the C.K. BRONSON. [3]

In the wardroom of the C.K. BRONSON, Lieutenant Patterson treated the rescued trio to the warmth of some brandy. Bush was tipping back his second shot when the C.K. BRONSON received word of the sighting of an enemy submarine off the starboard beam. Realizing that the submarine would have been his target, Bush lamented that he could not respond. After all, he had no airplane. Since November 1943 Bush had piloted "The Barbara" during 72 flights. Now it was in the watery depths of the Philippine Sea, about 20 miles west of Guam, the victim of failed oil pressure.

Overhead the fierce air battle continued to rage without pause all afternoon. By sundown June 19 over 395 Japanese planes had been shot down by American forces. It was the largest air battle of the Pacific War and became commonly known as the "Marianas Turkey Shoot."

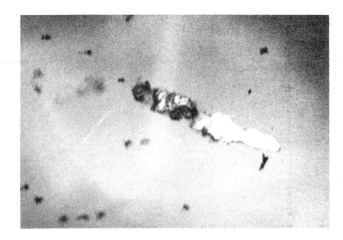

"The Barbara" Hit by Battle Debris

George Bush in "The Barbara" was catapulted from the USS SAN JACINTO at almost the same instant this Japanese "Judy" began a dive bombing attack over the Task Group. This "Judy" was one of 174 dive bombers launched by the Japanese carriers. As far as known, this is the only "Judy" to reach Task Force 58 on June 19.

USS SAN JACINTO photos by Robert Stinnett using F-56 camera with 40-inch telephoto lens. National Archives.

"The Barbara" and George Bush were hit by this battle debris as the Japanese "Judy," afire and trailing black smoke, plunged into the Philippine Sea off the Mariana Islands. At this moment, "The Barbara" was attempting to gain altitude and is somewhere between the USS ENTERPRISE (far left) and the horizon. USS SAN JACINTO at far right. *Source: USS LEXINGTON photo, National archives.*

Lost in the action was Ensign Thomas Hollowell, one of the SAN JACINTO photo pilots on the Bush photo team. Hollowell had been vectored to Guam during the "Turkey Shoot" to neutralize Japanese aircraft being staged through the island's air bases. He and his fighter were last seen entering a cloud bank over Guam. A few weeks later, his body was recovered when U.S. forces recaptured the island.

It was frustrating for Bush and his crew to be without a plane and sequestered on the C. K. BRONSON as the biggest carrier air battle raged around them. Because of the on-going fleet battle, the C.K. BRONSON could not return them to the SAN JACINTO. And it was a time when Captain Martin sorely needed aviators. When the orders were issued for the emergency launch against the Japanese carrier force, Captain Martin had only two bombers to put in the air. Japan's carrier fleet was finally located by navy search planes at 1615 (4:15pm) on June 20. The SAN JACINTO was short of bombers and pilots as Admiral Mitscher ordered a full strike on the enemy carrier armada. During a noon launch of bombers for antisubmarine patrol Bush's long time friend, roommate and wing man Lieutenant Richard Houle and his crewmen Charles Bynum and Walter Mintus experienced engine failure on takeoff and crashed into the water off the SAN JACINTO's starboard bow. Fortunately, Houle and the crew were immediately rescued by the destroyer USS HEALY but Houle's bomber joined "The Barbara" at the sandy bottom of the Philippine Sea.

Bush was following the action from the C.K. BRONSON, which was part of the defensive screen of the task group. During combat action the carriers would move to the center of a circle formation. The battleships, cruisers and destroyers of the task group would form around the flattops similar to the strategy of covered wagon days when American frontiersmen fought Indians. The battle circle customarily would be 15 miles in diameter with the carriers in the center and the destroyers on the outer fringe at seven miles. Bush watched as the SAN JACINTO launched Lieutenant Commander Donald Melvin and Ensign Jack Guy to join the massive attack on the enemy fleet. Both Melvin and Guy attacked the carriers and each was awarded the Navy Cross for scoring hits on a Japanese destroyer and carrier.

Bush's return to the SAN JACINTO was round-about. On June 21 he Delaney and Nadeau were transferred from the C.K. BRONSON by breeches buoy to the flagship of Task Force 58 the USS LEXINGTON for further transfer to the SAN JACINTO.

The Japanese carrier-based aircraft had been decimated in the "Turkey Shoot." As replacements for this devastating loss, Japan staged land-based aircraft from the Empire down the Chichi Jima slot in a persistent effort to attack and sink U.S. troop ships and supply vessels of the Saipan invasion force and the carriers of Task Force 58. George Bush witnessed one of these raids on June 23, 1944, while he and his crew were still aboard the LEXINGTON.

About June 22, the Hachiman Air Corps unit, using twin engine torpedo-bombers called "Bettys," departed from the Yokosuka Naval Air Station, flew down the Chichi Jima slot overnite and arrived at Iwo Jima. Among the pilots of the Hachiman Corps was Flying Petty Officer Second Class Shiro Toyota of the Imperial Japanese Navy. At 0632 on the morning of June 23, 1944, Toyota flew his plane off the Iwo Jima air strip. He was piloting one of seven planes sent out on patrol to discover and attack American war ships involved in the Mariana invasion. In his flight gear he carried a package of pills called soryukusen which translated to "fountain of power." Soryukusen was a drug available to Japanese pilots through the Yokosuka Naval dispensary. According to Japanese sources, the drug was intended to put the fliers on a high, making them feel all powerful and able to perform heroic acts. [4]

About noon on June 23, Flying Officer Toyota sent a message in the Japanese telegraphic code called kata kana to the radio command post on Iwo Jima. The radio operators entered the message in the log: "Enemy in sight, two battleships and cruisers." A little later: "Enemy airplanes in sight." Then silence. Officer Toyota was not heard from again. Not by the Japanese.

Officer Toyota was next seen by the destroyer USS HEALY on duty in the SAN JACINTO's task group. At 1210 hours (12:10pm) a lookout on the destroyer spotted the enemy plane off the HEALY's starboard quarter flying low over the water. Lieutenant W. L. Healy Jr., officer of the deck, focused his binoculars. He saw Toyota's plane being chased by the combat air patrol of the Task Group. The HEALY did not open fire because of the danger of hitting the American pursuer. At 1220 hours (12:20pm) Toyota's plane was shot down by the air patrol. It crash-landed into the water, breaking off its undercarriage. Approaching the crash scene, the HEALY saw there were survivors in the water clinging to the undercarriage of the bomber.

Frank Cody, a HEALY deck hand yelled out: "They are clinging to Goodyear tires." Once again, the Japanese were using American-made products to fight the Americans. Admiral Marc Mitscher, commander of Task Group 58, ordered the HEALY crew to take

A TBM sinks into ocean waters and the crew gathers in life raft. This photo is from USS SAN JACINTO photo file, but neither Lee Nadeau or George Bush are sure this is "The Barbara." Nadeau does not recall any other aircraft flying above them.

Source: USS San Jacinto photo files.

John Delaney.

George Bush made a successful water landing, ditching "The Barbara" at the edge of the Task Group. He, radioman John Delaney and gunner Leo Nadeau got into the life raft and were picked up by the destroyer USS CLARENCE K. BRONSON. Later Bush thanked Rear Admiral James L. "Reggie" Kauffman, commander of the Pacific Fleet's destroyers, for his rescue. Bush had a dual purpose in meeting Kauffman. The Admiral's daughter was engaged to and later married Bush's brother, Prescott.

Source: The White House.

Rear Admiral James L. Kauffman and Ensign George Bush

Leo Nadeau with "dunking cake."

June, 1944

Date	Type of Machine	Number of Machine	Duration of Flight	Character of Flight	Pilot		PASSENGERS		REMARKS
7	TBM-1c	25123	3.0	A/S	Ens. Bush		Self + Delaney	lct. lct.	San Jacinto
10	"	25137	3.5	A/S	"		" "	" "	San Jacinto
★ 12	"	16928	2.3	G	"		" "	" "	STRIKE ON SAIPAN
13	"	25123	3.0	A/S	"		" "	" "	SAIPAN AREA
13	"	16935	2.4	A/S	"		" "	" "	SAIPAN AREA
13	"	25137	.5	—	"		" "	" "	Emergency landing (PRE DAWN)
★ 14	"	25123	2.2	G	"		" "	" "	STRIKE ON ROTA
★ 14	"	"	3.0	G	Hit on Coastal gun.		" "	" "	STRIKE ON SAIPAN
★ 16	"	"	30	G	"		" "	" "	STRIKE ON GUAM
18	"	16931	2.9	A/S	"		" "	" "	SAIPAN AREA CLARENCE P. BRONSON
19	"	25123	1.5	A/S	"				(Picked up by destroyer U.S.S. BRONSON) CRASH LANDING NEAR GUAM
★ 25	"	25305	2.4	G	"		" "	" "	STRIKE ON ROTA
25	TBF-1c	48103	3.7	A/S	"		" "	" "	ROTA AREA

Total time to date,

10—18616

TORPEDO SQUADRON - 51

Brought Forward 123.8
This Month.... Pilot.... Pass 33.4 Total 33.4
Total to Date 202.2
I certify that the foregoing flight record is correct.

L. H. Nadeau
Signature

Approved:

George H. W. Bush
Lt. Comdr., USN Comdg.
10—18616

Leo Nadeau (right) flew 12 combat missions with George Bush in June 1944. His official log book (above) records the crash landing of "The Barbara" (plane #25123) on June 19, 1944. After their rescue, Bush, Delaney and Nadeau spent time on the USS LEXINGTON, awaiting return to the SAN JACINTO.

Courtesy Leo Nadeau, copies by Robert Stinnett.

the Japanese fliers into custody as prisoners of war and to bring them to his flagship the USS LEXINGTON so they could be interrogated. Mitscher wanted to know where they came from so he could dispatch bombers to knock out the air facilities.

At 1252 hours (12:52pm) the HEALY's motor whale boat was lowered into the water as the destroyer came to a full stop, becoming an easy target for any lurking Japanese submarine. Lieutenant (j.g.) F. C. Hill, in charge of an armed guard in the whale boat, came on the crash scene. There were three bodies in the water. Two of the men appeared to be alive. Cody, who was part of the guard detail, pulled the two Japanese aboard. One spoke some English and kept repeating, "You are going to kill me, you are going to kill me." Although Cody was carrying a rifle, he had no intention of killing him. His orders were to take them prisoners.

At 1317 hours (3:17 pm) the whaleboat with the prisoners was hoisted back aboard the HEALY. The deck log noted that two unnamed Japanese survivors were brought aboard, one with a head injury. The second prisoner died almost immediately after his rescue. Still wildly protesting that he was going to be killed, the injured survivor was restrained by Lieutenant Hill who used rope to bind his arms. Hill sent the POW to the HEALY's sick bay where Pharmacist Mate First Class John Tarrant examined his injuries. He found a large deep gash on his right forehead and minor abrasions over much of his body. Medic Tarrant noted the youth of the pilot, estimating his age between 19-20 years old. Tarrant sutured the gash and other pharmacist mates tended to the smaller cuts and bruises. All the while the Japanese POW was protesting in English, asserting that he was going to be killed. Ironically, only moments before the prisoner had tried to torpedo these Americans who were now giving him aid. [5]

"I had control of the prisoner," pharmacist mate Tarrant said later. "It was my responsibility as a humanitarian and a member of the medical profession to use all my skills to care for his wounds. He received the finest medical care we could provide." After completing the suture, Tarrant, who also served as the ship's official photographer, recorded the rare event with a picture of the bandaged POW on the operating table. [6]

The HEALY brought him immediately to the LEXINGTON. Word spread quickly that a Japanese pilot was coming aboard. At 1805 hours (6:05pm), Bush, Nadeau and Delaney saw the heavily bandaged prisoner taken by the LEXINGTON's Marine detail. He was marched to Admiral Mitscher's office for questioning by USN intelligence officers.

Back on the HEALY, coxswain Frank Cody, who had been part of the whale boat crew, had officially confiscated the life jackets, other clothing and belongings of the Japanese pilots. Before disposing of the items, he used his hunting knife to cut the Japanese name plate from one of the life jackets. Cody saved the name plate and the small container of pills. In 1989 a translation showed the items belonged to Flying Petty Officer Shiro Toyota of the Hachiman Corps and had been issued to him at the Yokosuka Naval Air Station.

In his Navy aviation log book, Bush recorded the four day period he spent on the LEXINGTON as "sack time." He and his crew were not returned to the SAN JACINTO and aviation duty until the morning of June 24, 1944, when the destroyer USS TERRY picked them up by breeches buoy and shuttled them to the SAN JACINTO.

The original plans of Operation Forager called for the invasion and liberation of Guam to take place on "W" day, a designation arbitrarily selected by the navy for June 18, 1944, three days after the Saipan landing. However, overly optimistic U.S. Navy and Marine Corps planners headed by Major General Howland M. Smith, the commander of ground forces of FORAGER, failed again to perceive the tenacious Japanese opposition. The Second and Fourth Marine Divisions took heavy casualties on D-Day, June 15th. Saipan was a tragic replay of Tarawa. The next day, June 16 at 1100 hours (11am) as the Marines encountered stubborn Japanese defenses, Admiral Spruance postponed the Guam invasion and sent the transports carrying the invasion troops of the Third Marine Division and the First Marine Provisional Brigade back to Eniwetok to await the outcome of the Saipan ground battle. [7]

General Smith, again blasted the lack of US Naval photo intelligence for the high Saipan casualties. He was soon joined by Brigadier General Lemuel Shepherd of the First Marine Brigade, who complained of the inaccuracy of navy aerial photos. General Shepherd was in command of the troops scheduled to land at Agat on Guam's west coast. None of the Bush photo team recalled hearing of the Marine Corps' complaints, but SAN JACINTO records showed aerial photography on Guam and Saipan was stepped up immediately after the battle with the Japanese Fleet on June 19-20, 1944. [8]

Upon George Bush's return to the SAN JACINTO on June 24, daily photo intelligence sorties were added to the carrier's flight operations. Ensign Dixie Mays flew these photo sorties targeting Guam's west coast

Tare One loses power, wing tip catches waves.

Bush Section Leader in Water Crash

Task Force 58, victor in the carrier air battle of June 19th, turned to the task of locating the warships of the Japanese Strike Force. From his perch on the C. K. BRONSON, George Bush and his crew could watch launching of search aircraft from the flight deck of the USS SAN JACINTO. To his horror, Bush saw one of the TBM's veer off the starboard side of the SAN JACINTO and crash into the Philippine Sea. He didn't know it then, but the plane was Tare One piloted by his section leader, Lieutenant Richard "Rich" Houle and crewed by Charles Bynum and Walter Mintus. This series of photographs illustrates the water technique of dunking and escaping from a TBM. George Bush and his crew used these same methods the day before.

Tare One photos taken from USS SAN JACINTO by Robert Stinnett; Rescue of Houle by John Tarrant, USS HEALY.

Houle can be seen on starboard wing, Bynum and Mintus exiting from turret canopy. USS CLARENCE K. BRONSON, with George Bush and crew aboard is shown on the horizon.

"Rich" Houle begins inflating life raft on starboard wing of Tare One. Parachute still strapped to back.

Lieutenant "Rich" Houle (below) lays aside raft's paddles and grabs lanyard from crew of USS HEALY. Charles Bynum is in bow of raft, Walter Mintus in center.

Crewmembers of USS HEALY give Rich Houle a helping hand.

Japanese carrier strike force under attack Battle of Philippine Sea, June 20, 1944.

U.S. Navy photo, National Archives

LCDR Donald Melvin.

The Navy Cross.

Sam Melton.

Lawrence Mueller.

Distinguished Flying Cross.

Ensign Jack Guy.

Fred D. Myers, Jr.

Wendell Tomes.

Japan's Fleet Routed
Awards for the Torpedo Squadron

The Japanese carrier force was finally located at 1615 hours
(4:15pm) June 20, 1944. With Bush and Houle's Avengers
at the bottom of the ocean and four others on anti-submarine patrols, the SAN JACINTO was short of bombers
and only could launch Don Melvin and Jack Guy to attack
the Nippon carriers. Melvin and Guy bombed the enemy
warships and were awarded the Navy's highest honor, The
Navy Cross. Melvin's crew, Sam Melton and Fred Myers
Jr., Guy's crew, Lawrence Mueller and Wendell Tomes were
awarded the Distinguished Flying Cross.

Vice-President of the United States, George Bush con-
gratulates Jack Guy for his Pacific War bombing feats.
Courtesy Lee Nadeau.

Navy Cross winner, Don Melvin is returned to the
SAN JACINTO via breeches buoy from the destroyer
USS MARSHALL. *USS SAN JACINTO photo, National Archives.*

invasion beaches. During his bombing strikes on Guam
and nearby Rota, Bush augmented the Mays' photos
with obliques taken from his bomber. All of the photo
intelligence was delivered by SAN JACINTO aircraft flying directly from the carrier to Saipan's Marine Corps
command post. Mays later recalled landing on Aslito
Airfield shortly after its capture to personally deliver the
photographs. "If the Marine Corps didn't want to look
at the photos that was their problem," Mays said.

Bush rejoined his squadron and participated for ten
successive days in the bombing of Japanese targets on
Guam and Rota. During these bombing strikes, which
lasted until July 5, Bush wasn't flying in " The Barbara."
Half the time he did not have his turret gunner Nadeau.
There was no permanent "Barbara" since none of the
remaining Avengers of Squadron 51 were equipped as
photo planes.

Nadeau was off the flight list because he was in captain's mast trouble for expressing his strong substitution theories. In filing charges against Nadeau, the
squadron's senior chief petty officer (CPO) accused him
of "insubordination," a minor transgression. Nadeau
recalled he was brought before Captain Martin but
neither he nor Bush were allowed to present a defense.
Martin sided with the CPO and ordered Nadeau to serve
extra duty hours.[9]

By mid-July, 1944, Task Force 58 had ended its support of the Mariana Islands operation. On July 21,
1944, the postponed Guam invasion by U.S. Marines
went off well—at first. But with the Japanese dug into
caves and battlements in the island's highlands, the
Marine's Third Division and First Provisional Brigade
suffered heavy casualties. By August 10, the island was
declared liberated from Japanese control.

Wreckage of the "Betty" kept afloat by Goodyear tires.

Hachiman Corps
Bush Crew Sees Japanese POWs

Though defeated in the carrier battle, Japan continued a tenacious defense of the Mariana Islands by shifting aerial forces from the Empire. On June 23, 1944 several land based torpedo-bombers called "Bettys" belonging to the Hachiman Corps of Yokosuka Naval Air Station attacked the SAN JACINTO's Task Group. George Bush and crewmembers John Delaney and Lee Nadeau watched from the USS LEXINGTON as the "Bettys" were shot down by the antiaircraft guns of the Task Group. Survivors were seen in the water and Admiral Marc Mitscher ordered the destroyer, USS HEALY, to pick up the Japanese crewmembers for intelligence questioning. The HEALY's whaleboat located survivors and one was treated in the sickbay by medic John Tarrant, who was also the ship's official photographer. Tarrant recorded his patient's rescue and humane treatment on the operating table. Bush viewed the transfer of the POW to the LEXINGTON and in two months would face the same situation when he was targeted as a POW by Japanese forces on Chichi Jima.

Official U. S. Navy photos by John Tarrant, USS HEALY. Intercept from SRN series, National Archives.

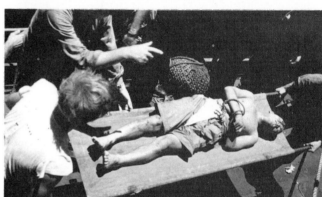

Japanese pilot, gash on forehead, taken by stretcher to sick bay.

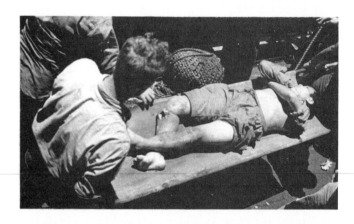

This Japanese pilot died from injuries, according to USS HEALY records.

Both Japanese pilots are shown in the HEALY's whaleboat after rescue. Pilot in bow was treated in sick bay and transferred to USS LEXINGTON.

(anp)

                  Summary   PK
NA RA E
DE   Sent Out Coper-Cond
O HA KA   Cmas 05.1236
NI SA 231   SHAPE UP
WL21 A MA   P   SJE

From   MA 0 7   Yokosuka Air Group-Sta   LC
Action: KU 0 7   Air Base #52, Iwojima   NONE   NO
Info: RA MA E   Northeast Area Fleet CinC   RELS
        I SA 7   Vice Chief Nav Gen Staff
        HI HA 0   GF Cin C   75gu
        TO A 5   Yokosuka Nav Dist Comdt   lg

06/201830/I 1944   (TOI 06/202210)

TO: Commander HACHIMAN Air Attack Force.

27 type-0# fighters, 13 Comets, 5 ----, 7 Tenzans and 5 landbased

attack planes depart for Air Base #52 today - - - - - - - - - -

- - - - - - - -. 6 landbased attack planes of YOKOSUKA Air Group

and 7 from Air Group 1001 will be used as transports.

COMMENT: "HACHIMAN" is the JAPANESE God of War and "HACHIMAN
Air Attack Force " is the tactical title of the force
composed of AirFlot 27 and Air Group 301. It was
organized on 15 June on which date the Eastern Operations
became effective.

JP-4: 5270-C (MR)   (Japanese)   (I)Navy Trans. 07-061010/.(?)

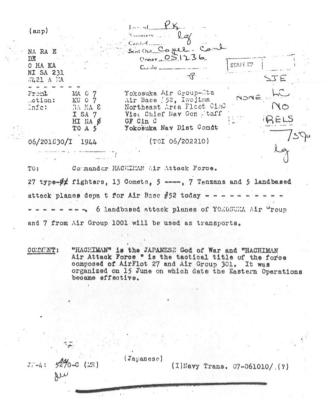

Intercept from Station Hypo provided advance intelligence on movement of the Hachiman Corps to Iwo Jima.

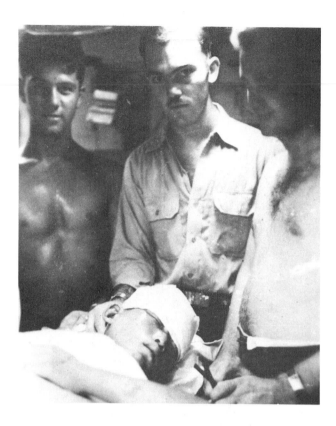

Medics of the USS HEALY watch over injured Japanese pilot.

George Bush and crew were part of the throng on fantail of USS LEXINGTON when POW was brought aboard by breeches buoy. On horizon, rear, is USS SAN JACINTO.

John Tarrant, senior medic on the USS HEALY, treated Hachiman Corps pilot.

Remembering The China Clipper
Bush in Guam Bombing Raids

George Bush and his crew were returned to the SAN JACINTO on June 24 by the USS TERRY after a five day hiatus during which they were moved to various warships of the Task Group. On the same day he resumed bombing missions using a replacement Avenger from the USS ENTERPRISE. For the next two weeks, the Bush crew participated in photo missions, bombing strikes and patrols in preparation for the July 21, 1944, recapture of Guam. Ensign Thomas Hollowell (left), one of the Bush photo pilots, was killed while on a mission attacking the Japanese airbase on Guam's Orote Peninsula (below) former site of the Pan American China Clipper base (upper).

The fighter and bomber pilots of all the INDEPENDENCE class light carriers of Task Force 58 resented being assigned to routine anti-submarine patrols while the pilots of the big ESSEX class were given the majority of "choice bombing missions." Vice Admiral John S. McCain was sent around to the light carriers to placate the pilots and assure them they would be given their share of strikes against Japanese forces. McCain pointed out the smallness of the light carriers allowed for versatility in rapid launching during varied tactical battle situations. McCain, also a naval pilot, won over the aviators. Upon his arrival on the USS SAN JACINTO, McCain was greeted by Captain Harold "Beauty" Martin.[10]

USS SAN JACINTO photo by Edward Tinsley, National Archives.

Bush and Pilots
Protest to the Admiral

Admiral Mc Cain confers with "Beauty" Martin on the bridge of the SAN JACINTO.

USS SAN JACINTO photo by Richard Names, National Archives.

President George Bush greets Admiral McCain's grandson, Senator John McCain of Arizona in the Oval Office.

White House photo by David Valdez.

PART VI

Admiral Nimitz was determined to end persistent Marine Corps complaints about the pre-invasion naval photo intelligence. The criticism by Marine Corps Generals Smith and Shepherd had reached the Admiral directly as he personally toured the Saipan and Guam battlefronts in late June and early July 1944. His solution was unprecedented. Nimitz ordered the entire Task Force 58 to a massive photo mission. He called it Operation Snapshot. Ironically SNAPSHOT is regarded as a derogatory term by professional photographers. Like all wartime navy operations, it was to be a top secret—so secret that its name could not be written in any communique!

Operation Snapshot would supply General Smith and the Marine Corps with the most extensive and most inclusive photo reconnaissance possible of the next objective in the Pacific island hopping strategy. The target was Peleliu, an island at the southern end of the Chichi Jima defensive barrier. The invasion would begin September 15 when the First Marine Corps Division would land on Peleliu.

In Task Force 58's operation plans, the SAN JACINTO— including the Bush photo team—were given prime responsibility for obtaining detailed aerial photography of the island's terrain and near-shore reef environment. The other eight carriers of the Task Force augmented the Palau coverage.

The SAN JACINTO was still in the same task group but with a new commander, Rear Admiral Alfred E. Montgomery, who had been in charge of the Wake Island raid of May 23. Montgomery's flagship was the USS BUNKER HILL, one of the large Essex class carriers. Rounding out the group was the USS LEXINGTON with Admiral Mitscher, the commander of Task Force Fifty-Eight aboard, five battleships, four cruisers and 15 destroyers.

Admiral Montgomery, who was aware of the Marine Corps photo intelligence complaints, drafted the Operation Snapshot orders to the 27 warships under his command: "ATTENTION IS INVITED TO THE FACT THAT THE PRIMARY OBJECTIVE OF THIS OPERATION IS PHOTOGRAPHIC COVERAGE OF ASSIGNED AREAS. UNLESS COMPLETE AND THOROUGH COVERAGE IS OBTAINED THE ENTIRE OPERATION WILL HAVE BEEN A FAILURE." He said the operation would start on Yoke minus three day (Y-3) which was set for July 25, 1944. Bush and the SAN JACINTO had participated in the Saipan-Guam intelligence photog-

Bum Photo Intelligence
Tell it to the Marines

General H. M. "Howlin Mad" Smith, stung by media criticism of the Mariana invasion, blamed lack of U.S. Navy intelligence photography for high casualty rates on Saipan and Guam.

raphy, but not in the pre-invasion stages. Operation Snapshot would be different. Under guidance of Lieutenant (j. g.) Jerome Pasto, the SAN JACINTO's photo interpretation officer, the Bush team was geared to provide the Marine Corps with every possible aerial photo look at Peleliu's military terrain.

Colonel Thomas L. Ridge, a member of the headquarters staff of the Fleet Marine Force during the Pacific War discussed the importance of pre-invasion reconnaissance: "Photography is critical during planning for an amphibious landing operation. The amphibious commander's problem is to get his troops and equipment from the sea to land and then establish a sustainable supply system over the routes." Ridge who later commanded military landings at Inchon, Korea, said, "Marine Corps doctrine developed over decades

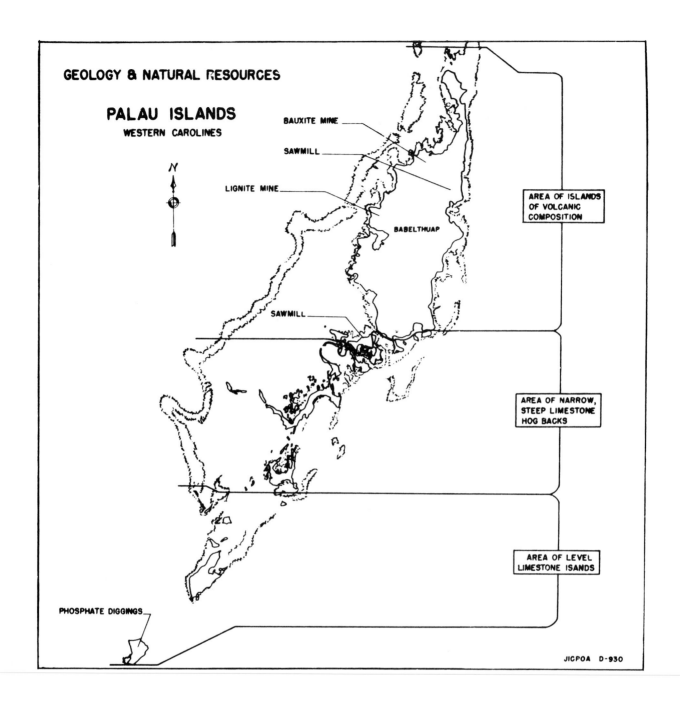

GEOLOGY & NATURAL RESOURCES

PALAU ISLANDS
WESTERN CAROLINES

N

BAUXITE MINE

SAWMILL

LIGNITE MINE

BABELTHUAP

AREA OF ISLANDS
OF VOLCANIC
COMPOSITION

SAWMILL

AREA OF NARROW,
STEEP LIMESTONE
HOG BACKS

AREA OF LEVEL
LIMESTONE ISANDS

PHOSPHATE DIGGINGS

JICPOA D-930

Background of
The Marines' Complaint

These intelligence monographs of Peleliu tend to support Marine Corps complaints concerning the pre-invasion photography intelligence of Peleliu. Naval intelligence mislabeled Peleliu as an "area of level limestone islands" (above) in a JICPOA bulletin of June 1, 1944 used for the initial invasion planning. Compounding the error, JICPOA focused on the Japanese installations in the central Palau Islands and minimized information on the actual invasion target, Peleliu (opposite page). The geology error was continued in subsequent revisions. *Source: JICPOA Bulletin #87-44.*

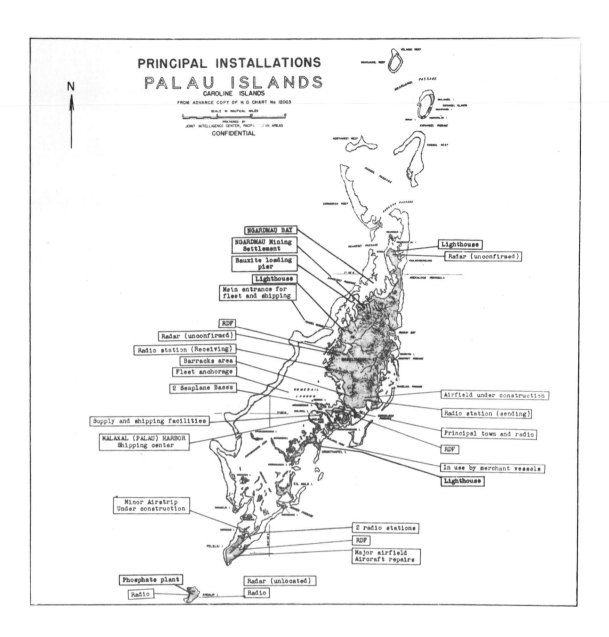

PRINCIPAL INSTALLATIONS
PALAU ISLANDS
CAROLINE ISLANDS
FROM ADVANCE COPY OF H.Q. CHART No. 12003

SCALE IN NAUTICAL MILES

PREPARED BY
JOINT INTELLIGENCE CENTER, PACIFIC OCEAN AREAS
CONFIDENTIAL

N

NGARDMAU BAY

NGARDMAU Mining Settlement

Bauxite loading pier

Lighthouse

Main entrance for fleet and shipping

RDF

Radar (unconfirmed)

Radio station (Receiving)

Barracks area

Fleet anchorage

2 Seaplane Bases

Supply and shipping facilities

MALAKAL (PALAU) HARBOR Shipping center

Minor Airstrip Under construction

Phosphate plant

Radio

Lighthouse

Radar (unconfirmed)

Airfield under construction

Radio station (sending)

Principal town and radio

RDF

In use by merchant vessels

Lighthouse

2 radio stations

RDF

Major airfield Aircraft repairs

Radar (unlocated)

Radio

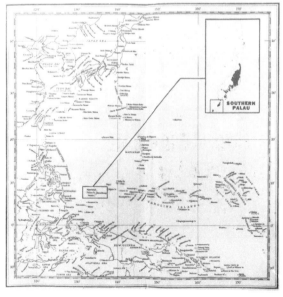

SOUTHERN PALAU

Naval Photo Teams Ordered:
Get the Pictures

The Marine Corps photo complaints caught the attention of the Navy's top brass, Admirals Chester Nimitz, Ernest King and Raymond Spruance (above). They ordered Task Force 58 on a Peleliu photo mission and called it Operation Snapshot. The word quickly got to the SAN JACINTO where pilot Dixie Mays' photo plane, Fox 13, was ready to go (left).

Photo source: Admirals: National Archives. Fox 13, courtesy Dixie Mays.

Admiral Marc Mitscher, commander of Task Force 58, sent out the word on Operation Snapshot: "Do not fail."
Photographers surround the Admiral (second from right with goggles on head) aboard his flagship, USS
LEXINGTON. J. R. Eyerman, LIFE Magazine focuses a twin-lens reflex (second from left), and navy
photographer, E. S. Cornwell uses a Kodak Medalist (right). *USS LEXINGTON photo, National Archives.*

Lieutenant (j.g.) Jerome Pasto (left in photo) planned the SAN JACINTO
photo flights of the intended Peleliu invasion beaches with Dixie Mays
(right) whose "lucky" Fox 13 was equipped with vertical and oblique
cameras. George Bush, in the slower Avenger, participated in search and
destroy missions in north portion of the Palau Islands.
Source: USS SAN JACINTO photo, courtesy Dixie Mays.

Opening day of Operation Snapshot on July 25, 1944. Here the USS SAN JACINTO flies the Lone Star Flag of Texas as George Bush in Tare Two (lower right) moves up the flight deck to the catapult. Bush, as usual, is in last or "sniffer" position for the torpedo–bombers. Hellcat (F6F) fighter escort (aft) used a deck launching.

USS SAN JACINTO photo by Robert Stinnett, National Archives.

required aerial photography to provide data on underwater obstacles and learn details of the tactical situation facings invaders on the beach. Vertical and oblique aerial photography work together to furnish this type of data as well as provide intelligence on defensive positions of the enemy."

To meet these basic invasion intelligence requirements, Lieutenant Pasto planned 12 photo sorties that covered every square foot of Peleliu's land area and the adjacent reef. Pasto wanted a photo look at the reef to locate any obstacles placed by the Japanese to block movement of American landing craft coming in from the sea. Included in the sorties were the west coast landing sites which the Marine Corps code-named, Orange, White and Amber beaches. The SAN JACINTO's aerial photo duties were divided between Ensigns Dixie Mays and George Bush. All photo sorties using fixed-cameras were flown from Hellcats piloted by Mays and Ensign Douglas Bramhall, who had replaced Ensign Hollowell, killed in combat during the Marianas Turkey Shoot. Bush and his aircrewman-photographers were responsible for all aerial scouting photography using hand-held cameras during Operation Snapshot.

On July 25 at 1400 hours (2pm), the SAN JACINTO hoisted the Texas Lone Star Flag signaling that the carrier was ready for combat action. Operation Snapshot was underway as a deck load of fighters and bombers was launched for sweep-and-search missions over the entire Palau chain of islands.[2]

George Bush's first assigned combat mission for Operation Snapshot was the northern tip of Palau at Kayangle Atoll and nearby Velasco Reef.

The Bush air crew of John Delaney in the radio/bombardier spot and Leo Nadeau in the gun turret were flying from a "new" Tare Two. The replacement bomber had been obtained from the USS BELLEAU WOOD, another light carrier of the SAN JACINTO's class. Deck crews had painted "X-2" on the tail section obliterating the recognition number issued by the BELLEAU WOOD. Nadeau regarded the "used bomber" as a clunker, not worthy to be called "The Barbara." Nevertheless, George Bush christened the bomber "The Barbara Two."

Bush was flying wing to the Division commander, Lieutenant Richard Houle. They were escorted by a section of Hellcat fighters led by Lieutenant Bayard F. Griffin Jr., and Lieutenants Leo A. Bird Jr., Rufus

Henderson Jr., and Ensign Nathaniel J. Adams.

As the search group reached Velasco Reef, Lieutenant Griffin spotted a Japanese float plane called "Jake" by USN recognition procedures. The "Jake" was escorting what Griffin believed to be a Japanese destroyer. Later it was determined that the warship was the Japanese coastal minelayer SOKUTEN, loaded with 120 mines. Griffin and his wing man Nat "Blackie" Adams, shot down the "Jake," then turned their attention to the SOKUTEN which was under strafing attacks from the .50 caliber machine guns of Lieutenant Bird and Ensign Henderson. The fighters were softening up the minelayer for a bombing attack by Bush and Houle. As Ensign Adams went into his strafing dive, a terrific mushrooming explosion blew the munitions-loaded ship apart. It literally "vaporized," Adams recalled.[3]

Circling above the action at 5000 feet, Bush saw the explosion and tipped his right wing, allowing Delaney, using the hand-held K-20 camera, to snap one of the most spectacular pictures of the Pacific War. Adams flew through portions of the explosion's aftermath. As he did so, shrapnel and debris from the massive detonation of 120 mines pierced his fighter, severely damaging the left stabilizer. Adams control of the Hellcat was crippled by the damage. He decided to try an emergency return to the SAN JACINTO, about 100 miles away.

While en route to his emergency landing, his fighter began to stall and became difficult to maneuver. Nearing the operational area of the task group, he saw the USS HEALY, a plane guard destroyer. He decided to try a ditch in the ocean alongside the vessel. Ever so gently he pancaked the Hellcat on the water. The ditching was successful. Quickly he climbed from his cockpit and inflated his life raft and paddled clear of the doomed fighter. Hearing of the ditching and rescue on his radio circuit, Houle grimmaced as he thought of Adams in the water. The HEALY had pulled him and two crew members from the drink a month earlier.

Back at the SOKUTEN explosion scene, Bush looked for traces of the warship. There was no debris, no survivors, no life rafts. The minelayer had completely disappeared.

Bush and Houle turned their bombers south and continued on their search mission. They found more Japanese navy targets in the lagoon of Kayangle Atoll.

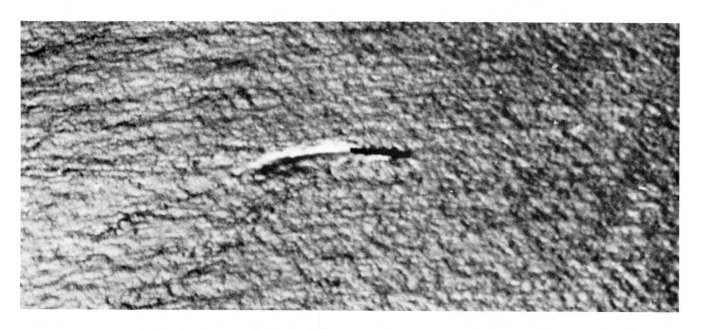

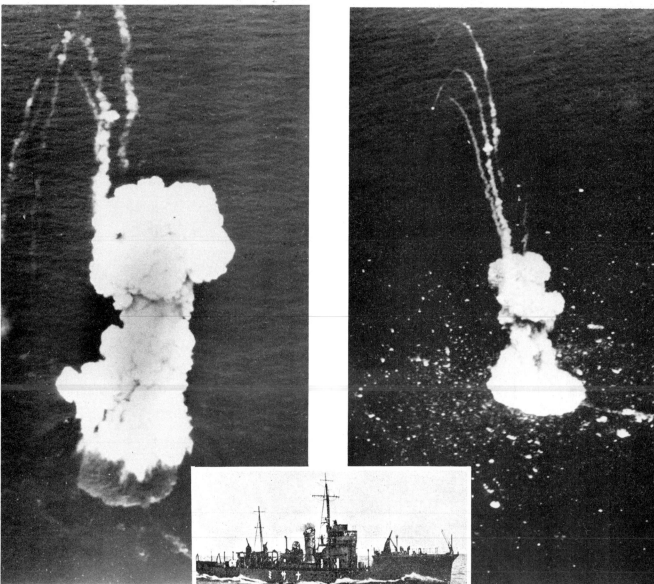

Wingman Destroys Minelayer
Bush Sinks and Photographs Japanese Warships

The Japanese coastal minelayer, SOKUTEN, loaded with 120 mines, vaporizes in the series of photos (opposite page) taken from George Bush's Tare Two. Bush, along with wingman Richard Houle and a fighter escort, was looking for Japanese warships in the north portion of Palau Islands on the first day of Operation Snapshot. At Velasco Reef (see map) the fighters, piloted by Leo Bird, Bayard F. Griffin Jr., Nat "Blackie" Adams and Rufus Henderson, began strafing the minelayer (top opposite page) in preparation for a Bush-Houle bombing attack. Blackie Adams' 50-cal machine guns set off this explosion. Debris hit Adams' Hellcat forcing him to ditch near the USS HEALY where he was safely rescued. (Inset on opposite page shows Japan minelayer class.) Moving on to Kayangle Lagoon, Bush and Houle found three small Japanese cargo ships. Bush got credit for a direct hit (bottom) and brought back the photographs to prove the sinking. This was their last combat mission together. Houle and crewmen were killed two days later by Japanese AA fire.

SOKUTEN and Kayangle Lagoon photos taken from USS SAN JACINTO bomber piloted by George H. W. Bush. National Archives and author's files.

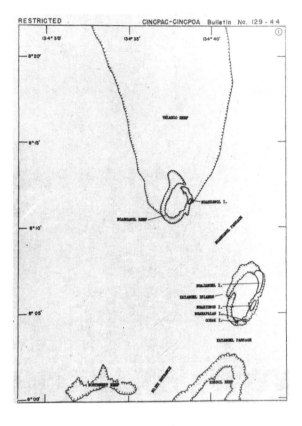

Richard Houle

Nat Adams

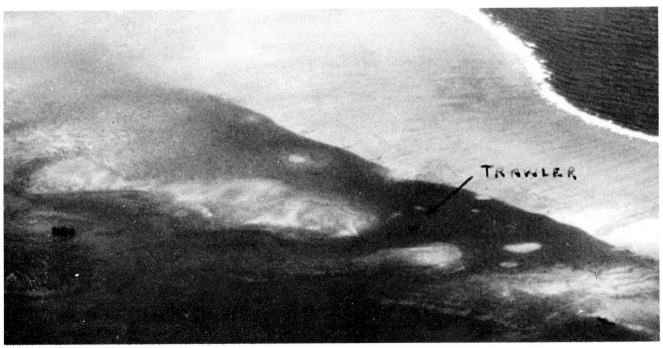

TRAWLER

During Operation Snapshot, the torpedo–bombers of the SAN JACINTO engaged in strikes on Japanese military installations located within the islands of the Palau chain. Tare One was usually flown by VT-51 skipper Lieutenant Commander Donald Melvin. Photo missions were also flown over Anguar, an island just south of Peleliu. Tare 6 (below) is shown flying above Anguar. The lack of a painted "X" on the tail indicates this Avenger was a temporary replacement. *Source: USS SAN JACINTO photos. National Archives.*

President George Bush gets reacquainted with the K–20 aerial camera he used in 1944 during a visit by the author (right) in November 1990 to the Oval Office. *Official White House photo by David Valdez.*

Navy Photographs Rebut Marine Corps

Marine Corps history files contain original photo prints taken by the Bush photo team during Operation Snapshot. Dixie Mays (below) holds up an oblique of the Peleliu radio station which he took on July 26, 1944.

Photo by Robert Stinnett, 1990

Hidden Japanese caves of "Bloody Nose Ridge" were located in this vertical photo taken by Mays, July 26, 1944. It is same subjecct as above. The radio station is shown at upper left. Bomb crater, just off beach, shows in both pictures. Trails (center) lead to underground Japanese cave system on Bloody Nose Ridge. West Road, (horizontal through center of photo) connects cave systems of Bloody Nose Ridge with the Peleliu Airfield complex. Marine Corps general William Rupertus said the US Navy did not provide him with photo intelligence of Peleliu. *USS SAN JACINTO photo by Dixie Mays located by author in Marine Corps History Library, Navy Yard, Washington, D. C.*

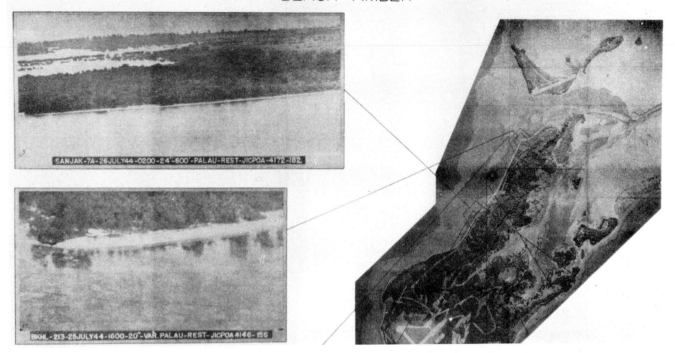

The SAN JACINTO aerial photos of Operation Snapshot were used in the pre-invasion analysis of the Peleliu beaches (top). Elevation contours of Bloody Nose Ridge are included in this official U.S. Marine Corps map (lower) of Peleliu prepared by the Intelligence Section of the First Marine Division based on the Operation Snapshot aerial photos. In the post attack critique, the US Marine Corps said US Navy intelligence failed to provide information on Peleliu's hilly terrain. *Source: Maps and photos located by author in U.S. Marine Corps History Section, Navy Yard, Washington, D. C.*

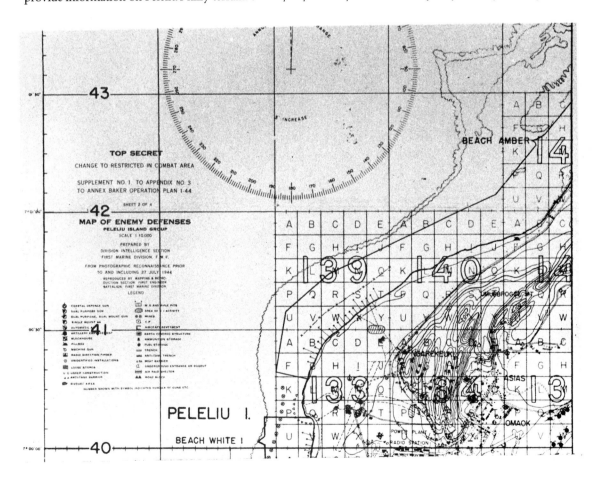

Caves Found on Bloody Nose Ridge

The caves of Bloody Nose Ridge were located by Jerome Pasto, the SAN JACINTO's photo interpretation officer. Pasto's warnings, based on the stereo aerial photos taken by the Bush photo team, were included in this special topography monograph issued August 15, 1944, 30 days in advance of the Peleliu landings. *Source: JICPOA Bulletin #124-44.*

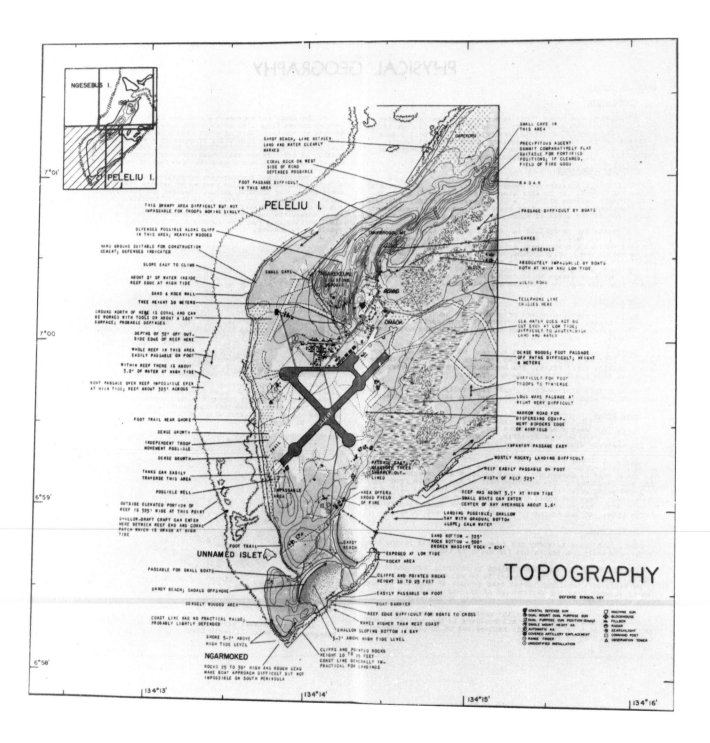

There were three small intercoastal warships inside the lagoon. Two of about 3,000 tons each were beached on the reef and unserviceable. The other was a 150-foot armed trawler anchored in the deeper water of the lagoon. The bombers began their first run, each aiming one 500 pound bomb at the trawler. Both bombs missed. In the second try, Bush scored a direct hit on the trawler's stern and Houle landed one near the bow. The trawler sank within five minutes. Its crew took to the life boats, which were strafed by the escorting SAN JACINTO fighters.

After pulling out of his bombing run, Bush again tilted his wing to allow Delaney to get pictures of the sinking trawler. The vessel was Bush's first Japanese Navy trophy. While the sinking did not rate much attention, it chipped away at the ability of Japanese forces to reinforce their Central Pacific garrisons. One less armed trawler lessened the chance of future American casualties on Peleliu.

During the next two days, July 26-27, the SAN JACINTO's photo planes focused on Peleliu's invasion beaches and the land areas that concealed Japanese defenses. All nine carriers of the huge Task Force 58 were assigned aerial photo missions throughout the Palau Island group. Admiral Nimitz wanted to provide comprehensive photo coverage of all Japanese military installations in case the Marines decided on a target other than Peleliu. The widespread bombing and strafing also served to disguise the true target, Peleliu. The photo planes were surreptitiously included in these attacks to keep Japanese commanders on Palau guessing as to the strategic intentions of the United States Navy.

Lieutenant Pasto called upon his pre-war experience in using aerial photos as base maps for delineating soil boundaries and upon photo interpretation schooling provided by the Navy at the Anacostia Naval Air Station. Stereo pairs can be obtained when the same scene is photographed with one camera from two different but adjacent positions, or simultaneously with two cameras mounted side by side. When the prints are viewed through special optical equipment three dimensional pictures spring forth. Stereo photography was modeled after turn-of-the-century "3-D" travel scenes.

SAN JACINTO metalsmiths installed "side by side" cameras in Dixie Mays' fighter Fox 13. They cut holes into the port fuselage and mounted two F-56 aerial cameras. Each camera was fitted with a 24-inch telephoto lens. Varied flight lines and altitudes which distort the photo interpreters look at enemy terrain are to be expected in combat aerial photography. To overcome these distortions, Pasto relied on a new (for 1944) science called photogrammetry. "Even more sophisticated for the time, was photogrammetry, using mathematics to iron out variations in scale, determine elevations, distances, etc.," Pasto recalled. He briefed photo pilots Mays and Bramhall on their Peleliu missions while Bush outlined photo targets to the aircrewmen-photographers of the bombing squadron. Mays and Bramhall, using their "3-D" stereo-optical cameras, were to "dice" the beach at about 50 foot elevation. Mays explained that "dicing" meant a gamble: "The photo run was a throw of the dice. We knew the guns would be aimed at us, maybe hit us, maybe not. Most of the time we went into the runs at slow speed so as to obtain sharp photographs with sufficient overlap and not to miss any of the target." Like some other aviators, Mays held superstition theories involving flight but in a different way than Leo Nadeau, who associated the number "thirteen" with hexes. Mays numbered his photo plane "Fox 13" and called it the "Hoblin Goblin." Mays said, "It was my lucky number. We were never hit by the Japanese gunners and I was really stuffing the camera up their noses."

During the two days of aerial photography of Operation Snapshot, the Bush team produced 1,017 different photographs of the Peleliu landscape from the near shore reef areas to inner hilly terrain region called the Umurbrogol. When he viewed the stereo twin pairs, Lieutenant Pasto could literally look into the Japanese defenses hidden in the contours of Peleliu's Umurbrogol. He located and marked the military caves on the photo prints.[4]

"Camouflage perhaps can confuse a pilot who has but a few minutes to observe all the detail on the ground and also pay attention to flying. But to the interpreter, who can study the photos in stereo for hours if need be, camouflage can be revealed, and rather easily," Pasto wrote.

Japanese military positions revealed by the photography were pinpointed by Lieutenant Pasto on many of the photo prints. He warned of beach and reef obstacles and located military emplacements in the limestone hillocks of the Umurbrogol.

Each day's photo sorties were processed immediately upon return of the photo planes from their missions. Bush and Pasto watched the photo print development in the SAN JACINTO's darkrooms, selecting certain prints for examination by Captain Martin. While some photos were still fixing in the hypo, Pasto took the photo trays directly to Captain Martin. He wanted instant assurance that the "no failure" edict issued by Admiral Montgomery was carried out. The scene was

The hillocks of Bloody Nose Ridge clearly show in this one-dimensional photo of the west coast of Peleliu taken during Operation Snapshot. When this photo was paired in stereo, Jerome Pasto saw the secret Japanese cave system. These embattlements contained extensive Japanese artillery which hit U.S. First Marine Division invasion troops on September 15, 1944 (opposite page). *USS SAN JACINTO photo by Dixie Mays.*

Japanese artillery hidden in the cave system of Bloody Nose Ridge took heavy toll of U.S. Marines' invasion force during D-Day, September 15, 1944. This is nearly the same view shown on opposite page.

USS SAN JACINTO aerial photo by Dixie Mays.

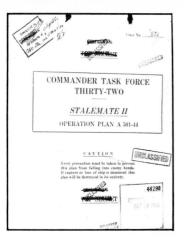

William Ewing, war correspondent.

The General Lost a Bet

General William Rupertus (center above), commander of the First Marine Division on Peleliu, confers with (left) Colonel Lewis J. Fields and General Roy S. Geiger. In a pre-invasion bet with war correspondents (left) covering the Peleliu invasion, Rupertus predicted the island would be secured in four days. Rupertus was wrong. The island was not declared secure until January 1945. Rupertus was relieved of his command by Geiger, two weeks after D-Day.

U.S. Marine Corps photo, National Archives.

Salvos of phosphorous smoke bombs were hurled at Bloody Nose Ridge in attempt to screen off U. S. Marine landing craft. *U.S. Marine Corps photo, National Archives.*

Tare Nine flies over same scene as above on September 15, 1944. *USS SAN JACINTO photo. National Archives.*

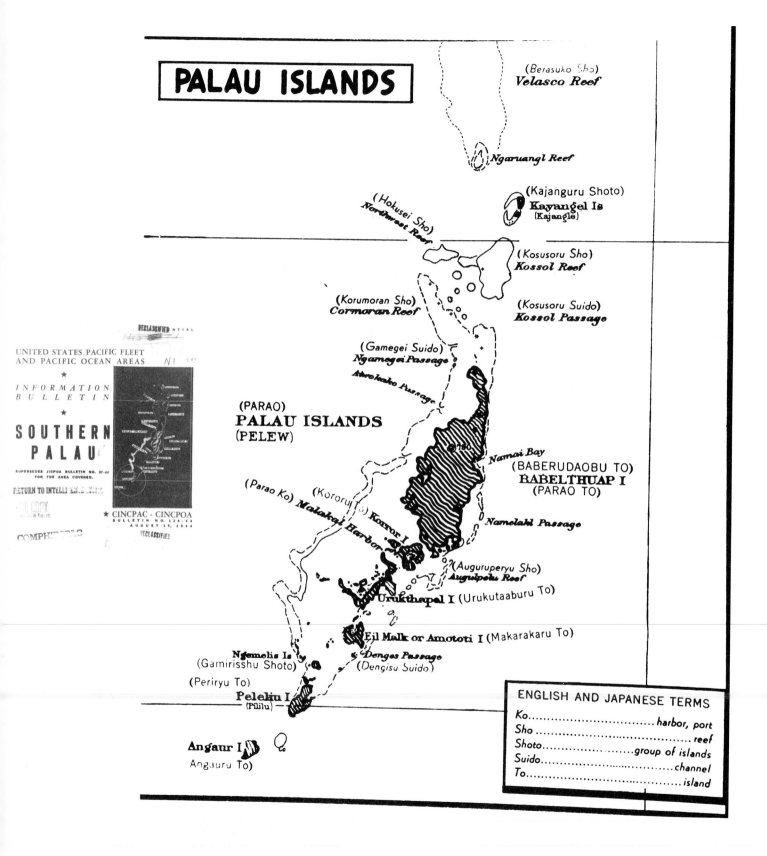

PALAU ISLANDS

(Berasuko Sho)
Velasco Reef

Ngaruangl Reef

(Kajanguru Shoto)
Kayangel Is
(Kajangle)

(Hokusei Sho)
Northwest Reef

(Kosusoru Sho)
Kossol Reef

(Korumoran Sho)
Cormoran Reef

(Kosusoru Suido)
Kossol Passage

(Gamegei Suido)
Ngamegei Passage

Atolesho Passage

(PARAO)
PALAU ISLANDS
(PELEW)

Namai Bay
(BABERUDAOBU TO)
BABELTHUAP I
(PARAO TO)

(Parao Ko)
Malakal Harbor

(Kororu)
Koror I

Namelakl Passage

(Auguruperyu Sho)
Auguipelu Reef

Urukthapel I (Urukutaaburu To)

Eil Malk or Amototi I (Makarakaru To)

Ngemelis Is
(Gamirisshu Shoto)

Denges Passage
(Dengisu Suido)

(Periryu To)

Peleliu I
(Pililu)

Angaur I
Angauru To)

ENGLISH AND JAPANESE TERMS	
Ko	harbor, port
Sho	reef
Shoto	group of islands
Suido	channel
To	island

Iwo Jima Was Mild
Toughest Marine Fight

"Burn 'em out" was practically the only way Marines could get at the Japanese defenders of Peleliu (below). At left, Corporal C. E. Cross and Pvt. E. L. Manfort of the Third Battalion, First Marine Division. After the battle, JICPOA intelligence officers found a labyrinth of 500 caves on Bloody Nose Ridge.

U.S. Marine Corps photo, National Archives.

Members of the First
Marine Division salute as
the U.S. flag is raised atop
the former Japanese radio
station tower.

U.S. Marine Corps photo. National Archives.

General William Rupertus
(lower right with cane)
watched casualties from the
Peleliu battle evacuated to
hospitals. After being
relieved of his command,
Rupertus was sent back to
mainland where he suffered
a heart attack and died at
Bethesda, March 1945.

U.S. Marine Corps photo. National Archives.

reminiscent of a newspaper city room where "scoop" pictures of news events are rush-previewed by editors.

At daybreak the next morning a SAN JACINTO fighter flew a package containing the Peleliu intelligence photos directly to Admiral Montgomery on the USS BUNKER HILL. Another set was rushed by USN air guard mail to Admiral Nimitz' joint intelligence center at Pearl Harbor. The Pacific Fleet photo interpreters and those of the Fleet Marine Force Pearl Harbor headquarters reconfirmed the Pasto findings. Minute intelligence studies and special bulletins concerning Peleliu defenses were issued based on the "3-D" photo coverage of Operaton Snapshot. Additional photos taken by the U. S. submarine BURRFISH during patrol off Peleliu July 29-August 4, 1944, augmented the Operation Snapshot sorties.

All of the photographs and special joint intelligence bulletins were sent to Major General William Rupertus, the commanding general of the First Marine Division. He was in command of the ground forces at Peleliu. From this intelligence an operation plan called Stalemate II was devised by Marine Corps headquarters for the September 15 invasion.

General Rupertus was confident Peleliu would be an easy conquest. Prior to D-Day he presented news correspondents with sealed envelopes. Inside was his prediction: The battle would be tough but his Marines would conquer the enemy in four days or less. He was too optimistic. Hostilities were not declared ended until November 27, 1944. And pockets of fierce resistance continued until early 1945.[5]

Although the island was seized from the Japanese, the human toll was devastating to the Marine Corps. Admiral William F. Halsey, overall commander of the invasion, said the Marine assault troops suffered a 46% loss—6,786 men were killed, missing or wounded. Of this number 1300 were killed.[6]

Again the Marine Corps command blamed their Peleliu tactical problems on the navy's aerial photography. Referring to the Peleliu casualties Marine Corps Colonel William F. Coleman wrote: "Prior to D-Day the aerial photo coverage of our objective (Peleliu) was inadequate and incomplete."

Peleliu's "Bloody Nose Ridge," also known as the Umurbrogol Mountains, was the scene of the Marine Corps' ordeal. Colonel Coleman said the U. S. Naval aerial photo coverage failed to "make interpretations of both terrain and enemy installations." Japanese defenders of Peleliu had constructed an elaborate underground fortress in the limestone ridge of the Umurbrogol which they labeled the "jack-in-the-box" system. From these cave bastions the U.S. Marines were easy targets for Japanese gunners who popped up from the "boxes" with deadly fire.

Official Marine Corps reports charged that the U.S. Navy intelligence and photo interpreters failed to discern the hillocks of "Bloody Nose Ridge" prior to D-Day, September 15, 1944. The Navy's official historian, Admiral Samuel Eliot Morison, joined in the Marine Corps denunciation, writing in his extensive naval history that the aerial photos of Peleliu were defective, giving the general impression that Peleliu was low and flat.[8]

These accusations that U. S. Navy photo interpreters were derelict in their duty do not stand scrutiny. It is true Admiral Nimitz' Joint Intelligence Center erroneously reported Peleliu "was generally level" and "an area of level limestone islands" in the special bulletin issued on June 1, 1944. How this faulty information crept into the bulletin is a mystery because the photos taken during Task Force 58's first attack on Palau, March 31, 1944, distinctly show the hilly terrain of the Umurbrogol. Nevertheless, subsequent joint intelligence reports and bulletins expressly labeled the caves and defenses of the Umurbrogol.

In his examination of the aerial photos taken by the Bush team during Operation Snapshot Lieutenant Pasto located numerous caves in the Umurbrogol and associated them with munitions storage. Underwater obstacles of trenches and barbed wire were found when Dixie Mays "diced" Peleliu's invasion beaches. On August 15, the Joint Intelligence Center, using Lieutenant Pasto's interpretation of the SAN JACINTO photos, indicated the caves and pointed to extensive military bastions in the Umurbrogol. A full-page topograph map outlined the cave system and warned of a 200-foot-high summit at the north end of the Umurbrogol was suitable for fortified positions.[9]

Also providing the Marines with intelligence about Peleliu was the Engineer Battalion of the First Marine Division which produced two series of grid maps entitled "Map of Enemy Defenses, Peleliu Island Group." Series #1 was based on the Operation Snapshot photos of July 26; then revised as the photos of July 27 arrived. These maps, produced by Rupertus' own staff, detail Japanese defenses in the invasion beaches and point to the cave ramparts of the Umurbrogol.

Terrain contours show clearly in the maps which were available to the troops of the Division on September 1, 1944 as annex B to the Stalemate II operation order.

Beach studies using aerial photos produced by the Bush photographer team in Operation Snapshot provided clear low angles of Orange and White Beaches,

The "S" Word
Reprimand Warning for Bush and Squadron

Admiral Marc Mitscher (in photo at left with cap) hit the bulkhead when he saw the words "Operation Snapshot" written in the official reports from Bush's squadron. A written charge citing "violations of instructions" was sent under the Admiral's name by his chief of staff, Arleigh Burke (right) to the "Snapshot Four" (below). All were required to use razor blades and delete the forbidden phrase from the records.

USS LEXINGTON photo, National Archives.

The Accused

Rear Admiral Alfred Montgomery

Captain Harold Martin

Lieutenant Commander Don Melvin

Ensign George Bush

The Charge

COMMANDER FAST CARRIER TASK FORCES

3698

12 AUG 1944

FOURTH ENDORSEMENT to
VT51 ltr. VT-51/A16-3
dated 31 July, 1944.

From: Commander, Task Force FIFTY-EIGHT.
            (Commander, Fast Carrier Task Forces, Pacific)
To :   Commander-in-Chief, U. S. Pacific Fleet.
            Commander, FIFTH Fleet.

Subject: Aircraft Action Reports - Operations 25 July
            1944 through 27 July 1944.

Reference: (a) Cominch restr. ltr. serial 2714, 6 April,
                1944.

1.   Forwarded.

2.   A code name appearing in the basic letter, and
second and third endorsements, in violation of instructions contained in reference (a), has been deleted from all copies received by Commander, Task Force FIFTY-EIGHT. By copy hereof,
Commander, Torpedo Squadron FIFTY-ONE, the Commanding Officer
U.S.S. SAN JACINTO and the Commander, Task Group FIFTY-EIGHT
POINT THREE are requested to make similar deletions from copies
in their possession.

A. A. BURKE,
Captain, U. S. Navy,
Chief of Staff.

The Evidence

VT-51/A16-3   TORPEDO SQUADRON 51

SECRET   ℅ FLEET POST OFFICE,
                    SAN FRANCISCO, CALIFORNIA

                                        31 July 1944

From: The Commanding Officer.
To :   The Commander in Chief, U. S. Pacific Fleet.

Via :   (1) Commander Carrier Air Group FIFTY ONE.
            (2) The Commanding Officer, U.S.S. SAN JACINTO.
            (3) Commander Task Group FIFTY EIGHT POINT THREE.
            (4) Commander Task Force FIFTY EIGHT.
            (5) Commander Fifth Fleet.

Subject: Aircraft Action Reports - ▇▇▇ Operations, 25 July 1944
            through 27 July 1944.

References: (a) CominCH Serial 7152 of 29 Oct. 1943.
            (b) Pacific Fleet C/L 2-CL-44, 1 January 1944.

Enclosures: (A) through (H) - Aircraft Action Reports, VT-51, "1▇▇▇
            through "8▇▇▇▇▇".

1.   In accordance with references (a) and (b) enclosures (A)
through (H) are forwarded herewith.

Copy to: ComAirPac.

D. J. MELVIN.

- -
FIRST ENDORSEMENT: Carrier Air Group FIFTY ONE
CAG-51/A16-3   ℅ Fleet Post Office
                                 San Francisco, Calif.

                                        31 July 1944

From: The Commanding Officer.
To :   The Commander in Chief, U. S. Pacific Fleet.

Via :   (1) The Commanding Officer, U.S.S. SAN JACINTO.
            (2) Commander Task Group FIFTY EIGHT POINT THREE.
            (3) Commander Task Force FIFTY EIGHT.
            (4) Commander Fifth Fleet.

1.   Forwarded.

C. L. MOORE, Jr.

34

The Result

(self-typed)

★ ★ ★   THE VICE PRESIDENT
★ ★ ★   WASHINGTON

                9-20-84

Dear Mr. Stinnett,

Shirley Green passed along to me your
Sept. 3rd letter.

I had not returned to the San Jacinto
by October 25, 1944- to the best of
my recollection.

I was the photographic officer for
our squadron (VT-51). I do recall having
camera equipment issued to me, and I
have some of my snapshots in a scrap
book at home.

I will keep the items you sent me as
souvenirs unless you need them back.

Sincerely with thanks,

the code names for the initial invasion targets.

These studies were also included in the September 1 operation order. A number of historians writing in the immediate post war period for the Marine Corps Historical Section failed to report on the photo intelligence produced by Operation Snapshot. Example: The 1950 official Marine Corps history entitled "The Assault on Peleliu" condemns the navy aerial photography of Operation Snapshot. "Photographic coverage, however, was incomplete and generally unsatisfactory for planning purposes," wrote Major Frank Hough in a monograph published six years after the battle. Hough failed to mention Operation Snapshot but did publish one of the SAN JACINTO's photos taken of the Ngesebus air strip. Hough's critique is similar in language used by the Marines in condemning the navy photography at Tarawa, Saipan, and Guam.

Because naval historian Admiral Morison did not describe the events of the photo operation, this official American history omits important information about the Peleliu invasion.

The omissions by the Marine Corps historians and Morison can be explained, however, because in the summer of 1944 Operation Snapshot was top secret throughout the U.S. Military. It was not to be spoken or written about by any person except those with special security clearance. At the time, naval regulations called for a court martial of anyone revealing the code name of any military operation.

Enter George Bush, Commander Melvin, Captain Martin and Admiral Montgomery. They inadvertently incurred the wrath of Admiral Marc Mitscher when they revealed the forbidden phrase in Squadron 51's secret aircraft action reports of Operation Snapshot. Selected aerial photos taken from Bush's bomber and written descriptions of the combat action were combined in the reports and signed by Melvin on July 31, 1944. The reports were addressed to Admiral Nimitz but had to flow through a naval chain of command in an endorsement process involving Melvin's superior officers.

Melvin violated the orders by mentioning Operation Snapshot eight times in his Action Reports. Captain Martin and Admiral Montgomery each repeated the prohibited phrase during their endorsement process. When the reports and endorsements reached Admiral Mitscher he found 24 technical violations of the Operation Snapshot prohibitions. Mitscher fired off reprimands to Martin, Melvin and Montgomery. In the order signed by Mitscher's Chief of Staff, Captain Arleigh A. Burke, all officers were directed to remove the 24 violations from copies in their files. They complied. The original reports containing the violations are in the Naval Archives in Washington, D. C. and show razor blade cuts in the text which removed the wording. Apparently Admiral Mitscher was satisfied.

Reminded of the incident in 1989, retired Admiral Arleigh A. Burke confirmed that he sent the reprimand on direct orders of Mitscher. Informed that George Bush was the aerial squadron's photo officer on the SAN JACINTO during Operation Snapshot, Burke hinted with tongue-in-cheek that the indictment should have included George Bush. "It's unfortunate we couldn't foresee the future achievements of our associates, and as a result there are thousands of interesting events not recorded."[10]

The Operation Snapshot controversy seems subliminally embedded in Bush's memory. He has referred to his wartime aerial photos as "snapshots."[11]

PART VII

Japanese commanders of Chichi Jima were worried. The American military success at Saipan and the Mariana Islands of Guam and Tinian had broken down the door of the Chichi Jima Defensive Arc like cops busting in for an arrest. Now the door was open for sustained B-29 bombing raids of the home islands from airfields being developed in the Marianas.

In Tokyo, the military command believed the northern portion of the Chichi Jima arc was the "great hope" for ultimate victory over the United States and her allies. Japan still controlled the 680 miles of the arc which stretched from Iwo Jima north to Tokyo Bay. Reinforcements in manpower and supplies were dispatched from the Empire down the Chichi Jima slot, a chain of small volcanic islands extending off Tokyo Bay to Iwo Jima.

Major General Yoshio Tachibana and Vice Admiral Kunizo Mori had been in charge of the army and navy defenses at Chichi Jima since late spring 1944. During their command the victorious Americans had opened the way for attacks on their home islands. General Tachibana and Admiral Mori shared the enmity expressed from the high command in Tokyo. American fliers were "kichiku," or evil beasts equivalent to the devil.

In a sickening attempt to brighten the day for the general and admiral, a series of cocktail parties featuring sugar cane rum and hors d'oeuvres was organized by junior officers of the Chichi Jima command. A report on these parties is in the transcript of the Tokyo War Crimes Trial. What follows here is the actual testimony of defendant Major Sueo Matoba, (M) commanding officer of the 308th Brigade on Chichi Jima; the prosecutor is Captain James J. Robinson (R) of the U. S. Navy:[1]

R: Relate the circumstances of the first case of cannibalism on the island.

M: I went to the Divisional Headquarters and I personally reported to General Tachibana that the flier would be executed at the Suyeyoshi Tai.[2] While I was still at Divisional Headquarters, a telephone call came through from the 307th Battalion headquarters and it was said we should come to a party which Colonel Kato prepared for General Tachibana and myself. We walked to Colonel Kato's quarters, and when we arrived, we found that Colonel Kato did not have enough drinks and things to go with the drinks. On account of this

fact, the general was not satisfied and the question came up where to get something to eat in line of meat and more sake. The general asked me about the execution and about getting more meat. Therefore, I telephoned personally to my headquarters that meat and ten sho of sugar cane rum be delivered to the 307th Battalion Headquarters. I do not recall now if the sugar cane rum was delivered or not, but I know the meat was. The meat was cooked in Colonel Kato's room and everyone present had a taste of it. Of course, nobody relished the taste.

R: They all knew that it was human flesh?

M: Yes.

The prisoners of war referred to by Major Matoba were American carrier pilots of the Pacific Fleet who were carrying out bombing missions on Chichi Jima. All were captured by Tachibana's forces when anti-aircraft fire immobilized their planes, forcing an emergency parachute jump or water landing. Admiral Mitscher was fully aware of the danger facing American aviators taken prisoner by the Japanese. Reports had reached him of Japanese cruelties and violations of treaties concerning treatment of prisoners of war. To avoid this possibility, he ordered that United States submarines be stationed as "life guards" near each island during navy raids. If hit by anti-aircraft fire, the pilots had three options: (1) Make a water landing near the "life guard" sub; (2) Bail out by parachute and risk capture by Japanese forces; or (3) Ride the plane down to instant death. During the course of carrier raids on Chichi Jima, according to the Tokyo War Crimes Trial transcript, eight American fliers chose option number two and were taken prisoner by Tachibana's troops.

As an example Lieutenant (j.g.) "X" was one of the carrier pilots choosing option number two. Major Matoba, commander of the 308th battalion on Chichi Jima, told the War Crimes Tribunal what happened to Lieutenant "X" after he bailed out of his U. S. fighter during an attack on the Mt. Yoake radio complex. (The name of Lieutenant j.g. "X" is being withheld by the author.)

R: (Captain James Robinson, U.S. Prosecutor): How many executions were there at the Yoake wireless station?

M: (Major Sueo Matoba of the Imperial Japanese

Beer Party on Eniwetok

There was no "city lights" liberty for the aviators or crew of the USS SAN JACINTO who remained in the Pacific combat zone from May 1944 until return to Alameda Naval Air Station in September 1945. During the 16 months of continuous war duty, the only "R&R" came via a sporadic beer party staged by the Navy at one of the fleet anchorages. Captain "Beauty" Martin, the affable skipper of the carrier, enjoys a talk with two sailors (opposite page). Crew members (lower opposite page) loaded onto landing craft for journey to the "beer beach" where they waited in line for their two beers. Carriers of Task Force 58 ride at anchor in the background. The massive water area of the Eniwetok Lagoon sheltered the SAN JACINTO (below), Task Force 58, plus all the auxiliaries needed to supply the fleet. *USS SAN JACINTO photos, author's files.*

No Bomber Pilots
Awards to Fighter Pilots

For their heroic air actions against Japanese forces, fighter pilots of Air Group 51 received air medals from Captain Harold Martin during August 1944 ceremonies aboard the USS SAN JACINTO. Awaiting presentation are (left to right): Lieutenant Bayard F. Griffin Jr., Lieutenant (j.g.) Rufus Henderson Jr., Lieutenant (j.g.) Leo A. Bird, Ensign Nat J. "Blackie" Adams, Lieutenant William L. Poland, Lieutenant (j.g.) William H. Hile Jr., Lieutenant (j.g.) Dixie Mays, Ensign Douglas Bramhall. Though nominated for both the Air Medal and Distinguished Flying Cross, George Bush did not receive his awards until after the war ended. Bush is shown in this picture standing "at ease" directly behind Rufus Henderson. At Bush's right is LCDR Donald Melvin.

USS SAN JACINTO photo by Robert Stinnett, National Archives.

Army): I do not know, either one or two. The execution was performed by an officer who was present with his sword.

R: Do you know Sergeant Furushika?

M: Yes.

R: Why was it that Sergeant Furushika was scheduled to perform the execution?

M: Out of the personnel there were some who volunteered and wanted to perform the execution, and Furushika must have been one of them. Sergeant Furushika was sharpening his sword and polished it up and was expecting to execute Lieutenant "X." It was not the custom of the Japanese to order an execution. Therefore, only volunteers could do the job. The responsibility lies with me and I am willing to take full responsibility for what happened."

Major Matoba explained that General Tachibana regarded Lieutenant "X" as a war criminal for his attack on the Mt. Yoake radio station. When his fighter had been hit by the anti-aircraft batteries, Lieutenant "X" had bailed out and upon landing been taken prisoner of war by Japanese military police on Chichi Jima. After interrogation by Major Yoshitaka Horie, Tachibana's Chief of Staff, Lieutenant "X" was taken to the Mt. Yoake wireless complex where he was forced to view the scene of his attack. Then his Japanese captors tied his hands, placed a blindfold over his eyes and forced him to kneel on the ground before the transmitter building. Next, Sergeant Furushika stepped forward and with a swoop of his polished sword beheaded Lieutenant "X."

The three-option choice was about to be faced by George Bush. On September 2, 1944, he was assigned the bombing run on the Mt. Yoake radio labyrinth.

In August 1944, after completing Operation Snapshot, the U. S. carrier task force retired to the Eniwetok Naval Anchorage for rest and replenishment. The task force also started loading supplies for Operation Stalemate II, the Peleliu invasion.[3] As part of the replenishment, Bush, Nadeau and Delaney flew the substitute "Barbara" off the deck of the SAN JACINTO to the Naval Air Station on Eniwetok and exchanged the "clunker" for a brand new bomber. Bush also had a new rank. He was promoted to Lieutenant junior grade.[4]

The Bush flight crew was proud of its new airplane. It was informally christened "The Barbara" as Bush, Delaney and Nadeau were photographed standing alongside. During the photo session, Nadeau saw what he regarded as a hex sign. He noticed the new "Bar-

bara" was not Tare Two, but Tare Three. This was not tradition. Ever since he joined Bush, their official fuselage number had been Tare Two. But rather than complain and possibly face another discipline hearing, he remained silent. Besides, Bush didn't care if the bomber was Tare Two or Tare Three.[5]

Operation Stalemate II (the Peleliu invasion) called for units of the Fast Carrier Task Force to carry out search and destroy missions on what remained of the Chichi Jima defensive arc. Admiral Mitscher scheduled three days of strikes on the island from August 31 to September 2, 1944. Determining to reverse its defeat at Saipan, Japan had begun sending reinforcements to Chichi Jima and Iwo Jima. Staged from Japanese air bases on Iwo Jima, these reinforcements were used in August 1944 to hassle U. S. forces who were now developing the Marianas into major air bases for operations of the B-29 bombers.

General Tachibana and Admiral Mori were responsible for maintaining the supply line and thwarting the construction of the American air bases. Japan delegated to the two commanders the task of converting Chichi Jima into a strategic military center for one of the most fanatical defenses of modern time. Chichi Jima's pivotal role in Japan's final defense was clearly described in orders sent from Tokyo. It was to be the last stronghold of the Nipponese Island Empire.[6]

By August 1944, 15,000 Japanese troops were on the island with 166 "suicide" boats poised to strike American warships. Offshore, mines were floated 10 feet below surface to prevent U. S. landings. To underscore his nation's determination, Emperor Hirohito sent his own palace guard of anti-aircraft gunners to Chichi Jima. Transferred from the Akasaka Imperial Palace and environs, the gunners were part of the Tokyo Air Defense Regiment, Japan's most elite anti-aircraft unit.

On Chichi Jima the unit was organized into grossbatteries to aim concentrated 75mm (3-inch) fire at American flight formations. Usually containing 18 guns, the grossbatteries were established throughout the island and especially on Mt. Yoake on Chichi Jima's east coast. Japanese gunners were told to fire at the American lead plane as it began its bombing or strafing run.[7]

American fliers could not mistake Mt. Yoake. The rugged volcanic peak was part of a small chain of mountains which rose abrubtly from the Pacific waters to about 1,000 feet in height. Its summit and slopes were distinguished from the other peaks by the forest of radio antennae towers which served the radio transmitters and receivers of the Imperial Japanese Navy.

Bush Celebrates New Bomber

The Bush bomber crew, John Delaney, Leo Nadeau and Bush, were all smiles (below) as they posed before the new TBM Avenger torpedo-bomber on the flight deck of the USS SAN JACINTO in late August 1944. This aircraft, Bureau #46214, was first permanent replacement for "The Barbara" which was ditched on June 19. In 1988 (left), George Bush hugs Leo Nadeau who introduced the future president to the Republican National Convention in New Orleans.

Crew photo: USS SAN JACINTO by Richard P. Names. Convention: Courtesy Lee Nadeau.

George Bush and radioman John Delaney pose before Tare Three in their last photograph together.

USS SAN JACINTO photo by Richard P. Names. Courtesy Lee Nadeau.

Tare Three proved to be a popular new bomber with many of VT-51's aircrewmen who wanted to pose before it. Front row, left to right: John Richards, Wendell Tomes, UNID (rear), Donald Gaylien, Sam Melton, John Delaney, George Stoudt. In the rear (left to right): Al Maxwell, George Griffith, Leo Nadeau, Lawrence Mueller, Tom Burns, Harold Fuchs (leaning), UNID, Denzel A. Ryboldt. The fuselage number "three" is painted on cowling and inside folded wing assembly. *USS SAN JACINTO photo by Richard P. Names. Courtesy Leo Nadeau.*

Japan's Top Secret
The Mystic Kiyose Vaults

During the bombings of Chichi Jima in 1944 and 1945 Pacific Fleet intelligence officers were unaware of the elaborate vault-bunker system dug into the volcanic terrain of the island. A Marine Corps study team was startled to discover the caverns in December 1945. Immediate speculation arose: Were these "treasure vaults" to house art treasures of Japan or a Hitler style "bunker" to be used by the Imperial family or other high personages? Major Yoshitaka Horie (left) said the copper lined chambers were built in 1939 to serve as "the final stronghold of the Niponnese Island Empire." The main chamber (below) was a vault within a vault and measured 120 feet long by 16 feet wide.

Photo of Major Horie, USS DUNLAP photo, National Archives. Vault photos from JICPOA Bulletin #2-46.

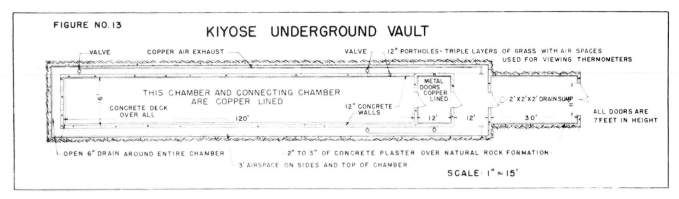

FIGURE NO. 13

KIYOSE UNDERGROUND VAULT

VALVE   COPPER AIR EXHAUST   VALVE   12" PORTHOLES- TRIPLE LAYERS OF GRASS WITH AIR SPACES
                                                    USED FOR VIEWING THERMOMETERS

THIS CHAMBER AND CONNECTING CHAMBER
ARE COPPER LINED

METAL
DOORS
COPPER
LINED

CONCRETE DECK
OVER ALL   120'   12" CONCRETE   2'X2'X2' DRAIN SUMP
                                    WALLS   ALL DOORS ARE
                                          12'   12'   30'   7 FEET IN HEIGHT

OPEN 6" DRAIN AROUND ENTIRE CHAMBER   2" TO 3" OF CONCRETE PLASTER OVER NATURAL ROCK FORMATION

3' AIRSPACE ON SIDES AND TOP OF CHAMBER   SCALE: 1" = 15'

The Marine Corps requested further detailed examination into the purposes of the Kiyose Vaults.
Source: Plot plan JICPOA Bulletin #2-46.

The unpretentious entry to the Kiyose vault.
Source: U.S. Marine Corps photo, JICPOA Bulletin #2-46.

Copper lined bank-vault doors protected Kiyose
chambers. *Source: U. S. Marine Corps photo, JICPOA Bulletin #2-46.*

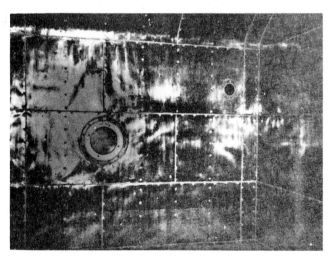

Elaborate air intake and ventilator system of Kiyose
vaults. *Source: U. S. Marine Corps photo, JICPOA Bulletin #2-46.*

Secret Bunkers or Treasure Storage?

Marine Corps Colonel Thomas Ridge (left) was mystified upon discovery of the Kiyose vaults. Unlike common storage areas he found on the island, (below) the chambers of Kiyose were elaborately constructed of burnished copper suggesting a possible bunker system (lower) for the Imperial family of Emperor Hirohito or others of high rank. *Photo of Colonel Ridge by Robert Stinnett, 1990.*

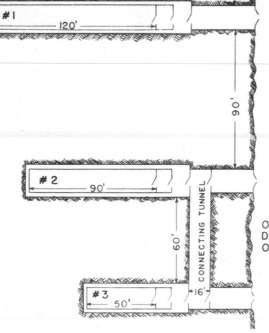

#1 120'

KIYOSE VAULTS
SCALE: 1" = 40'

90'

#2 90'

CONNECTING TUNNEL

60'

OTHER DIMENSIONS AND DETAILS ARE AS SHOWN ON DIAGRAM OF VAULT #1

#3 50'

16'

FIG. NO.12

The main towers were tripod masts which stood 200 feet tall piercing the Pacific sky like masts of tall sailing ships. Protecting the radio towers was a nest of anti-aircraft guns and radar facilities which could hone in on American aircraft. This ordinance had an effective range of 20,000 feet.

One of the most intriguing mysteries of the Pacific War was secreted on Chichi Jima and not discovered until after the war had ended. The mysteries centered on three underground bunkers of immense size, dug into the volcanic rock and located in a small hillside village called Kiyose.

An astonished intelligence team from the Fleet Marine Force of the Pacific discovered the bunkers in December 1945, four months after the Pacific War had ended. Speculation arose immediately on the purpose of the subterreanean facilities according to Marine Corps Colonel Thomas L. Ridge, head of intelligence for the Marines and editor of a final report on the Kiyose mysteries.

Ridge and his staff considered the uncovering of the bunkers a "fantastic find" and chronicled the discovery in a special report in February 1946: "Only as one passes further into the antechamber does one's interest rise. Superior workmanship, modern materials, chaste design and cleanliness impress one first. Then when the center handwheel is spun, drawing the peripheral bolts, and the ponderous strongroom door swings slowly outward revealing the glittering interior of a long chamber lined throughout with flawless sheets of burnished copper, one is dumbfounded."

Stunned by their discovery, Ridge's team wondered at the purpose of such elaborate underground quarters. They were told by Japanese interpreters that the subterreanean chambers were for storing arms and ammunition. The Marine Corps' investigators found it difficult to accept the description. "The whole system seems too grand and costly to be intended for the protection of any military commodity or equipment," said Colonel Ridge. The skepticism voiced by Ridge appears to be justified. Chichi Jima had scores of other storage areas for ammunition and military supplies. Each of these storage spaces were of crude construction, hollowed out of the volcanic rock or built of concrete.

The Kiyose bunkers were chambers within chambers. Each had its own controlled ventilation system to supply fresh air. Bunker number one was a long room with inside dimensions of 120 × 16 feet. The sides and curved ceiling were completely lined with burnished copper. This bunker was set inside an excavation which measured 149 × 24 feet. Entry to the chamber was via three ante-rooms each protected by heavy steel doors which Ridge estimated weighed at least two tons each.

Nearby were two smaller copper lined bunkers which were interconnected by a separate underground tunnel. Each had the same massive steel door security system. Entry to all three underground bunkers was through an unpretentious concrete portico which effectively belied the glitter which lay inside.

Seeking the real purpose of the subterranean bunkers, Ridge's investigators quoted Major Yoshitaka Horie, chief of staff to General Tachibana: "They were built between 1939–1942 under a regime which held that Chichi Jima was one of the final strongholds of the Nipponese Island Empire. Ridge was not satisfied with any of the offered explanations and officially requested further inquiry be conducted by General Douglas MacArthur who was head of the American occupation forces in Japan. Ridge said he never received a reply from MacArthur.[8]

During an interview with the author in February 1990, Colonel Ridge discussed the various speculations concerning the Kiyose mysteries:[9]

S: Colonel you said you had personnaly ventured inside the Kiyose vaults and found two surprises there.

R: Yes. I think it was the only Japanese installation on Chichi Jima which gave surprise to anyone on our staff, particularly me. The discovery was my first surprise. The Japanese had installed a large bank-type vault door at each entrance to the three Kiyose chambers. The door was similar to the type seen in large United States bank installations. These entry doors must have weighed a couple of tons each. Once I passed through the vault door, I went into a very, very long room. Then I discovered the second amazing find. Copper shielding covered all the walls and ceiling. It was burnished copper of a very high luster which had been fabricated and installed inside the chambers with enormous technical skill.

S: You say the vaults were copper lined on ceilings and walls?

R: Yes. The walls and also the ceiling. I think the photographs also show copper on the ceiling. An automatic question came to my mind: Was this vault system intended to keep out radio interference or to prevent radio emissions from leaving the interior of the vaults? But we could never develop any leads along that theory.

S: You believed this copper might have been an electronic shield. That was your first assumption because you had previous experience and interest in electronics as a hobby?

R: Yes, that is right. Therefore, it appeared the copper lining of the vaults was placed there to confine electronic emissions to the interior of the vault. It would be a shield. But we found no lead whatsoever to that thought. It was just an initial idea I had as to the copper lining's purpose as I entered the strange chamber.

S: When you entered and first saw this vault did you think it could have been living quarters?

R: That never occured to me because of the way the thing was built. First if it was for living purposes you would not want a big bank vault door on it. Those doors must have weighed a couple of tons each.

S: You mentioned earlier that the door was similar to a device that drives a ship with a huge type of wheel.

R: When the door was partially opened it had a big metal wheel which you would have to turn to get all the bolts out of the sides.

S: This was extraordinary security for the vault and its contents.

R: Actually I tried moving the door but I could not move it with a light push. It would take all your might to swing against it once it was unlocked.

S: You mean it took two or more people to open the door?

R: No. One person could do it, but you would really be tugging against a lot of weight.

S: Another speculation on this vault system concerns possible storage of art treasurers of Japan. You mentioned this possibility earlier to me. Could you elaborate?

R: Yes. There was speculation among my staff personnel who were researching this project and writing the report. The storage of art treasurers was one speculation. However, as far as we could tell nothing had been stored inside. There would have been some type of debris or something leftover.

S: Did your group discuss the possibility these vaults might have been a bunker or bomb shelter for high Japanese officials?

R: Well, it certainly did not look like it was meant as a place to live. It would have been difficult to live there.

S: You indicated the vaults did have air vents, is that correct?

R: Yes. Each vault had one vent that brought in outside air.

S: What about sanitary facilities?

R: We found none inside. Of course there could be outside.

Colonel Ridge said the Kiyose vaults were unprecedented. Neither he nor any members of his experienced staff saw anything of similar nature constructed by the Japanese in either the South or Central Pacific areas. Japanese scholars in the United States find the Kiyose vaults as puzzling as Colonel Ridge. Kiyoko Yamada of the Asian Library at University of California, Berkeley, was skeptical that the vaults were slated for a last-ditch defense as reported by Major Horie. "Japan's leaders expected total victory. Therefore, a last-ditch defensive command bunker would never have been part of their strategy," Yamada said.

While finding the copper lining of the vaults intriguing, Yoshiko Kakudo, curator of the Asian Art Museum, San Francisco, said the metal is not architecturally associated with Japanese royalty or deities. Both Asian experts sided with Colonel Ridge's best guess: "Probably a secret electronic facility of some sort."

Still unresolved are the statements of Major Yoshitaka Horie, Chief of Staff to General Tachibana, who insisted to Colonel Ridge that the bunkers were built for the final battle of the Nipponese empire. During the post war period, Major Horie served "most outstandingly" by contributing to John Toland's Pulitzer Prize winning book, *The Rising Sun*. In the book, Toland pays tribute to Major Horie for his services as his representative in Japan.

Atrocity Secrets

Both Lieutenant General Yoshio Tachibana and Vice Admiral Kunizo Mori, Japan's commanders on Chichi Jima in 1944 and 1945, were treated with dignity following the surrender of the island, September 3, 1945. Later U.S. Naval war crimes prosecutors charged both commanders with war atrocities involving mayhem against aviators of the Pacific Fleet. *National Archives Photos.*

PART VIII

Operation Stalemate II's first phase was Chichi Jima.

In the squadron ready room of the SAN JACINTO, Lieutenant (j.g.) Bush was briefed on the formidable weaponry on Chichi Jima. Commander Donald Melvin would lead the September 2 attack on the Mt. Yoake radio stations. He and Ensign Doug West would hit the southern end of the complex while Bush and Ensign Milton Moore were directed to drop their bombs on the radio buildings a quarter mile north of Melvin's target.[1]

Leo Nadeau was present for the 6 a.m. briefing but not as a September 2 flight member. He was bumped from the Mt. Yoake strike to make room for Bush's childhood friend, Lieutenant (j. g.) William "Ted" White. White was the gunnery officer of the squadron and asked Bush for a bombing ride to check out the equipment under actual combat conditions. Although Lieutenant White, like Nadeau, was an original member of the squadron, the two had never met.

Nadeau's "substitution" jitters were now back and growing feverishly. First, the change of "The Barbara" from Tare Two to Tare Three and, then, Lieutenant White supplanting him in the gun turret. Nadeau could not stop the substitution after Bush asked him to relinquish his seat and the change was approved by Commander Melvin.

At 0715 (7:15am), a frustrated Nadeau watched as "The Barbara" was catapulted from the SAN JACINTO's flight deck. Lieutenant (j. g.) Bush was at controls, Lieutenant (j.g.) White was in the gun turret and John Delaney, Aviation Radioman Second Class, was in the bombbay, looking after the four 500-pound bombs which were destined for the Mt. Yoake radio facilities.[2]

Once airborne, Bush joined the other aircraft pilots of Strike Baker—flight leader, Commander Melvin, Lieutenant (j. g.) Doug West and Ensign Milton Moore. Melvin's crew consisted of Chester Mierzejewski in the gun turret, Sam Melton as radioman.[3]

Doug West had Joe Foshee as gunner and Harold Nunnally as radioman. Moore's crewmen were Charles Bynum as turret gunner and Richard Gorman as radioman. Melvin led the four SAN JACINTO bombers to a rendezvous with dive bombers from the USS ENTERPRISE which also participated in the raid. The bombers of Strike Baker, together with their fighter escort, proceeded to the Mt. Yoake radio station target on Chichi Jima's east coast. The time was about 0730, September 2, 1944. On the southeast coast of Chichi Jima, the KATO radar unit picked up the approach of Strike Baker which showed as "pips" on their radar screens. Second Lieutenant Kato of the Japanese Army (not to be confused with Colonel Kato of the 308th Battalion) was in command of the radar squad which had been expanded on August 2 with the arrival of the advance units of Emperor Hirohito's anti-aircraft gunners of the Tokyo Air Defense Regiment. The Hirohito gunners actually were en route to Iwo Jima, about 140 miles south of Chichi Jima, but American air attacks on the convoy carrying the regiment forced a retreat to Chichi Jima. The several hundred members of the Air Defense Regiment were dispersed to various mountaintop anti-aircraft batteries on the island.[4]

One member of the regiment was Superior Private Yoshiji Urazaki of Tokyo who described Japanese preparation to shoot down the approaching U.S. naval aircraft: "When enemy planes were picked up, the information was passed on to the Chichi Jima Naval headquarters, which also had under it a Navy radar unit located approximately in the center of the island."[4]

In the next step, according to Urazaki, the anti-aircraft guns of the grossbatteries would be immediately alerted to the approach of American aircraft. These radar warnings also triggered an island-wide air raid alarm sounded by buglers blasting the warm September day with continuous three-minute warning cycles.[6] The Japanese had installed 75mm anti-aircraft guns in the grossbatteries on Mt. Yoake. The gunners were under orders to concentrate their fire on the lead plane of each American flight formation. Commander Don Melvin gradually climbed to 8,000 feet as he led his bomber division on the 71-mile journey.

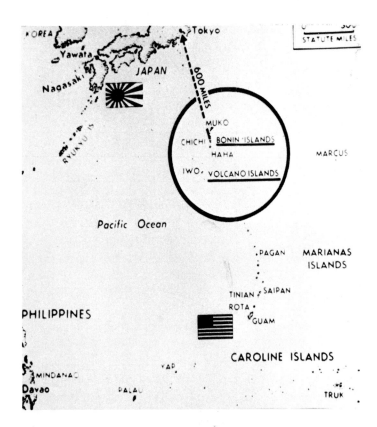

Tragedy at Chichi Jima

Chichi Jima is part of the Ogasawara Islands (Bonin Islands) which, during the Pacific War, initially served Japan in the offensive phase (1941-43) then in defense (1944-45) when U. S. forces brought the war to the Empire's home islands. The JICPOA intelligence map depicts Japanese embattlements on Chichi Jima (father island) below.

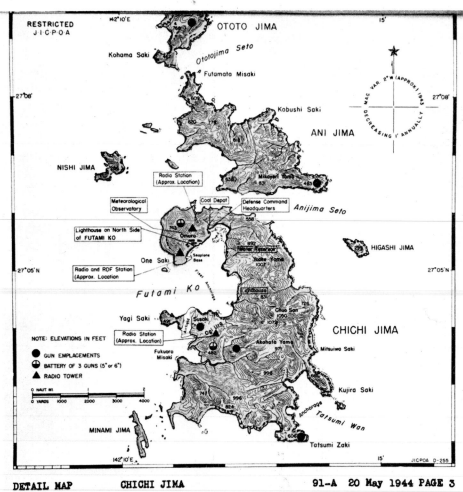

DETAIL MAP   CHICHI JIMA   91-A 20 May 1944 PAGE 3

A US Navy "Helldiver" SB2-C dive bomber flies over the irregular geography of Chichi Jima. Futami Bay, the Japanese Fleet anchorage is directly below the SB2C. At far right, Ani Strait separates Chichi Jima from Ani Jima (elder brother). *USS YORKTOWN photo, National Archives.*

Chichi Jima
Intelligence Briefing

Japanese naval radio facilities on Chichi Jima were on ridge tops of the island's east coast. Radio station #7 was Mt. Yoake, Radio #6 was Mt. Asahi. Distance between Asahi and Yoake is about 1000 feet. *Source: JICPOA Bulletin #122-44.*

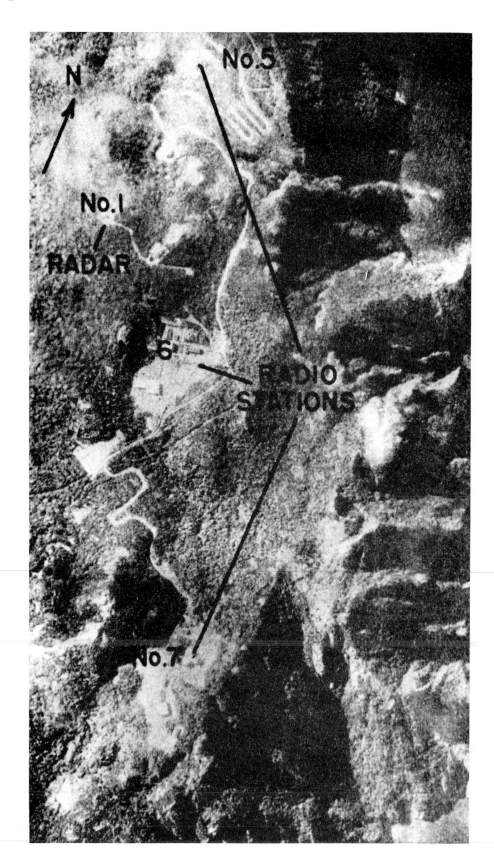

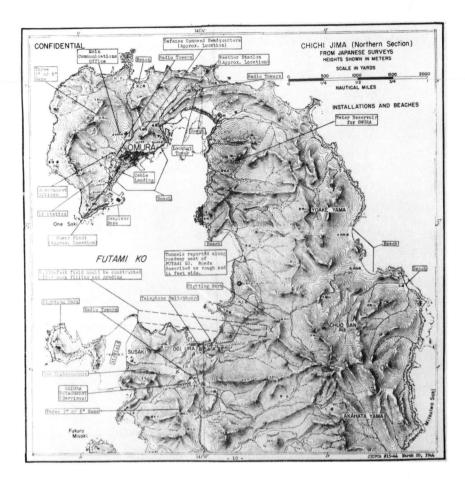

U. S. Navy intelligence prepared this map of Chichi Jima based on Japanese sources. The strategic radio facilities on Mt. Yoake and Mt. Asahi were unknown to USN on March 20, 1944 when this diagram was published.

Source: JICPOA Bulletin #15-44.

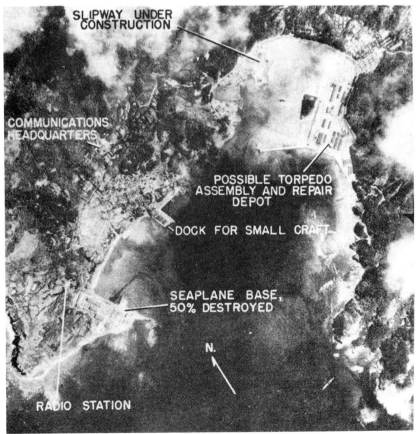

Japanese military facilities near the town of Omura (center left) are pinpointed in this aerial photograph of Chichi Jima prepared by USN intelligence.

JICPOA Bulletin #122-44.

Chichi Jima Defenses

Radar shack and "mattress"

Track vehicle surrendered on Chichi Jima.

A Japanese dual 25mm AA gun.

Japanese "suicide" boats were found hidden in caves.

From the air, this dummy gun looked real.

Mobile searchlights served Chichi Jima defenses.

Hirohito Gunners Obtain USN Flight Formation Plans

These captured Japanese documents indicate extensive knowledge of the U. S. Navy's combat flight formation of Hellcats, Avengers and Helldivers (right). Japanese AA gunners were advised Avenger bombers would start their bombing attack from 2000–3000 meters (approx 6000 to 9000 feet) approaching at a glide angle of 45. *Source: JICPOA Interrogation #28.*

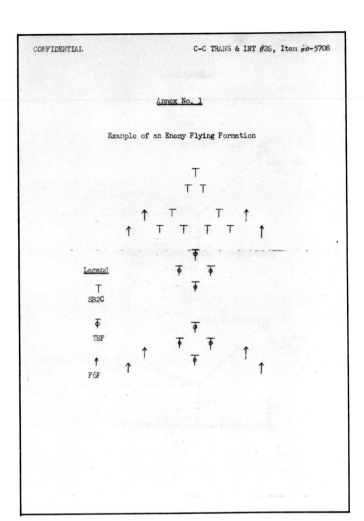

Annex No. 1

Example of an Enemy Flying Formation

Legend

T
SB2C

Φ
TBF

↑
F6F

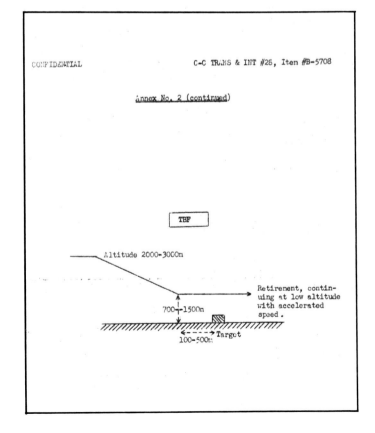

Annex No. 2 (continued)

TBF

Altitude 2000-3000m

Retirement, continuing at low altitude with accelerated speed.

700–1500m

Target
100-500m

Lieutenant (j.g.) George H. W. Bush sits in the cockpit of "The Barbara" making notes on his JICPOA "8 × 8" intelligence bulletins. He wears his parachute harness over the "Mae West" life jacket and a dye marker packet for attracting attention in water. The radio headset enabled him to communicate with the USS SAN JACINTO and his crewmen. *USS SAN JACINTO photo by Robert Stinnett.*

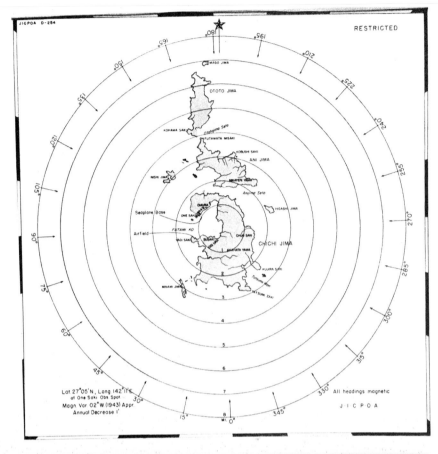

George Bush used this approach map and a heading of 315 from the SAN JACINTO to make his landfall over Kujira Saki. *Source: JICPOA Bulletin #91-A.*

Japanese naval radio facilities on crest of Mt. Asahi included nine stick masts and three towers.

USS YORKTOWN photo from National Archives.

The Mission For Bush

Communication Center, Mt. Asahi

Bombs from George Bush and his wingman, Milt Moore, hit the Mt. Asahi radio facility (lower). In distance is Mt. Yoake. The 200-foot towers (left) were not hit in the raid and survived the war. A bank of radio receivers line the wall (right top) and were operative at time of surrender. A two-story concrete building (opposite page, lower) housed extensive spare parts for Japanese naval communications.

U. S. Marine Corps photos from JICPOA 2-46.

George Bush had strapped the target approach map to his knee for reference. He and Milt Moore would bomb Radio Station #6 on Mt. Asahi, which was about 1,000 feet north of the Japanese main radio facility on Mt. Yoake, a peak of 1,018 feet. Don Melvin and Doug West had the Mt. Yoake radio, known to American intelligence at #7, as their target. The time was now about 0820 (8:20am).

Melvin's attack plan was to circle at the 8,000 foot level with the bombers forming an echelon pattern, allowing for a scattered push over to avoid the anti-aircraft bursts. Then the bombers would begin their glide bomb run, expecting to reach speeds of more than 350 miles per hour. The approach to the targets was on a south to north tack. The time was now 0825 hours.

The Asahi station #6, the Bush/Moore target, was a high frequency long range radio facility responsible for electronically guiding Japanese naval aviation units from the Empire to the South Pacific air bases.

Asahi also provided all electricity for the radio complex from two 50 kilowatt power plants. Bush's target map indicated the principal structures of Asahi were the 6,400 square foot power plant and the 3,600 square foot transmitter building surrounded by the 200-foot high radio antennae. The radio antennae were easy to spot because they cast long shadows in the early morning sun.

The Hirohito anti-aircraft batteries of the Kato Unit focused on the 8,000 elevation as Bush and the other aircraft of Strike Baker prepared to push out of their echelon formation. Just a fraction of a second after Bush pushed over for his glide bomb attack on the Asahi radio complex, "The Barbara" was hit in the engine by the accurate and intense anti-aircraft fire put forth by the Hirohito gunners.

Bush chronicled the hit: "Suddenly there was a jolt, as if a massive fist had crunched into the belly of the plane. Smoke poured into the cockpit and I could see flames rippling across the crease of the wing, edging

CAVE ENTRANCE—AUX. POWER PLANT

ABANDONED AA PO

RADIO STATION NO. 7 (200 FOOT TOWERS)

Grossbatterie AA Guns Surround Radio Stations

The Mt. Yoake radio facilities (below) were hit by bombs dropped from the Avengers of Don Melvin and Doug West. At far left one of the 200-foot towers damaged in the raid rests against cave entrance. Abandoned AA positions, marked on the panoram, were probably the locale of guns which hit Bush's bomber. At right, Lieutenant (j.g.) Jerome Pasto examines a 25mm dual purpose Japanese AA gun. The same type of gun, arranged in clusters (grossbatterie) was found on Chichi Jima

Source: Mt. Yoake U. S. Marine Corps photos from JICPOA Bulletin #2-46. Pasto photo by USS SAN JACINTO, National Archives

A PANORAMIC PHOTOGRAPHIC TERRAIN STUDY.

SITION   ABANDONED AA POSITIONS   MT.KASA

Hellcat fighters (opposite page) provide cover for the
USS SAN JACINTO.
Source: USS SAN JACINTO photo by Edward Tinsley, author's collection.

Bombs for Strike Baker

George Bush dropped four of these 500-pound bombs on the Mt. Asahi radio complex. This photo (lower) taken September 2, 1944, shows SAN JACINTO ordnance men wheeling bombs for loading in the Avengers. Bombs were set to explode a fraction of a second after impact. Such timing permits greater destruction to the target. *USS SAN JACINTO photo, National Archives.*

George Bush heads towards Chichi Jima seconds after
this catapult launch. Full flaps provide maximum lift
during this critical stage. *USS SAN JACINTO photo by Robert Stinnett*

Helldivers from the USS ENTERPRISE fly over south
eastern coast of Chichi Jima on September 2, 1944.
George Bush made landfall at point in lower right and
then proceeded north (right) to target.
USS SAN JACINTO photo, National Archives.

Participating in the Chichi Jima raid with George Bush were flight leader Don Melvin (above center) shown with his crewmen Sam Melton (left) and Chester Mierzejewski. *Courtesy Chester Mierzejewski*

Doug West and his crew (upper right) Harold Nunnally (left) and Joe Foshee. *Courtesy Jacqueline Forshay*

At the lower right, Milt Moore (in center) is joined by his aircrewmen, Richard Gorman (left) and Charles Bynum. *Courtesy of Mrs. Jeanne Moore.*

In the diagram above, Bush begins his glide bombing run, is hit, then with "The Barbara" afire and smoking heads out to sea. He parachutes from the plane and eventually is rescued by USS FINBACK. Ani Jima is at left. *Diagram by Skip Rains.*

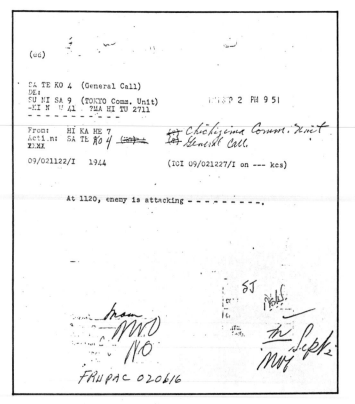

Chichi Radios Enemy Is Attacking

Using the radio call sign HI KA HE 7, Chichi Jima broadcast a general call of the air raid by George Bush and his squadron mates on September 2, 1944. This intercept (left) is by Station Hypo.

Source: SRN series, National Archives.

Chichi Jima's naval base under attack on September 2, 1944 (above). In lower left smoke pours from the Japanese seaplane base. At Special Naval Base (center right) American POW's were held as human shields and tied to trees during these attacks. The Yoake-Asahi radio complex is on ridge at top left.

USS SAN JACINTO photo, National Archives.

The Bush photo team continued to function and brought back pictures of Japanese torpedo boats stashed in this cove adjacent to village of Ogiura.

USS SAN JACINTO photo, National Archives.

The Veep Says Thanks

A joyous Vice President George Bush, in 1984, again thanks Milton Moore for protecting him from would-be Japanese captors during the Chichi Jima raid. Moore and his turret gunner, Charles Bynum, drove off Japan gun boats attempting to take Bush as a POW and human shield. *Courtesy Lee Nadeau.*

The tragic listing in Lee Nadeau's aviation log book (below) records the loss of John Delaney and Ted White on September 2, 1944 . After returning to the SAN JACINTO George H. W. Bush attested to the entry.

Courtesy Leo Nadeau. Copy by Robert Stinnett.

September, 1944

Date	Type of Machine	Number of Machine	Duration of Flight	Character of Flight	Pilot		PASSENGERS	REMARKS
★ 1	TBM-1c	16955	2.7	G	Lt.(JG) Bush		Self + Delaney Icat Icl.	STRIKE ON CHICHI JIMA BONIN IS.
2	Lt. (JG) Bush shot down. Rescued.						Delaney + Lt.(JG) White Missing	
21	Arrived in the Admiralty Is.							
24	Left Admiralty Is.							

TORPEDO SQUADRON - 51

Brought Forward 262.6

This Month   Pilot   Pass 2.2 Total 2.2

Total to Date 270.3

I certify that the foregoing flight record is correct.

L.H. Nadeau
Signature

Approved:

George H.W. Bush
Lt. Comdr., USN, Comdg.

Total time to date,

16—18616

16—18616

toward the fuel tanks. I stayed with the dive, homed in on the target, unloaded our four 500-pound bombs and pulled away, heading for the sea. Once over water, I leveled off and told Delaney and White to bail out, turning the plane starboard to take the slipstream off the door near Delaney's station." Commander Melvin's official report tells what happened next: "Bush continued in his dive, releasing his bombs on the radio station to score damaging hits. He then turned sharply to the east to clear the island of Chichi Jima, smoke and flames enveloping his engine and spreading aft as he did so, and his plane losing altitude."[7]

According to Melvin's account, Bush advised him by radio that it was necessary to bail out. At a point four to five miles off Chichi Jima's north-east coast Melvin said he saw two chutes fall from the disabled bomber, which was then at about 3000 feet. One chute, later identified as Bush, opened and landed safely in the water. The chute of the other person who bailed out did not open. The time was now about 0840.

In his written narrative of the parachute jump, Bush borrowed a superstition line from Nadeau: "Trouble comes in pairs." He then detailed the trouble unfolding over the waters of Chichi Jima's east coast: "According to the book, you dive onto the wing; then the wind pulls you away from the plane. But something went wrong. The wind was playing tricks, or more likely, I pulled the rip cord too soon. First my head, then my parachute canopy collided with the tail of the plane. It was a close one. A fraction of an inch closer and I'd have been snagged on the tail assembly. I came down fast because of the torn canopy, faster than I wanted. Instinctively, I started unbuckling on the way down and easily stepped out of the harness when I hit the water."[8]

Bush had splashed down in the water about four miles northeast of Chichi Jima near a volcanic outcropping called Higashi Jima (Eastern Island). Melvin radioed the location to the rescue submarine, USS FINBACK, which was in position off the west coast of Chichi Jima awaiting just such an emergency.

In landing, Bush became separated from his parachute's collapsible life raft which had been carried away by the ocean swell. A choppy sea hid the raft package so Melvin, flying 500 feet above, pointed out the location by dipping his wing over the raft. Bush swam over and inflated the yellow one-man raft, which was about the size of a large sofa cushion, and climbed aboard. In evaluating his situation, Bush knew he had a chance to survive. "The question was whether my crew members had survived. Neither had responded after the order to bail out." From his bobbing ocean perch, and soaking wet from the ocean dunking, Bush scanned the horizon for signs of Delaney and White. He saw nothing.

The ocean currents were carrying him toward Chichi Jima's eastern shore line. Using his hands, he paddled furiously in the choppy waters just to stay afloat and avoid drifting toward enemy capture. Overhead, pilot Milt Moore saw the telltale wakes of Japanese small craft. They were heading toward Bush. It was to be a race against time. Charles Bynum, who was Moore's turret gunner, had a clear view of the action. He described the effort to save Bush from capture: "I saw those small boats heading his way and thought, oh he's a goner. But at that instant Moore, who was my pilot, and Melvin in the adjoining bomber took the initiative. Our two planes went down and strafed the boats and drove them off.[9] As we dove, Moore's 50 caliber machine guns fired on the Japs. Then as we passed over, the boats became my target. I fired my turret gun at them, but I can't recall if I hit them or not," Bynum said. SAN JACINTO ordnance records indicate 1,460 rounds of machine guns bullets were fired at the would-be Bush captors.[10]

Bush could not see the Japanese small craft and was unaware he was being chased as a POW. "My head still ached. My arm was burning from the sting of an angry Portuguese man-of-war (jelly fish). And to complicate matters, I'd swallowed a few pints of brackish water along the way, which meant I'd occasionally stop paddling to lean over the side." The FINBACK reached Bush at 1156 hours, (11:56am) two hours and 23 minutes after receiving Commander Melvin's radio call. The time lapse was much longer for Bush who had been struggling for survival since about 0840. When it received Melvin's alert at 0933 hours (9:33am) the submarine was on the Philippine Sea side of Chichi Jima maintaining the rescue station and always keeping 7½ miles from the Japanese coastal defense guns. Overhead, two Hellcats provided aerial escort and could shoot down any Japanese aircraft that might try to attack the FINBACK. The skipper Commander Robert R. Williams Jr. maneuvered the FINBACK around the southern tip of the island, then headed north to the reported position of the drifting pilot. Melvin's original report placed Bush as nine miles northeast of Minami Jima a small islet off the southwest coast of Chichi Jima that served as a navigational benchmark.

The time was four minutes to noon on September 2, 1944. Bush had been in the tiny yellow raft tossing on the ocean for nearly three hours. His fellow SAN JACINTO and ENTERPRISE pilots, running low on

Sent From Tokyo

Hirohito's Gunners Hit Bush

Smoke rolls skyward from the Yoake-Asahi radio complex on Chichi Jima following U. S. Navy raid. In foreground the rescue sub heads north toward Ani Jima (far right in photo). Since several aviators were rescued in the locality it is not certain this is the actual Bush rescue mission, but it is similar. This is the area where George Bush parachuted into the waters. His crewmen, John Delaney and William "Ted" White perished when "The Barbara" was hit by AA fire aimed by gunners dispatched from the Imperial Palace, Tokyo. Sea area between sub and the island was heavily mined by Japan.

Source: Rescue sub and White, U.S. Navy photos, National Archives. Delaney courtesy Mrs. Josephine Lee.

John Delaney.

Ted White.

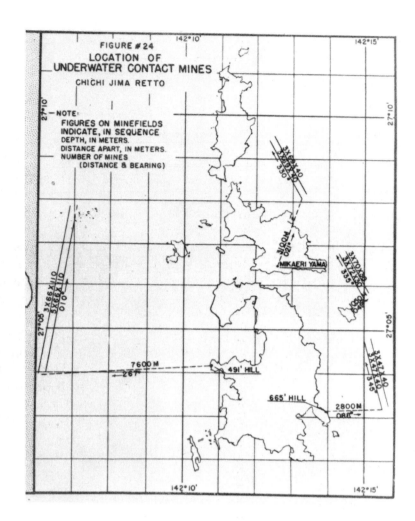

FIGURE #24
LOCATION OF
UNDERWATER CONTACT MINES
CHICHI JIMA RETTO

NOTE—
FIGURES ON MINEFIELDS
INDICATE, IN SEQUENCE
DEPTH, IN METERS.
DISTANCE APART, IN METERS.
NUMBER OF MINES
(DISTANCE & BEARING)

Minefields Endanger Bush and Finback

George Bush's parachute landed him near the Japanese minefield located at 142.15 × 27.06 or due east of Mikaeri Yama. When it heard the distress call that Bush was down in the water, the USS FINBACK was near position 142.10 × 27.02 at the SW corner of Chichi Jima. The sub's skipper navigated to clear these underwater mines. *Map from JICPOA Bulletin 2-46.*

Task Force 38 and 58 pilots were stationed above all rescue subs to prevent attacks by Japanese forces. Here (left) a rescue sub breaks the surface. *USS LEXINGTON photo, National Archives.*

Five members of the FINBACK's crew guide George Bush and his life raft to the starboard bow. This is an enlargement from 16mm movie film taken by Ensign Bill Edwards from the FINBACK's conning tower.
Source: The White House

Tragic News from Chichi Jima

The USS FINBACK notified the SAN JACINTO of the successful rescue of Bush, but the fate of his two crewmen John Delaney and "Ted" White were unknown. Squadron skipper Don Melvin brought back news when he landed Tare One followed by fighter escort (left). Milt Moore, Bush's wingman in the raid (bottom lower with goggles on head), reported Charles Bynum seeing "chutes" which gave hope one of the crew might have survived.

USS SAN JACINTO photos by Robert Stinnett

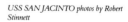

San Jac Sun

Restricted   Sept.   1944

the Back Page

VT-51   VF-51

VT - 51: September 2, 1944

Our torpedo planes flew four flights over Chichi Jima. They had over the target 12 planes, each carrying 4 500# bombs. They hit and destroyed 1 radio station with 8 hits. A second radio station was also hit. VT also hit an ammunition dump or storage place and a large explosion occured with heavy flames. The anti-aircraft fire was very heavy and intense.

Lt.(jg) Bush, while in a dive bombing attack over the target, was hit and his plane caught fire. Mr. Bush and one of the crewman bailed out some where near the target. Mr. Bush's chute opened and was later picked up by a rescue sub. Unfortunately the chute of the crewman failed to open. The crewmen in Mr. Bush's plane were Lt.(jg) W.C. White and J.L. Delaney ARM2/c.

In the afternoon at Haha Jima 3 VT planes with 4 500# bombs each hit one large building and scored many hits on a group of 12 to 15 smaller buildings.

VF - 51:

Today our fighters flew 3 target CAP's. All of them were over Iwo Jima. They likewise flew 5 CAP's over the force all through the operations. The final hop of the day included two photo planes piloted by Ens. Dixie Mays and Ens. Bramhall, who photographed the damage assessment of the raids, also covering the assessment of the shelling by the task unit headed by the

The SAN JAC SUN edition of September 3, 1944 reported Bush's plane was afire and two chutes were seen to exit the bomber, but only one opened. The SUN was one of a few daily newspapers published by a Pacific Fleet vessel. *Courtesy, Lou Grab*

Bomb Damage Confirmed by Photos

At a 1990 Fort Lauderdale reunion Charles Bynum recalls how he drove off Japanese gun boats (middle) who were attempting to take George Bush as a POW. Some of the boats were hidden on rail tracks inside caves at Chichi Jima's seaside (bottom).

Bynum photo by Robert Stinnett. Others by U.S. Marine Corps from JICPOA Bulletin #2-46.

The Avengers from the SAN JACINTO scored direct hits on the Yoake/Asahi radio facilities. Skipper Don Melvin's bombs hit one of the 200-foot radio towers which collapsed over a cave entrance. George Bush was officially credited with hits on the two concrete buildings which housed transmitting equipment.

fuel, had returned to their carriers. They knew the rescue submarine was on the way. Their machine guns had either sunk the POW boats or driven them back to the island.

Bush suddenly saw what appeared to be a black dot emerge from the water about 100 yards away. He recalled the scene: "The dot grew larger. First a periscope then the conning tower, then the hull of a submarine emerged from the depths." Bush prayed it was not a Japanese sub. He saw a large bearded figure standing on the bridge of the conning tower holding a black metal object. It didn't take long for photo officer Bush to identify the object as a Cine Kodak 16mm movie camera. The beard decorated the friendly face of Ensign Bill Edwards, the FINBACK's photographer who recorded the rescue on motion picture film. He was soaking wet, bareheaded, bleeding from a head wound and sitting legs folded as the FINBACK nosed its starboard bow alongside the raft. Five FINBACK sailors, led by Ralph Adams, gathered at the starboard bow and threw Bush a line, pulling him and the raft to the side of the submarine. Adams then reached over the side, grabbed Bush's hands and with the rest of the sailors pulled him aboard. The FINBACK was at a near stop and lurching in the Pacific swell. The five sailors steadied Bush on the pitching forward deck and helped the exhausted but grateful aviator to the inner-quarters of the sub.[11]

Anxious to clear out of the range of Chichi Jima's coastal defense guns, Skipper Williams then submerged the FINBACK to periscope height and headed for the safety of deeper water. Bush told Williams how his plane had been hit by the Chichi Jima gunners. He urged a further search of the waters to look for White and Delaney. Using his periscope, Williams then combed the area hoping that the crew had successfully bailed out. Bush's spirits soared at 1236 hours (12:36pm) when the FINBACK received a report from USS ENTERPRISE planes of spotting a rubber raft and one occupant. Maybe, Bush prayed, it was either White or Delaney. At 1620 hours (4:20pm) the FINBACK reached the rubber boat and rescued Ensign James W. Beckman, fighter pilot of the USS ENTERPRISE who had also been shot down by the intensive anti-aircraft fire from the Japanese gunners. Beckman said he saw the Mt. Yoake attack and only one parachute emerged from Tare Three. "This decided us to discontinue any further search of that area, particularly as our air cover had left," Williams said in his report.[12]

By 1700 hours (5pm) the bombing raid on Chichi Jima was over. On the Mt. Yoake radio complex grounds the Japanese broadcast personnel emerged from their shelters and surveyed the bomb damage. One of the 200-foot transmitting antennae had collapsed from a direct bomb hit. Several buildings in the area were severely damaged. Bomb shrapnel had severed communication lines which linked the various transmitters and receivers that broadcast to the Japanese fleet and shore stations. Rather than risk the remaining radio equipment and men to future bombing danger, the Japanese abandoned the exterior Mt. Yoake complex.[13]

They moved their radio operations into hillside caves where the men and equipment would be immune from U. S. bombing attacks.

Safely back in the SAN JACINTO ready room, pilots Melvin, West and Moore together with their aircrewmen, Bynum, Nunnally, Gorman, Mierzejewski, Melton and Foshee were relieved to hear of the rescue of Bush. But sorrow and gloom silenced the room when they realized Delaney and White would not be coming back. Although the crew members were officially listed as "missing in action," Melvin wrote: "Both were killed as a result of the action."

PART IX

For 44 years, George Bush's attack on the Mt. Yoake radio complex and subsequent shootdown was considered one of many heroic but tragic events in the Pacific theater. For this heroism in action, he was decorated with the Distinguished Flying Cross, an award presented in the name of The President of The United States. The recommendation for the award originated with Rear Admiral Ralph Davison, who was Commander Carrier Division Two during the Chichi Jima attack in September 1944![1]

Admiral Davison cited Bush for "heroism and extraordinary achievement" in the bombing attack on the Mt. Yoake radio complex. The Admiral said Bush's torpedo bomber was hit and set afire at the beginning of his dive. "His courage and devotion to duty were in keeping with the highest traditions of the United States Naval Service," he added.

Then during the presidential campaign of 1988 a different perspective was raised that challenged the official account of the Chichi Jima attack. Chester Mierzejewski, who had been turret gunner in Commander Melvin's bomber, accused Bush of lying about his need to bail out. Mierzejewski was substitution gunner on the raids on Chichi Jima September 1 and 2, 1944, because Fred Myers, the regular gunner was in the Eniwetok Naval Hospital for surgery.

Mierzejewski created a tempest when he said: "That guy (meaning Bush) is not telling the truth." He told reporters for the New York Post that he had seen Bush's plane and it was not smoking nor was it afire when Bush bailed out. Referring to the lost crew members White and Delaney, Mierzejewski said: "I think he (Bush) could have saved those lives if they were alive. I don't know that they were, but at least they had a chance if he had attempted a water landing." From his turret gunner position, Mierzejewski said, he could see clearly into Bush's bomber. He told The Post he was about 100 feet ahead of Bush's plane, so close he could see into the cockpit.[2]

Mierzejewski's charges against Bush were discounted completely by four of the six surviving aircrewman who were on the mission. These eye witnesses were interviewed by the author during 1989 and 1990. One has since died and Sam Melton, radioman for Commander Melvin, did not respond to written inquiries.

Meierzejewski stood by his charges in an interview with the author in July 1990. "The others were not in a position to see Bush. In the attack on the target we were in a tandem dive, each plane behind one another. I knew it was Bush who got hit for he was with us on the dive as Melvin's wing man."

Mierzejewski said he was first to see Bush hit. He said: "I got on the intercom and told Melvin, Bush had been hit. Then Melvin ordered all planes out of the area, so not to draw Japanese attention to Bush in the raft. We didn't want him captured." Reports that they were bombing a radio station are all wrong, according to Mierzejewski. "It was a radar station. Japan didn't need radio facilities for anyone with a transmitter set could send a radio message."

After the war ended, Mierzejewski returned to civilian life and worked in quality control for Pratt & Whitney, aircraft engine manufacturers. He saw the aircraft industry move from piston to jet engines. He and his wife had seven children and 17 grandchildren. Mierzejewski was awarded the Distinguised Flying Cross for his role in sinking the last of Japan's Pearl Harbor day carriers on October 25, 1944 during the Battle off Cape Engano.

Recollections of the surviving four fliers of the Chichi Jima raid refute Mierzejewski on all of his major contentions. They say he is wrong on six major points:

1. The glide bombing was in an echelon or scattered mode, not tandem.
2. The target was two radio stations, one on Mt. Yoake, the other 1,000 feet north on Mt. Asahi.
3. Bush was the leader, Moore the wing man on Mt. Asahi radio station.
4. Melvin was leader and West was the wing man on Mt. Yoake radio.
5. The bombing grid maps used on the raid confirm Bush hit Mt. Asahi and Melvin hit Mt. Yoake.
6. Eyewitnesses including those from the USS ENTERPRISE squadron said Bush's bomber was smoking and afire.

The essence of Mierzejewski's charges boil down to this concept: All four bombers were together in a tandem dive on the Japanese radar station on Chichi Jima. Melvin was in the lead followed by Bush, West and Moore. As turret gunner, Mierzejewski was facing to the rear and could clearly see Bush's bomber which, he says, was 100 feet away. The gunner saw Bush's bomber get hit, but except for a brief flareup there was no smoke or fire. In Mierzejewski's opinion,

Flames and smoke bellow up from bomb hits on the Mt. Asahi radio facilities as Lt (j.g.) George Bush heads for open sea off east coast of Chichi Jima. Wingman Milton Moore is in Avenger at lower right. Skipper Don Melvin and his wingman Doug West attacked Mt. Yoake radio at lower left. *Rendering by Skip Rains based on eyewitness accounts.*

White House presidential assistant, Don Rhodes (second from right) with Torpedo Squadron 51 members at Fort Lauderdale reunion in 1990. Left to right: Harold Fuchs, Leo Nadeau, Charles Bynum, Rhodes and Joe Foshee. Both Bynum and Foshee were eye witnesses to the Bush shoot-down. *Photo by Robert Stinnett.*

Charles Bynum looked out his turret gun hatch and saw parachutes leave "The Barbara" on September 2, 1944. Bynum (above) recreates his position in an Avenger at Fort Lauderdale, March 1990. *Photo by Robert Stinnett.*

Joseph Foshee   Harold Nunnally   Chester Mierzejewski

Rear Admiral Ralph Davison
(Recommended Bush Award)

Vice Admiral Marc A. Mitscher
(Approved Bush Award)

Bush could have attempted a water landing just as he did on June 19 and possibly saved the lives of Delaney and White. The official reports of the USS SAN JACINTO, Torpedo Squadron 51, USS ENTERPRISE, USS FINBACK, The White House and the SAN JAC SUN (the carrier's newspaper at the time) do not support the gunner.

Affirming Bush's account and official documents were two eyewitnesses to the Chichi Jima shootdown—Charles Bynum and Joe Foshee, who were turret gunners on Strike Baker. They said they had a direct view of "The Barbara" when it was hit. Foshee was in the turret seat of Doug West's bomber which was flying left wing on Melvin. As all turret gunners in the TBM's, Foshee sat in his seat facing toward the tail and constantly scanned the sky so as

to be able to spot any attacking Japanese aircraft. He said he probably had the best view of Bush's plane at the time of the hit by Hirohito's gunners.

"I saw Bush get hit. Immediately a blackish brown smoke began trailing from the tail of the plane. It reminded me of aerial dog fights I'd seen in the movies back home. You know, where a stream of smoke starts coming out the back," Foshee said in an interview with the author in 1990.

"Of course I didn't know who it was at the time. Just that the plane was one of ours. I did not see any fire, just smoke. He kept going down, kinda like we were, then as we got out over the water he leveled off. Then he turned the nose down again trying to keep up flying speed. I assumed the flak hit his engine, but I wasn't sure."

Foshee, who was Doug West's gunner, then related how Bush struggled to keep the bomber in the air by using undulating motions of dipping the nose, leveling off, then dipping again. "He was just trying to keep the plane up and flying as long as he could trying to give his crew a chance to get out."

Radioman Richard Gorman, who was in Milt Moore's bomber, recalled how he was concentrating on the release of the 500 pound bombs when he heard Bush holler "hit the silk" over the radio earphone. Gorman said he recognized Bush's voice and was startled. He quickly peered out his small window: "Bush's plane was smoking like a two-alarm fire, then I saw a chute blossom out." Gorman said he followed the chute down and saw Bush "hit the drink." At almost the same moment, Gorman said he saw a "huge ball of fire." He knew it was Bush's bomber exploding.

Yet another witness was Harold Nunnally, radioman for Doug West who was manning the radar/bombing controls directly under Joe Foshee's gun turret. The restrictive compartment limited his view of the outside action so he did not see the hit on Bush's plane and was unaware of the emergency until West moved over the water after the release of bombs on the Mt. Yoake target. Nunnally's memory of the Bush predicament was somewhat hazy but he recalled the debriefing in the SAN JACINTO ready room clearly: "We were pretty sure there was only one person rescued from the Bush plane. It was my understanding at the time that only one person bailed out. This meant the others did not get out and we were not too happy. It is something you accept."

Turret gunner Charles Bynum was in the glide bombing of the Mt. Ashai radio station with Bush. He outright disputed the Mierzejewski allegations, particulary his claim of being within 100 feet of Bush's bomber. As the turret gunner in Milt Moore's plane Bynum said he was in a better position to witness the plane's trouble than Mierzejewski who was 1,000 feet south attacking the Mt. Yoake installation.

"At the start of our bomb runs, the two flights separated. The Mierzejewski flight with Melvin and West aimed at Mt. Yoake. Our flight (Bush and Moore) went for Mt. Asahi, 1000 feet north," Bynum said. "He (Mierzejewski) couldn't see us distinctly. We were quite a bit apart, quite a bit apart. Now I think that is a bunch of malarky that Mierzejewski has been putting out."

"He may have seen Bush's plane, but it would have been just a small speck. I don't think he could distinguish at that distance. He would know it was a plane, but could not tell if it was a TBM or not."

Bynum said he could see Bush's frantic maneuvering as he attempted to level the crippled bomber. "I knew he was hit because he leveled off. He came out of his dive, leveled his plane momentarily, then the plane started going down. About this time he bailed out. By trying to keep the plane level he was giving his crew an opportunity to bail out. Bynum said in attacking Mt. Yoake and Mt. Asahi the bombers were at dive speeds of 300 miles per hour and Bush had to gain level flight to permit successful exit from the plane. "It's kinda hard to bail out of an airplane while in a 300 mile an hour dive," Bynum said.

Ensign Milt Moore was in the cockpit just forward of Bynum's turret. "We were flying wing on Bush on the (Mt. Asahi) strike and saw the hit on the bomber followed by smoking. "I pulled up to him, then he lost power and I went sailing on by him. My gunner (Bynum) was the only one who could see behind us and he called out, "Chutes!" Moore said.[3]

All reports of the Bush mission issued from the USS SAN JACINTO in 1944 were based on the ready room debriefing of the members of Strike Baker. Each of these nine aviators was questioned by Lieutenant Martin Kilpatrick, the squadron's intelligence officer and Lieutenant Commander Brewster Righter, the SAN JACINTO's intelligence officer. From the debriefing, Kilpatrick prepared Aircraft Action Reports which noted these main points: Bush's plane " was hit and caught fire," and "two parachutes were seen to leave the bomber, but only one opened."

In a separate Action Report, Captain Martin, the SAN JACINTO skipper, said Bush's plane "was hit by AA fire over northeast side of Chichi Jima and the plane dived in flames. Two parachutes were seen to leave the plane, only one opening." Martin sent the report which was prepared by Commander Righter, to Admiral Ernest J. King, Chief of Naval Operations in Washington, D. C. after it had been approved by Rear Admiral Ralph Davison, the Task Group commander, Admiral Marc Mitscher, Task Force Commander and Admiral Chester Nimitz, Commander of the Pacific Fleet. The SAN JACINTO's War Diary for September 2, 1944, based on the eye witness accounts conducted by Commander Righter, said Bush's bomber was "flaming" when he released his bombs on the radio station. "The plane was leveled long enough for the pilot and one other crewman to bail out. The crewman's parachute failed to open, however." The War Diary was signed by Captain Martin and forwarded to Admirals King and Nimitz.

The FINBACK rescued five aviators during the first phase of Operation Stalemate II. They are (kneeling left to right): Ensign Thomas Keene, Lt. (j.g.) George Bush, Ensign James W. Beckman, James. T. Stovall, AOM 3/c and John R. Doherty, ARM 3/c. Standing are crewmembers of the FINBACK (left to right): Lt. James Griswold, Lt (j.g.) William Parkman, Lt (j.g.) Jack Peat, Ensign William Edwards, LCDR Dean Spratlin, LCDR Robert Williams, Lt. J. L. Lawrence, Lt. Lawrie Heyworth, Lt. Jerry Redmond and Lt (j.g.) Ollie Brostrom. Keene, Stoval and Doherty, were Avenger crew members from USS FRANKLIN and were picked up off IWO JIMA. Bush and Beckman (an ENTERPRISE fighter pilot) were rescued off Chichi Jima. *Photo taken September 30, 1944 by NAS Midway.*

Chichi Jima's naval radio was back on the air, September 16, 1944, still using call sign of HI KA HE 7.

Source: SRN series, National Archives.

```
(dh)

A  FU HE 2    (KISARATSU Air Base)
HE TO RU FU   (MARCUS Island Guard Division)
MA RI WE Ø    (YOKOSUKA Comm. Unit)
DE:
HI KA HE 7    (CHICHIJIMA Comm. Unit)
W41
- - - - - - - - - - - - - -

From:      HO HE A YO       (Air Base 52 IWOJIMA)
Action:    SA TE KO 4       (Concealed Identity)

09/160942/I 1944               (TOI 09/160954/I on ----- kcs)  ga


Secure for air alert.
```

Emperor Hirohito's gunners had turned George Bush from a naval aviator to an undersea submarine warrior. Once rescued, Bush fully expected to be returned to the SAN JACINTO within a few days. That had been his experience during the June 19 Marianas Turkey Shoot when the destroyer, USS CLARENCE K. BRONSON fished him out of the drink. But the FINBACK wasn't a destroyer and could not travel with the Fast Carriers of Task Force 38. It was out of the question for Commander Williams to move forth into the Fast Carrier operation area because his vessel could be easily mistaken for an enemy sub and attacked with depth bombs by anxious U. S. Navy air patrols.

Instead, Williams put Bush to work, along with other rescued aviators, standing midnight watches from the conning bridge of the submarine. The FINBACK was on its 10th war patrol and its prime mission was to attack and sink Japanese vessels carrying reinforcements to Chichi Jima and Iwo Jima.

Bush and his four air compatriots got their first taste of undersea warfare as the FINBACK patrolled along the 140 east longitude line at the northern portion of the Chichi Jima defense arc. For 20 days from September 3 to 23, the FINBACK was under air and surface attack from Japanese naval units as it attempted torpedo attacks on convoys. The concussion from Japanese depth bombs exploding about the FINBACK caused anxious moments for Bush and his fellow airmen. "As the sub shuddered from these explosives, we sought assurances from the crew," Bush wrote. "Not even close, they told us."

On the night of September 10-11, 1944, the entire crew and Bush were at general quarters. A Japanese convoy of six ships had been identified on the sub's radar screen. As Bush watched, Skipper Williams ordered: "Up periscope." He sighted two small oilers and three small cargo ships escorted by the sub chaser CHIDORI. The convoy was about 100 miles northwest of Chichi Jima and had been seen earlier in the day by navy patrol planes.

Commander Williams calculated the convoys' speed at 11 knots, then edged the FINBACK toward the group of ships. What followed was an 11 hour cat-and-mouse game as the FINBACK attempted to position itself for a torpedo attack on the Japanese vessels. The skipper of the CHIDORI heard the propellers of the sub on his sonar gear and briefly chased the FINBACK away.

But Williams was not one to give up. He resumed the stalk and at 2336 hours (11:36 p.m.) fired six torpedos at the convoy. All missed, but their wakes alerted the CHIDORI and set off a hornet's nest of activity from the convoy. The Japanese sailors fired depth charges to all parts of the compass. A wide-eyed Bush, feeling the explosions reverberate throughout the submerged FINBACK's steel hull, cast a furtive look at the composed Williams who said, "They're dropping them here and there". Translation: Relax, the bombs are not even close. The sub temporarily retreated to the depths of the Philippine Sea, hiding from the CHIDORI's search sonar. Midnight came and the date changed to Monday, September 11, 1944. The seconds ticked away to 0115 hours (1:15 a.m.). A full moon lighted the scene as the FINBACK's periscope sliced through the waters stirring up a luminous wake. Williams kept the sub "up moon," avoiding a silhouette which might be seen by the CHIDORI. Unaccountably the subchaser seemed to be daring the FINBACK to attack.

Commander Williams was eager to oblige. At 0137 hours (1:37 a.m.) he sent six more deadly torpedoes racing toward the Chichi Jima convoy. Three hits were scored on two ships. Williams' 11-hour battle had paid off. The FINBACK torpedos had sunk the 886-ton oiler HAKUUN MARU #2 and the 536-ton cargo vessel, HASSHO MARU![1]

The FINBACK was now foremost on Japan's most wanted list. Japanese patrol aircraft and sub chasers from the home islands to Iwo Jima were alerted to the sub attacks by the Mt. Yoake radio station now back on the air using the call letters HI KA HE 7. The tables had been turned. Bush was hunted by the very radio station he had bombed only days earlier.[2]

The radio transmitter silenced by Strike Baker on September 2 was back on the air. Japanese technicians had repaired the equipment and were broadcasting again from caves dug into the summits of Mt. Yoake and Mt. Asahi.

On September 24, the sub ended its patrol and headed for Pearl Harbor. It refueled at Midway Island where Bush and other aviators were transferred to Navy transport planes for faster return to their squadrons.

During this phase of his war career, Bush was outside the command of the Fast Carrier Force and came under the jurisdiction of Vice Admiral John Hoover, who was commander of the Central Pacific Islands called the Forward Area Command. Admiral Hoover was kept abreast of the FINBACK's exploits by his air intelligence officer, Lieutenant Henry Fonda, the famed actor, who like Bush, was serving in the Pacific Fleet.

Henry Fonda
Looks After Bush

Lt. (j.g.) Henry Fonda (far right) monitored status of Bush and other downed naval aviators for Vice Admiral John H. Hoover, (left). Fonda was Air Intelligence Officer for Hoover, the Commander of Forward Areas in the Central Pacific. Standing alongside the Admiral is his aide, Jack Breed. *USS CURTIS photo, National Archives.*

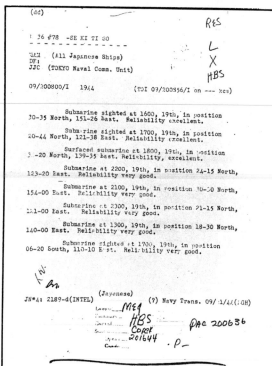

William Edwards presented the original motion picture film he took of the Chichi Jima rescue to Vice President George Bush in 1984. Naval intelligence returned the film to Edwards noting, "It had no intelligence value."
White House photo by David Valdez.

Japan Tracks
U.S. Navy Subs

George Bush was aboard the FINBACK when the sub took a depth bomb attack from the Japanese sub-chaser, CHIDORI (above).

Japanese communication intelligence reported location of U. S. submarines to all its vessels. It appears the FINBACK with Bush still aboard was located by a Japanese radio direction finder (RDF) near 139.35 east longitude September 19, 1940, at 1800 hours (6 pm). The position given by Japan coincides with the FINBACK's operation schedule during this time frame. The Tokyo Communication Unit (JJC) used phrase "in position" which probably means a RDF fix on the FINBACK when the sub made a report to Pearl Harbor.
Station Hypo intercept from SRN series, National Archives.

PART XI

When the FINBACK's war patrol concluded September 30, at Midway, Bush was flown to Pearl Harbor. Under U.S. Naval policy his tragic shootdown at Chichi Jima qualified him for the Rest and Relaxation center operated by the navy at Waikiki Beach's Royal Hawaiian Hotel, followed by extensive shore duty. He chose, instead, to return to his squadron and the USS SAN JACINTO. First the navy wanted to reaffirm his aviation skills. He was temporarily assigned to Torpedo Squadron 100 and for several weeks in October 1944 was flying Avengers at the Barbers Point Naval Air Station near Pearl Harbor.

Meanwhile the SAN JACINTO and Task Force 38 were preparing to support General Douglas MacArthur's return to the Philippines. The successful invasion of Guam, Saipan and Peleliu had opened the doors of the Chichi Jima barrier permitting the Fast Carriers of the Pacific Fleet to maneuver in the Philippine Sea without opposition. From October 7 to 21, 1944, the Fast Carriers raided Japanese bases which were supporting the Philippine defensive buildup, hitting Okinawa, Formosa and the Manila area. The SAN JACINTO photo team continued with its reconnaissance missions, obtaining aerial photos of Okinawa which were used for planning the invasion scheduled for the island in 1945.

General MacArthur's troops invaded the Philippines on October 20, 1944, landing on the island of Leyte. The Imperial Japanese Navy, anticipating such a move, had amassed warships at Borneo for a last ditch "do or die" effort to stop the U. S. Navy. Upon confirmation of the MacArthur landing, the Japanese warships headed for Leyte to destroy the American forces.

Station Hypo's radio code breakers intercepted the Japanese naval attack plans and alerted Admiral "Bull" Halsey, who then ordered the Fast Carriers and battleships of Task Force 38 to prepare for the oncoming battle. On October 22, 1944, at Pearl Harbor, George Bush heard of the massing of naval forces and was determined not to miss the battle. He personally flew a naval transport plane from Pearl Harbor to Guam hoping to rejoin the SAN JACINTO. The 19½ hour flight was made via Johnson and Kwajalein Islands. It was an extra long day for Bush since he crossed the international Date Line on the Johnson-Kwajalein leg of the hop.[1]

Bush expected to partcipate in the sea battle but lost the opportunity when he learned his squadron and the SAN JACINTO were operating off Leyte Island. There was no way for him the reach the carrier. He missed out on the Battle for Leyte Gulf but his squadron mates scored big by participating in the sinking of the last of the Japanese Pearl Harbor day carriers: The ZUIKAKU which hit Oahu on December 7, 1941, and the ZUIHO whose bombers attacked the Philippines.[2]

Following the battle, which turned out to be the last major naval engagement of the Pacific War, Bush rejoined his comrades on November 2 at the Ulithi Fleet Anchorage northeast of Peleliu. Lee Nadeau couldn't have been happier to see his pilot. Since September 2 he had been assigned to the squadron's substitute pool and had only flown three missions. Now he and Bush were reunited to fly again. Joining them as replacement for John Delaney who was killed at Chichi Jima, was radioman Joe Reichert. The new Bush crew was all smiles as they posed for pictures alongside their bomber. As they moved into position for the photograph Nadeau noticed the tail section was painted "X-2," the SAN JACINTO's code name for Tare Two. Nadeau had won the substitution jinx war.

Hex signs were now forgotton as the trio flew from "The Genuine Barbara," targeting Japanese military positions in and around Manila Bay. On Monday, November 13, 1944, at 1300 hours (1p.m.) Nadeau flew his final bombing mission with Bush. They were credited with hits on a Japanese cargo vessel. As they pulled away from the burning warship, Reichert took pictures of the long trail of smoke pouring forth from the vessel. As they left Manila Bay, Bush flew over Corregidor Island, symbol of a heroic but lost American battle to superior Japanese forces in the opening days of the war. Reichert's K-20 camera photographed the island as the Bush photo team took their last wartime pictures. On November 30, 1944, the SAN JACINTO anchored in Apra Harbor, Guam. Air Group 51 was transferred to the USS BOUGAINVILLE for return to the U.S. mainland.

After flying 58 combat missions, Bush was ordered home for a 30-day leave. "I arrived Christmas eve, December 24, 1944. No reunion could have been scripted more perfectly. There were tears, laughs, hugs, joy, the love and warmth of family in a holiday setting," Bush recalled.

Two weeks later—on January 6, 1945—George Bush and Barbara Pierce were married at First Presbyterian Church in Rye, New York. A wedding guest was Ensign Milton Moore, Bush's wingman on the fateful day over Chichi Jima.

The heroic actions of the fighter and bomber pilots of Air Group 51 earned the respect of the officers and crew of the SAN JACINTO and Task Force 58. SAN JAC SUN artist E. C. Strych said it all in this operation cover: "Boy We Sure Can Patrol This Range."

Aboard The Finback
Bush Misses King Neptune

Following the Peleliu Invasion duties, the SAN JACINTO and its Task Group were sent to the Manus Anchorage in the Admiralty Islands for replenishment. En route the carrier crossed the equator and came within the realm of King Neptune and his aide Davy Jones. Captain Harold "Beauty" Martin saluted King Neptune and party when they came aboard to initiate the polywogs of the SAN JACINTO into the ancient shellback mysteries of the Neptune Kingdom. Davy Jones wearing cross skull hat (Ganet Lloyd) and Long John Silver (Richard Laskarin) began formal inspection of the polywogs. (below) Fighter and bomber pilots, dressed appropriately in polywog heavy winter gear, stand in awe, upper left in photo.

USS SAN JACINTO photo by Howard Rowe, National Archives.

Air Group 51 celebrated its first birthday on September 23, 1944.

U. S. Navy art work by E. C. Strych, USS SAN JACINTO. Courtesy Lou Grab.

Last of Pearl Harbor Carriers Sunk

In the Battle off Cape Engano, October 25, 1944, Stan Butchart (inset) found his Avenger was hit in the starboard wing tip. This did not prevent his radioman, Richard "Ike" Kolstad from incorporating the damage within this photo of a Japanese battleship of the "ISE" class.

USS SAN JACINTO photo, National Archives.

Tare Four (left) and Tare One awaiting loading of torpedos for the fleet battle, October 25, 1944. The 16mm gun camera, usually mounted atop the engine, is missing from Tare One. *USS SAN JACINTO photo, National Archives.*

In 1984, Vice President George Bush (right) hears about the sinking of Japanese Pearl Harbor carriers from VT-51 veterans (left to right) Legare Hole, Stan Butchart and Jack Guy. *Courtesy Leo Nadeau.*

This massive explosion is believed to be a hit on the Japanese light cruiser, TAMA shown lower right in the Battle off Cape Engano. Battleship of ISE class appears in the left center.
USS SAN JACINTO photo by Don Gaylien from Avenger flown by Howard Boren, National Archives.

VT-51 Airmen Obtain
Startling Photo Intelligence

First intelligence hint of the Japanese kamikaze strategy was revealed in battle photos taken by the Bush photo team during the Battle Off Cape Engano, October 25, 1944. Captain Wilfred J. Holmes points to the conversion of the Japanese battleship ISE to a "one-way" aircraft carrier, in photo (left) with the author in 1982.

Photo by Peggy Stinnett.

A warning of possible Japanese suicide missions against Pacific Fleet units was dispatched by Holmes including the U.S. Navy's intelligence publication, Recognition Journal of January 1945, which contained the ISE photo (below).

Mongrel Ise Class BB-XCV shows carrier stern as it wheels around under aerial attack. A Terutsuki curvets at the right. Rebuilt Ises have dropped casemate guns but still retain the towering foremast structure and substantial mainmast. AA is concentrated around the hangar deck

One of two kamikaze suicide planes dive on the USS SAN JACINTO, October 30, 1944. In background, smoke rises from the light carrier, USS BELLEAU WOOD, target of an earlier kamikaze. *U.S. Navy photo by USS SOUTH DAKOTA, National Archives.*

The kamikazes missed the SAN JACINTO crashing into the sea off the port and starboard bows. *U. S. Navy photo by USS ENTERPRISE, National Archives.*

Members of the SAN JACINTO's flight deck crew pick up debris from the kamikaze explosions and near miss. *USS SAN JACINTO photo, National Archives.*

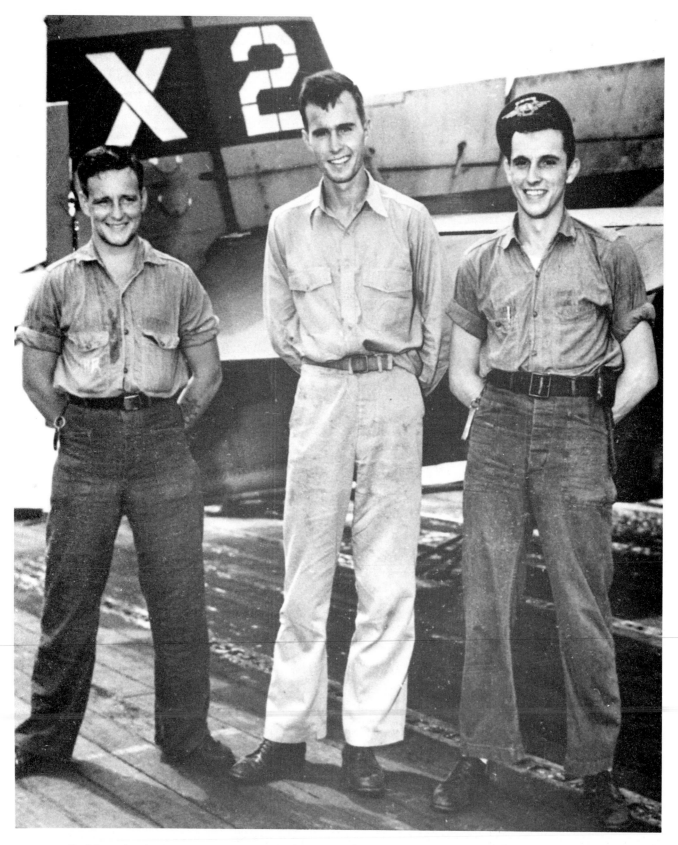

On November 2, 1944, Lt (j.g.) George Bush (center) returned to the SAN JACINTO. The date was exactly 60 days after his shoot down at Chichi Jima. He was welcomed aboard by turret gunner Leo Nadeau (right) and radioman Joe Reichert. *USS SAN JACINTO photo by Robert Stinnett, National Archives.*

"Just one more operation," was the promise to Air Group 51, then you can go home. The SAN JACINTO's busy bakery gave the pledge an extra sweet meaning (right).

The last combat mission for Air Group 51 and George Bush was the Manila Bay Area on island of Luzon in the Philippines. The SAN JACINTO heads for the target area accompanied by the USS BUNKER HILL (below).

Photo by USS ENTERPRISE, National Archives.

George Bush's final combat missions were called "The Manila Strikes" on November 13, and 14, 1944. He shared credit in bomb damage to Japanese war ships and brought back these photographs taken by Joe Reichert.

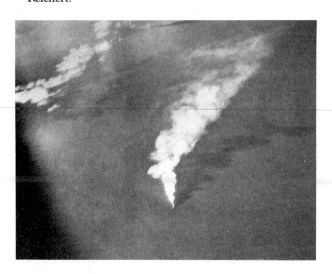

Lee Nadeau's flight log for November 1944 (above) records his last flight with Bush as an anti submarine patrol as the SAN JACINTO was en route from the Ulithi Anchorage to Guam. *Courtesy Lee Nadeau, copy by Robert Stinnett.*

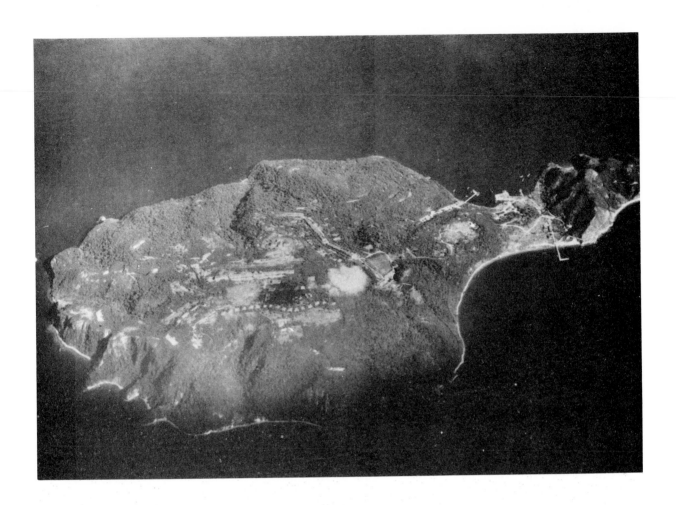

Air Group 51 Says Goodbye to the Pacific War

The last photographs taken from Bush's Avenger were of Corregidor Island (top) scene of heroic battle in opening months of the war. Air Group 51's battle score was recorded on the SAN JACINTO's island with downing of 51 aircraft, 1 carrier, 2 warships, and 5 cargo vessels. *USS SAN JACINTO photos, National Archives*

George Bush returned to the mainland and with fiance Barbara Pierce toasted the newlyweds his brother and sister-in-law, Mr. and Mrs. Prescott S. Bush Jr. *Courtesy Prescott Bush Jr.*

Lt (j.g.) and Mrs. George Bush walk down the aisle of Rye Presbyterian Church, January 6, 1945 (left) and enjoy their first dance at right. *Photos from The White House.*

```
(anp)

SA TE KO 4     Any or All Ships or Stations
DE
NI MI NE     Tokyo Comm Unit
HI TU 70 1 SINU W76
Frequency 16700J    (Tokyo B C #1)
- - - - - - - - - - - - - - - - -
From:        ----
Action:      RO WA TO 1              Adees O Intell Rpts

08/080701/I      1945         (TOI 08/080722)    fi
```

"O" Intelligence Report #15.

Departures of MARIANAS-Based B-29's -----------

------- attack on the mainland? is expected.

```
(anp)                    OY-1 / 342558,362577,
                                  362550
NI MI NE     Tokyo Comm Unit
DE
SO NO NO     Kure Comm Unit
P 498 -RO RA RA    W88
- - - - - - - - - - - - - - - - -
From:      " YO NI YA 2    Comm Unit Kure
Action:    " ME MI SU 8    Grd Dist Hainan CinC
           " TO MI HI I    Comm Unit 31
           " O KU O 8      Mobile Command #16
           " RE RO YO 5    (RE HO YO) Unident Comm Unit #21
           "RU RI A 2      Comm Unit 8
           //" KA HE NO 5  Takao Comm Unit

08/081124/I      1945     (TOI 08/082200 on 6435/ kcs)   kg


Reencipherment  062258.

To: Navy Minister.
    First Section, Naval Staff, Imperial Headquarters.
    Supreme Commander Combined Naval Force.

        Flash Report regarding air raid damage on the
city of HIROSHIMA. (August 6).
(1.)        Two or three B-29 penetrated HIROSHIMA city at
high altitude about 0825, dropping several bombs vicinity HIROSHIMA
city ---------.

        A terrific explosion, accompanied by flame and smoke(?)
occurred at an altitude of from 500 to 600 meters.

        The concussion was beyond imagination, demolishing
practically every house in the city.
(2.)        Present estimate of damage.

        About 80% of the city was wiped out, (destroyed or
burned).  Only a portion of the western section of the town
escaped the disaster.
JN-5 / 2713-H    (BE)    (Japanese)    (FK) Navy TOP SECRET ULTRA
```

The War Is Over

By August 1945 LCDR Homer Kisner had moved his intercept operators to Guam where they heard the Tokyo Communmication Unit speculating on a B-29 bombing attack on the mainland. Next, the Kure Communication unit reported a "terrific explosion . . . beyond imagination," striking Hiroshima. The atomic bombing of Hiroshima and Nagasaki brought an end to the Pacific War. *Source: SRN series, National Archives.*

At the Oceana Naval Air Station, Virginia, Jacqueline West, Lt (j.g.) George Bush (standing) and (seated left to right) Barbara Bush, Lt (j.g.) Doug West, Bea Guy, Lt (j.g.) Jack Guy, unidentified Wave and Lt (j.g.) Milton Moore celebrated the war's ending. *Courtesy Jack Guy*

```
SA TE KO 4      Any or All Ships or Stations
DE:
CAI MINE        TOKYO Comm Unit
HI TU 2762
-NU NU                                    ULTRA
EI HI

FO RA A RA   F 101
- - - - - - - - - - - - -

From:   SA TE KO 4      Any or All Ships or Stations
Action: SI YU  RA99     Garbio (Cinc _____ ___ ____)
        YU RO RA 35     _____  RABAUL Comm Unit #8
        RA NO MA 26     Force Comb Nav Hq
Info:   KU YA KU Ø6·    All ND GD Flts CinCs GR Surf Esc
        RO HO RA Ø7     Gr Surf Esc For Hqtrs

08/161202/I 1945        (TOI 08/16/1725/G on 8950 kcs)   bt
```

Naval Staff, Imperial Headquarters Order #48 August 16, 1945.

Chief of Naval General Staff, TOYODA SOEMU.

Orders for:

KUSAKA, CinC Southeast Area Fleet.
OOKAWACHI, CinC Southwest Area Fleet.
OZAWA, CinC Combined Naval Forces.

1.   CinC Southeast Area Fleet, CinC Southwest Area Fleet and the CinC of Combined Naval Forces will have all Naval and Army forces under their commands suspend battle operations immediately. However, between now and the time that -------- for the cessation of fighting is established, in the event of enemy attacks you will, of necessity, and in self-defense engage in battle operations and fight back.

2.   When each Commander in Chief in the preceding paragraph has suspended battle operations, he will immediately report the date and hour of same to me.

3   With regard to ------ will have the 1st Section, Naval Staff Imperial Headquarters --------------------.

(_____)   (Japanese)

JN-5 #3444-H (Ogord)   (R) Navy Trans 28-16 45

Admiral Soemu Toyoda, commander-in-chief of the Imperial Japanese Navy, ordered the immediate suspension of battle operations at 1202 hours (12:02 pm), August 16, 1945. *Source: SRN series, National Archives.*

Six Avengers of the USS SAN JACINTO escorted by Hellcat fighters make their final flight at war's end during Operation Tintype.

USS SAN JACINTO photo by Edward Tinsley, National Archives.

After Surrender
The Vile Secrets of Chichi Jima

General Yoshio Tachibana surrendered Chichi Jima on September 3, 1945 aboard the USS DUNLAP anchored in Futami Bay. Standing behind Tachibana are Major Yoshitaka Horie, Captain Kimitomi Nishiyotsuji, Capt S. Terasawa, Major Sanichi Yokota, unidentified U.S. Army Sergeant and Cadet S. Oyama.

Lt. General Yoshio Tachibana is shown with aides (from left) Major Sanichi Yokota and Cadet S. Oyama (far right). Behind them is U.S. Navy Lt. David C. McMillan.

Commodore John H. Macgruder accepts Japanese surrender of Chichi Jima aboard USS DUNLAP.

Chichi Jima surrender ceremony aboard USS DUNLAP. Commodore John H. Macgruder is seated at table (left), General Tachibana between two interpreters at table right. *USS DUNLAP photos, National Archives.*

Gallows Justice for War Crimes

War crimes involving cannibalism of U. S. naval aviators were discovered on Chichi Jima after the surrender. Two of those charged and convicted of the atrocities are pictured here. Major Sueo Matoba (top left), a sector commander and navy Captain Shizuo Yoshii head of the Yoake Wireless Station complex (top right) are led to the gallows at Guam September 24, 1947. *U.S. Navy photos, National Archives.*

Tachibana Receives Death Sentence

Stripped to his shorts, Lt. General Yoshio Tachibana hears his death sentence from a military court on Guam, then accompanied by a Shinto priest is led to the gallows by U. S. Marines. *U.S. Navy photos, National Archives.*

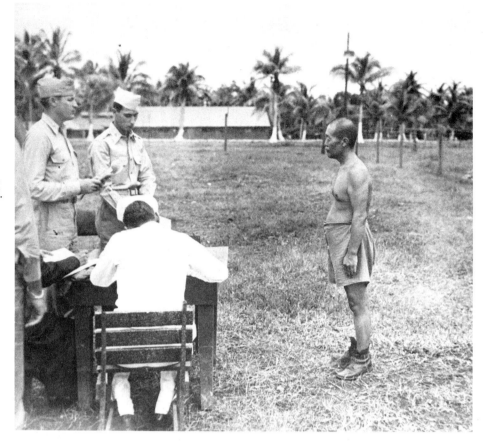

EPILOGUE

In early spring 1945, Bush was reassigned to Torpedo Squadron 153 and began preparations for the invasion of Japan. On August 15, 1945, at Virginia Beach, Virginia, George and Barbara Bush joined other aviators, sailors and their wives in a street gala, celebrating the news of the Japanese surrender. "Before going home we went to a nearby church filled with others giving thanks and remembering those lost in the war. After four years it was finally over," Bush wrote.

The SAN JACINTO and its crew remained in continuous operation with the Pacific Fleet and was near Tokyo on August 15 when cease fire orders were issued by Admiral Halsey. The carrier did not participate in the September 2, 1945, surrender ceremonies in Tokyo Bay and was ordered to its home base at Alameda Naval Air Station.

At Chichi Jima the Japanese naval radio stations on Mt. Yoake and Mt. Asahi continued to broadcast naval messages throughout 1945 from bomb proof underground transmitting rooms despite continued U.S. bombing raids. The radio stations served Japan's home islands as an early warning lookout post for Mariana-based B-29 raids on the homeland.

At Station Hypo, Commander Homer Kisner's radio code breakers intercepted a Mt. Yoake broadcast decoding an ominous message: *"DEPARTURE OF MARIANA-BASED B-29. ATTACK ON THE MAINLAND IS EXPECTED."* Later Kisner's men intercepted this report from the Communication Unit of Japan's major naval base at Kure: *FLASH REPORT, TWO OR THREE B-29 PENETRATED HIROSHIMA CITY AT HIGH ALTITUDE. A TERRIFIC EXPLOSION, ACCOMPANIED BY FLAME AND SMOKE OCCURRED AT AN ALTITUDE OF FROM 500 TO 600 METERS. THE CONCUSSION WAS BEYOND IMAGINATION, DEMOLISHING PRACTICALLY EVERY HOUSE IN THE CITY. PLEASE INVESTIGATE THIS NEW TYPE OF BOMB."*

On September 3, 1945, one year and a day after Bush was shot down, Lieutenant General Yoshio Tachibana surrendered Chichi Jima to U. S. naval forces. The ceremony was held aboard the destroyer USS DUNLAP anchored in Futami Bay, Chichi Jima's main harbor. U. S. Naval investigators later discovered Tachibana's war crimes. He was charged with war atrocities by a military tribunal, convicted and hanged on the island of Guam.

A Beautiful Island
Chichi Jima At Peace

Futami Bay dominates this photo of Chichi Jima taken in 1949. Susaki airstrip shows in top center. In center foreground was Special Naval Base commanded by Vice Admiral Kunizo Mori. Winding road at lower left leads to the Mt. Yoake radio complex. Bottom center is Hatsune Beach where boats were launched in effort to capture George Bush.

Photo looks southwest. U.S. Navy Photo by Ensign Braeuninger.

Best Preserved Battle Site
Chichi Jima in Time Warp

Unlike most other battle sites of the Pacific War, Chichi Jima was not bulldozed to make way for airfields or invasion depots. Consequently the military installations remain similar to the 1944 era as seen by George Bush. The Japanese naval seaplane base, target for Bush on September 1, 1944, still retains the ramp for the scouting aircraft. The hangars were destroyed but machine shop (against hillside left) still stands as does the operations building (near sea wall). A cave system can be seen at base of hill behind power plant. Circle structure at center left, originally intended for water storage, was used for a fuel dump during the war.

U. S. Navy photo taken 1954, National Archives.

Japanese seaplanes scouting the U. S. Pacific Fleet were directed from this building and its signal tower at the Chichi Jima seaplane base.

U. S. Navy photo by J. E. Hilty, National Archives.

Susaki Air Strip (center white area), target of VT-51 on September 1 and 2, 1944, would be easily recognized by George Bush. Never an operational air field, Susaki was used to ferry war planes from the Empire down the Chichi Jima slot. Mt. Yagi (lower left) housed Japanese anti aircraft and coastal defense guns.

U.S. Navy photo June 1954, National Archives.

The U. S. Navy administered Chichi Jima during years after war and used Futami Bay as an anchorage for warships such as the USS McCOY REYNOLDS (DE-440) in July 1952.

U. S. Navy Photo, National Archives.

Leo –
Thanks for be[...]
at my side then and [...]
Geo Bush

Loyalty for Crew

Delegates to the 1988 Republican
National Convention saw Leo
Nadeau and presidential candidate
George Bush reunited at the podium
as Barbara Bush looked on.

Courtesy Leo Nadeau.

Nadeau joins Bush alongside a
restored Avenger in Texas.

White House photo by Pete Souza.

Naval Honors

A restored Avenger forms the background of this U. S. Naval ceremony honoring "Flight 19" at Fort Lauderdale International Airport in March 1990. Air Group 51 held their annual reunion in conjuction with the observance which honors a group of Avengers lost in the Bermuda Triangle, December 1945.

Torpedo Squadron 51 veterans inspect the TBM flight line at Fort Lauderdale, Florida celebration, March 1990. Lou Grab (hat), William Fenger (dark glasses), Betty Lou and Art Horan, were joined by Tom Burns and fighter pilot Nat "Blackie" Adams (in rear). *Photos by Robert Stinnett.*

Avengers on Parade

"THE BARBARA," flys again in this demonstration TBM during the Fort Lauderdale Air Show in March 1990. Complete with gun camera on the engine mount, "The Barbara" replica is fairly accurate except for personal writings on the fuselage. Skipper Don Melvin of VT-51 would not have permitted inscriptions such as this for security reasons.

Tail section of "The Barbara" replica has the USS SAN JACINTO code "X" correctly marked on tail section. Tare Two was Bush's assigned number. At top of the "2" is the U. S. Navy's Bureau number #91598. According to Grumman records this TBM-3E was one of 646 built in this number series by General Motors. *Photos by Robert Stinnett.*

Camera Equipment of the Bush Photo Team

F-56 Camera with 40″ telephoto lens, Robert Stinnett photographer.

K-18 wide angle aerial camera, Edward Tinsley photographer.

Eyemo Model Q, 35mm motion picture camera with 400′ magazine, Robert Stinnett photographer; D. S. Murray, Jeep driver. F6F Hellcats in background.

F-56 camera with 20-inch lens, J. E. Haythorn photographer.

Kodak Medalist had roll film capacity, Robert Stinnett photographer.

K-20 aerial camera had rapid film advance for sequence photos, Robert Stinnett, photographer.

STATUS REPORT

People, Places, Airplanes & Warships

Many persons, places and warships were involved with George Bush in his war years. The following is a status listing as of July 1990:

- Adams, Ralph. Pulled George Bush aboard the USS FINBACK off east coast of Chichi Jima. Died in Honolulu April 21, 1989, at age of 76.

- Adams, Nathaniel. Pilot of fighter escort for George Bush during Operation Snapshot. Returned to civilian life after World War II and works as architect in Boise, Idaho. Attended inauguration of President Bush, January 1989.

- Allen, Ross G. George Bush's first Air Intelligence Officer, became an Episcopal chaplain and resides in New Orleans, Louisiana.

- Aslito Airfield, Saipan. Scene of George Bush's birthday bombing of June 12, 1944, is now the Saipan International Airport. The Operation Forager islands of Saipan, Tinian and Rota voted to join the Commonwealth of the Marianas and associated with the United States in a Convenant signed in 1975.

- Avenger torpedo-bomber. This aircraft is no longer in U.S. Naval service. Restored models can be seen at the Smithsonian Institution's Paul E. Garber Facility at Suitland, Maryland, the Naval Aviation Museum, Pensacola, Florida. Some flying versions can be seen at air-shows throughout the United States; others have been converted to serve as flying water tankers in forest fire situations.

- Bramhall, Douglas. Photo pilot of the squadron lives in Fayetteville, New York.

- Brewster, Edward C. Air Intelligence Officer for the SAN JACINTO's fighter squadron became a financial officer in New York City. He now lives in Locust Valley, New York.

- Burke, Arleigh A. Signed the Operation Snapshot reprimand letter on behalf of Admiral Mitscher. Named Chief of Naval Operations by President Dwight D. Eisenhower in 1955. With his wife, launched the USS ARLEIGH BURKE a U.S. Navy guided missile destroyer on September 16, 1989. Lives in Fairfax, Virginia.

- Bush, George. Elected President of the United States November 8, 1988.

- Bynum, Charles. Turret gunner for Ensign Milton Moore on September 2, 1944. Saw George Bush parachute from his stricken bomber. Lives in Scottsboro, Alabama.

- Chichi Jima. The Japanese-American treaty of 1951 placed Chichi Jima and the Bonin Islands under the administration of the United States and was occupied by U.S. Naval forces. The island was returned to Japan and is now part of the prefecture of Tokyo.

- CHIDORI, Japanese Navy motor torpedo boat of 600 standard tons. Dropped depth charges on George Bush, September 10/11, 1944, off Chichi Jima. Sunk by U.S. submarine TILEFISH on December 22, 1944, at northern end of the Chichi Jima defensive arc.

- Davison, Ralph E. Admiral. Was Commander of U.S. Navy Carrier Division Two at Chichi Jima, September 2, 1944. Recommended George Bush for Distinguished Flying Cross.

- Fonda, Henry. Air Intelligence Officer for the Pacific Fleet's Forward Area Command in 1944. Kept track of George Bush aboard USS FINBACK. Returned to motion pictures at conclusion of World War II. Died in 1987.

- Foshee, Joseph. Turret gunner for Ensign Doug West in Chichi Jima Raid of September 2, 1944. Saw George Bush's bomber smoking after being hit by Japanese anti-aircraft fire. Reports Bush leveled plane so crewmen could bail out. Lives in Lufkin, Texas.

- Gorman, Richard. Radioman for Ensign Milton Moore on Chichi Jima Raid, September 2, 1944. Saw George Bush's bomber "smoking like a two-alarm fire." Lived in Stayton, Oregon. Died in 1989.

- Grab, Lou. Original founding member of Torpedo Squadron Fifty-one. Trained with George Bush at Fort Lauderdale, Florida. Returned to civilian life after WWII and served as educator in Sacramento, California, public schools. Resides in Sacramento.

- Guy, Jack. Founding member of VT-51, Sept. 1943. Awarded Navy Cross and Distinguished Flying Cross for 1944 attacks on Japanese fleet units. Left active navy duty in Sept., 1945. Heads investment firm in Atlanta, GA.

- Halsey, William F. Fleet Admiral. Commander of United States Navy's Third Fleet during the Chichi Jima Raid of September 2, 1944. Died August 16, 1959.

- Emperor Hirohito. Imperial Ruler of Japan. Died January 1989.

- Hole, Legare. Executive Officer of VT-51 in 1943-45. Senior surviving officer of the squadron. Lives in Vineyard Haven, MA.

- Holmes, Wilfred J. Head of Pacific Fleet's Intelligence Center, Pearl Harbor. Aerial photos taken by Bush photo team sent to Holmes. Retired from U.S. Navy as Captain. Returned to educational pursuits at University of Hawaii as Assistant Vice President and engineering professor. Holmes Hall, the engineering college at the Manoa campus is named in his honor. He died in January 1986.

- Horie, Yoshitaka, Major. As Chief of Staff to General Tachibana on Chichi Jima, Major Horie interrogated American carrier pilots who were captured as prisoners of war. Major Horie returned to Japan after end of the war and served as research associate for John Toland, the Pulitzer Prize winning author of *The Rising Sun*.

- Kisner, Homer. Head of radio traffic interception at Station Hypo, Pearl Harbor (later Guam). Intercepted Japanese naval communications from the Mt. Yoake radio complex during World War II. Lives in Carlsbad, California.

- Martin, Harold M. Admiral. Commanding officer of USS SAN JACINTO from December 15, 1943, to October 14, 1944. Promoted to Rear Admiral and commanded Pacific Fleet carrier groups in 1945. Was named Vice Admiral and headed Seventh Fleet in 1951 during Korean War. Died December 1972 at Memphis, Tenn.

- Mays, Dixie Commander. Photo pilot assigned to the Bush photo team on USS SAN JACINTO. After World War II remained in U.S. Naval aviation up to and including the Vietnam War. He retired to become head of civilian aviation, State of Washington. He lives in Puyallup, Washington.

- Melton, Sam. Radioman for Lieutenant Commander Donald Melvin during Chichi Jima Raid of September 2, 1944. He resides in Richmond, Virginia.

- Melvin, Donald, Lieutenant Commander. Commanding officer of Torpedo Squadron Fifty-one from September 26, 1943, to departure of the squadron from USS SAN JACINTO on November 30, 1944. Received two Navy Crosses for attacks on Japanese Fleet. As skipper of the squadron appointed George Bush to post of photographic officer. Left U.S. Navy after World War II and became air traffic controller for FAA at Jacksonville, Florida. He died September 29, 1989.

- Mierzejewski, Chester. Turret gunner for Commander Melvin during the Chichi Jima raid of September 2, 1944. Disputes all accounts of the shootdown of George Bush. Returned to civilian life after WWII as quality control inspector for Pratt Whitney Aircraft Company. He lives in Cheshire, Conn.

- Mitscher, Marc Admiral. Commander of The Pacific Fleet's Fast Carrier Task Forces in 1944. Was George Bush's overall carrier commander. After World War II named to Commander-in-Chief Atlantic Fleet. Died at his post February 3, 1947.

- Montgomery, Alfred E. Admiral. Commander Carrier Division Three in May 1944 was in tactical command of George Bush's first combat against the Japanese at Wake Island. In 1943 presented Ensign Bush with his aviator wings at Corpus Christi, Texas. Retired from Navy in 1951.

- Moore, Milton. George Bush's wing man on the Chichi Jima raid September 2, 1944. Witnessed Bush struggling with bomber to keep it airborne long enough for his crew to bail out. Attended the wedding of George Bush and Barbara Pierce, January 1945. Moore died February 26, 1987.

- Nadeau, Leo. Turret gunner for George Bush in 1943 and 1944. Introduced Vice-President George Bush to the Republican National Convention held in New Orleans, August 1988. Returned to civilian life and is licensed general contractor in California. He lives in Ramona, Calif.

- Nimitz, Chester, Fleet Admiral. Commander-in-Chief of the Pacific Fleet from December 1941 to end of World War II. Named Chief of Naval Operations in December 1945. Retired to Berkeley, California. Died February 20, 1966.

- Nunnally, Harold. Radioman for Doug West on the September 2, 1944, raid on Chichi Jima. After leaving Navy at end of World War II, he served as deputy sheriff with the Alameda and Sonoma County Sheriff's Department in California. He lives in Santa Rosa, California.

- Pasto, Jerome. Photo Interpretation Officer of USS SAN JACINTO in 1944. Discovered hidden Japanese military positions in aerial photos taken by the Bush photo team. After World War II, Pasto taught at Penn State College where he is Associate Dean Emeritus and Professor Emeritus of Agricultural Economics. The Pasto Agricultural Museum at the University is named in his honor.

- Peleliu/Palau Islands. The island chain is known as the Republic of Belau. In February 1983 the people of Belau approved a Compact of Association with the United States. The Japanese airfield on Peleliu is now operated as a civilian field. Kayangle Atoll, where George Bush sank his first Japanese naval vessel, is open to visitors.

- Reichert, Joseph. Radioman for George Bush between November 2-30, 1944. Took place of John Delaney, killed during the Chichi Jima raid. Lives in Syosset, New York.

- Ridge, Thomas L. Colonel USMC. Intelligence officer of Fleet Marine Force Pacific and editor of a special study on Chichi Jima. The 1946 study photographed damage done in the September 2, 1944 raid by George Bush. Colonel Ridge lives in Potomac, Maryland.

- Rochefort, Joseph Captain USN. Co-founder of U.S. Naval crypto service and head of Station Hypo at Pearl Harbor at beginning of World War II. In November 1941, tracked Japanese submarines heading eastward toward U.S. possessions by intercepting Japanese Naval radio station on Mt. Yoake, Chichi Jima. Died in 1976 in Southern California.

- Sakaibara, Shigematsu Rear Admiral IJN. Was commander of Japanese garrison, Wake Island, during George Bush's first combat mission in May 23, 1944. Admiral Sakibara surrendered Wake Island on September 4, 1945. Later he was charged and convicted of war atrocities against American prisoners of war. He was hanged at Guam on June 18, 1947.

- Spruance, Raymond Admiral USN. Commander of the Fifth Fleet in 1944 and in charge of Operation Forager and Operation Snapshot. After war he was named to succeed Admiral Nimitz as Commander in Chief Pacific Fleet and Pacific Ocean Areas. Later Admiral Spruance was appointed president of the Naval War College.

- Tarrant, John. Pharmacist Mate on USS HEALY who treated injured Japanese naval pilot. He returned to civilian life and became an accountant with the Internal Revenue Service and retired in 1982 as Chief, Compliance Division.

- United States Naval Air Station, Fort Lauderdale, Florida. George Bush learned to fly the Grumman Avenger here in spring 1943. The site is now part of the International Airport complex. Only a few buildings of the World War II era remain. First formal reunion of Torpedo Squadron Fifty-one was held here in March 1990.

- USS ENTERPRISE (CV-6) Flagship of Rear Admiral Ralph Davison during the Chichi Jima Raid, September 2, 1944. Cut up for scrap iron, Kearny, New Jersey in 1959.

- USS FINBACK (SS-230). As rescue submarine in the Chichi Jima raid, pulled George Bush from life raft. Was decommissioned April 1950, sold for scrap 1959.

- USS HEALY (DD-672). Rescued Japanese naval pilots of the Hachiman Corps on June 23, 1944. Broken up for scrap 1976.

- USS LEXINGTON (CV-16). Flagship of Admiral Marc A. Mitcher, Commander of the Fast Carrier Force of the Pacific Fleet in 1944. Temporary home to George Bush June 19-24, 1944. Ship still in commission in 1991 as the training carrier for the U.S. Naval School of Aviation, Pensacola, Florida.

- USS SAN JACINTO (CVL-30) was retired to the Reserve Fleet and remained in moth balls until 1979 when the vessel was stricken from U.S. Navy roll and cut up for scrap.

- Wake Island. Site of George Bush's first combat mission on May 23, 1944, is now operated as an emergency landing field by the U.S. Air Force. From 1962-1972 the Federal Aviation Administration maintained the field and island. After 1973 there was no need for air facilities on the atoll because modern jets could cross the Pacific without refueling.

- West, Douglas. Fellow squadron mate of George Bush. Participated in the Chichi Jima raid of September 2, 1944. Left U.S. Navy after V.J. Day and became a news advertising executive. He died October 14, 1964.

- White, William "Ted." Gunnery officer of Torpedo Squadron Fifty-one. Was substitute gunner for his childhood friend, George Bush on the Chichi Jima raid, September 2, 1944. Was killed when Japanese aircraft hit George Bush's bomber.

- Williams, Robert R. Commander. Skipper of the USS FINBACK (SS-230). Rescued George Bush from waters off Chichi Jima's east coast on September 2, 1944. Retired, lives in Silver Spring, Maryland.

NOTES

PROLOGUE

1. Candidate Bush was speaking to the September 7, 1988, American Legion convention held at Louisville, Kentucky. "Today, you remember—I wonder how many Americans remember—today is Pearl Harbor Day. Forty-seven years ago to this very day we were hit hard, at Pearl Harbor. And we were not ready. In a Bush administration, that lesson would not be forgotten . . ."

The gaffe was again subject of media attention December 20, 1990, on the Evans-Novak report telecast on Cable News Network (CNN). Guest Art Buchwald, the syndicated columnist, discussed the 1988 presidential campaign with Robert Novak and Roland Evans:

Evans: "So you voted against George Bush. You say he's very bad copy."

Mr. Buchwald: "No, he wasn't as bad as Dukakis."

Novak: "Dukakis was worse?"

Mr. Buchwald: "Dukakis, from my standpoint. I weighed the two, and when George Bush said the Japanese bombed Pearl Harbor on September 7th, then I gave the nod to him."

2. Chichi Jima "last stronghold of defense": See JICPOA Bulletin 2-46, page 55 statement of Major Yoshitaka Horie chief-of-staff for Japanese Army 109th Division.

3. Units of Japanese anti-aircraft gunners were transferred from Akasaka Palace of Emperor Hirohito in summer and fall 1944. Their destination was Iwo Jima but transport vessels carrying the units were sunk by U.S. submarines and aircraft from Task Force 58. Survivors of the attacks made it to Chichi Jima via rescue vessels. Statement of Yoshiji Urazaki of the Tokyo Air Defense Regiment; JICPOA Interrogation #36 item #165, page 109 et al.

PART I

1. Chichi Jima and its naval radio complex was first linked to offensive operations against Guam during the Japanese Grand Fleet Maneuvers May-June 1930. USN radio intercept operators at Station Baker, Libugon, Guam, intercepted communications from the Japanese heavy cruiser ASHIGARA revealing Japanese naval strategy involving United States fleet defense of the Philippines. The messages gave a comprehensive outline of the Japanese estimate of the United States Navy's War plan. An analysis of the intercepted and decoded messages done by Captain Royal E. Ingersoll produced an astonishing discovery: "The Japanese had a very good idea of American War Plans as annually rehearsed at the Army and Navy War Colleges." For details see Special Research History #355, National Archives, Military Reference Branch, Volume 1 pages 71-77. (Note re: ASHIGARA: On December 10, 1941 Captain Colin Kelly pilot of a B-17 bomber attacked the heavy cruiser as it was participating in the Philippine invasion at Appari on north tip of Luzon. Kelly reported he hit a battleship of the Haruna class. There were no Japanese battleships at Appari. The ASHIGARA was not hit. The warship was sunk June 8, 1945, by a British submarine south of Singapore.)

2. Joseph J. Rochefort, then a Lieutenant Commander, took over command of Station Hypo about June 1, 1941. His immediate prior duty was aboard the USS INDIANAPOLIS attached to Battle Force Pacific Fleet, the officers who actually ran the fleet. As a cover, Rochefort's Hypo command was listed as "Combat Intelligence" on the Fourteenth Naval District's routing slips. In 1943 the facility was renamed Fleet Radio Unit, Pacific. The space which formerly housed Hypo was marked by historic plaque on March 11, 1983, on what is now building #1 Navy Base Pearl Harbor as suggested by E.B. "Ned" Potter, history professor emeritus at the U. S. Naval Academy.

3. Bush signed his name George H. W. Bush during the World War II period. See aviation log books of VT-51.

4. Murrow and Shirer: Edward R. Murrow was the CBS European Bureau Chief based in London. William L. Shirer was CBS bureau chief in Berlin and broadcast from the Nazi controlled radio facilities. Shirer was interned on December 11, 1941, by the Nazi's after German correspondents in the United States were placed in custody the same day by the US. In 1991 the rules of Persian Gulf war coverage were vastly different. CNN's Peter Arnett was permitted to telecast direct from Baghdad but under Iraq's censorship rules.

5. Secretly engaged August 1943. *Looking Forward* pg 31.

6. "Large scale screening maneuver": See Communication Intelligence Summary dated October 22, 1941, Station Hypo page 2 under Combined Air Force. See also Commandant 14th Naval District Secret Serial Z-2051 dated October 8, 1941 where Rochefort ordered that "every radio signal trans-

mitted in the Pacific Ocean will be observed and analyzed regardless of the time of day." Coincidental with Rochefort's assessment the October 16 ouster of Japan's civilian prime minister, Prince Fuminaro Konoye, took place. He was replaced the same day by General Hideki Tojo who immediately set in motion military events detected by Rochefort in his October 22 summary.

7. Rochefort's communication summaries were dispatched via Naval radio direct to Station US in Washington, D.C. encoded in a secure electronic machine cipher (ECM) called COPEK. The summaries, were processed into monographs then delivered on an " your eyes only" basis to President Roosevelt in the White House. The daily delivery by naval aide, Captain John Beardall was ordered by FDR November 7, 1941. Beardall and his assistant Lieutenant Lester Schulz received the COPEK messages from Captain Laurence F. Safford, the commander of Station US. During Roosevelt's journeys away from the White House Schulz, who accompanied FDR, was provided with a strip-cipher decoding device so he could receive the COPEK messages. Schulz said the Navy had no direct on the road presidential telegraphic delivery system and used Western Union facilities.

8. Kisner said he did not believe the Japanese Navy would attack the United States in 1941 but kept his personal opinions out of the reports. His job was not to make final assessment of the intercepts. For Rochefort's "war alert" see Commandant 14th ND SECRET serial 260110 of November 26, 1941, Rochefort Papers, author's file.

9. Torpedo Squadron 51 (VT-51) was commissioned as Composite Squadron 51 (VC-51) on September 22, 1943 and included nine SBD Dauntless dive bombers and nine torpedo bombers (TBM-TBF Avengers). The SBD's were detached November 8, 1943 and the squadron was re-designated VT-51.

10. Parade Magazine (April 23, 1989) and several east coast newspapers alleged Bush used his Avenger during aerial training in southern part of eastern Maryland in 1943 to buzz a traveling circus performance causing an elephant stampede. Both Bush and Lee Nadeau, his turret gunner, deny the buzzing took place. "We would never engage in such hi jinx and endanger our lives and others," said Nadeau. If Bush was involved in such an incident it had to be in November 1943. Lou Grab, who was wing man to Bush during many of the training flights said November in eastern Maryland is cold, wet and damp and not a time for a traveling circus tour. If such an event took place it had to be during the circus' summer or early fall touring schedule and involved another aviator and squadron. VT-51 was not operating in eastern Maryland at that time.

11. Flyaway cost of a TBM from Peter Kirkup, Grumman Corporation.

Part II

1. The SAN JACINTO was berthed at Philadelphia Naval Shipyard for fitting out.

2. George Bush flew "The Barbara" (BUNO 25123) from Atlantic City to Philadelphia for the commissioning of the carrier on December 15, 1943.

3. LCDR Thomas Bradbury had relieved the original Air Group 51 commanding officer, LCDR J. F. Adams in early November 1943 when SBD Dauntless dive-bombers were deleted from the aircraft complement. On March 20, 1944,

Bradbury was relieved by Commander Charles L. Moore Jr., who headed AG-51 through November 1944.

4. Kaneohe Naval Air Station was one of first targets hit by the Japanese bombers on December 7, 1941. In pulling out of their bombing dives, the aircraft circled over Station H, the key radio interception center at Heeia, Hawaii. Homer L. Kisner, the radio traffic chief at Station H, said he and his men grabbed rifles and fired at the attackers but were unable to hit any of the craft. Japanese naval spy, Ensign Takeo Yoshikawa, who had been secreted on the island of Oahu beginning in March 1941, failed to detect the purpose of Station H during his many auto forays around the island. "We had a perfect cover," said Kisner. "Our location was makai (toward the ocean) from the Kamehameha Highway and fronted by a series of typical green boarded, tin-roofed Hawaiian worker's homes. In one of them Mama-san operated a laundry. You couldn't see our buildings from the highway. Mama-san's wash was hanging on the clothes lines obscuring the view from the highway traveler," said Kisner.

5. Holmes, a naval academy graduate and a submariner, had been released from the USN in late 1930s because of arthritic problems. In summer of 1941 he was recalled to duty and was assigned to Station Hypo by Admiral Claude Bloch, the commandant of the 14th Naval District. Captains Holmes and Homer Kisner are both on the Battle of Midway Honor Roll awarded for their crypto efforts in May-June 1942.

6. With the arrival of the USS SAN JACINTO in the Pacific, Nimitz had a full complement of nine INDEPENDENCE class carriers. There were 14 ESSEX class carriers participating in the Pacific Theater (1943-45) plus the USS ENTERPRISE (CV-6) and USS SARATOGA (CV-3) a total of 25 fast carriers. There were eight ESSEX class delivered in 1945 but saw no war service; another eight were either scrapped or construction suspended. Note: British fast carrier groups also operated with the Pacific Fleet, but not directly with Task Forces 38 or 58.

Part III

1. Military feints: see Hoffman page 43. "Feints," similarity to Operation Desert Storm where General Norman Schwarzkopf, commander of the Coalition Forces, described his "Hail Mary" feint. The Schwarzkopf strategy used a force of U.S. Marines poised in amphibious vessels off Kuwait's coast as a lure while his main body of troops and equipment made an end run cutting off Iraq rear guard troops.

2. Ross Allen was first Air Intelligence Officer for VT-51. He was transferred to the USS LEXINGTON (CV-16), May 30, 1944. Martin Kilpatrick took Allen's place and remained with VT-51 through November 30, 1944.

3. There were two ready rooms on INDEPENDENCE class carriers: one for fighters, the other for bombers.

4. For the message to NOKAZE see the SRN series, National Archives for May 16, 1944 #193391.

5. For Admiral Nagumo's dispatch see SRN #193208, May 20, 1944 at 1340 hours. For Nagumo dispatch of May 12, 1944, see SRN #025512 at 2045 hours.

6. Pan American World Airways. See photo-essay, *WINGS TO THE ORIENT* published by Pictorial Histories Publishing Co., 1985. PAA operated a radio direction finder network in the Pacific during China Clipper Days. In 1941 this network was available to the USN's intelligence networks centered at Stations Cast (Corregidor) and Hypo (Pearl Harbor).

7. Jarvis breaks radio silence: see May 23, 1944 photo of SAN JACINTO fighter ready room where PANZER radio code assigned to Jarvis.

8. USS WASP is CV-18. The first WASP (CV-7) was sunk by Japanese forces September 15, 1942.

9. Yokosuka message of May 25, 1944. See SRN #026336 at 0730 hours. UNKAI MARU sunk Aug 4, 1944 near Chichi Jima: see Japanese Naval and Merchant Shipping Losses (JANAC) page 64.

10. Manchurian transfer: The submarine, USS TROUT, sank the SAKITO MARU on February 29, 1944 with loss of over 2,000 Japanese troops and all their equipment including tanks and heavy artillery. See JICPOA interrogation #38, page 80 et al.

11. Japanese Mandates: a series of German-owned Central Pacific Islands from Palau in west to Marshalls in east awarded to Japan by the League of Nations following World War I. Japan was allied with U.S., England and France.

12. For challenges to the reported fortification of the Mandates prior to December 7, 1941 see pages 26517 (et al) of Tokyo War Crimes Trial; statement of Yuzuru Goto; see also pages 26511, Commander Suguru Suzuki IJN. (Vol 7, Transcript of the Proceedings in Open Session. Garland Publishing Co., New York 1981). All Japanese names in this book are presented western style, i.e. given name first, followed by family name.

Part IV

1. Photo requests from Marine Corps; criticism of Navy: See Hoffman page 25 et al.

2. Navy photographs were "fuzzy" and "very poor in quality." See Hoffman, page 277 note #4.

3. Five intelligence bulletins: See JICPOA listings.

4. Bush Saipan target, see JICPOA Bulletin 66-44 page 31.

5. During World War II each U.S. Navy aircraft was assigned a Bureau Number issued by the Bureau of Aeronautics. For record keeping purposes all pilots and aircrew personnel used the Bureau Number to record their flight hours in their individual aviation logs. This Bureau Number was affixed to the instrument panel in the cockpit and also painted in small figures on the rudder. The Bureau Number is different from the fuselage number. A separate number was assigned each aircraft engine.

6. For log of Japanese radio on Saipan see JICPOA special translation Item #9438 published in Bulletin #21-45. Provides daily reports concerning Japanese communications on Saipan, June 1-27, 1944.

7. In June 1944, Ensign George Bush, as bomber and photo intelligence officer, was engaged in missions supporting U.S. landings on Saipan's west coast conducted by the 2nd and 4th U. S. Marine divisions. In 1991 Commander-in-chief George Bush ordered the same 2nd and 4th Divisions into battle in the Persian Gulf War.

8. Ratio of US ground forces facing Japanese on Saipan in June 1944 was approximately 1.3 to 1 (40,000 US Marines vs. approximately 30,000 Japanese). When the Navy force of about 150,000 is added the ratio becomes 5 to 1 in US favor. During buildup of troops in Operation Desert Shield in 1990-1991 Congress debated the merits of a coalition force of approximately 500,000 troops facing an estimated 1,000,000 Iraqis, a ratio of two to one favoring Saddam Hussein.

9. Charan Kanoa lookout in smoke stack: See page 37 where Hoffman contradicts, "Japanese are not inside"; then see page 38 where photo caption states ingenious Japanese used the stack for an observation post; page 80 where a Japanese lookout, who was directing fire at the Marines, was dragged from the stacks. (Note: Similarity to Persian Gulf War February 1991, when Iraqi forces were discovered by U. S. Marines of the Second and Fourth Divisions directing fire at coalition forces from a tall tower in Khafji. The same Marine Divisions were also involved at Charan Kanoa in 1944).

Part V

1. Code name for Saipan was TEARAWAY; Tinian, TATTERSAILS. See Operations chart, Annex A, CTF 52 Attack Order #A11-44. Battle of Philippine Sea, June 20, 1944: USN aircraft returned to their carriers in darkness. To orient the pilots Task Force 58 turned on all warship running lights and searchlights as beacons. A Japanese Val dive-bomber managed to slip into the returning USN formation and tried to land aboard the USS SAN JACINTO. Landing signal officer Ralph Bagwell believed he was guiding a SAN JAC pilot, but noted the on-coming plane did not have proper wing-tip lighting. A hand-held spot light was focused on the rapidly approaching plane to confirm the position of the tail-hook. At this instant, according to Bagwell, the light beam picked up the rising sun emblem of Japan on the port wing and fuselage. Bagwell waved off the Val but the pilot was determined and tried a second approach pattern. By this time the SAN JAC alerted Admiral Mitscher who ordered all lights of the Task Force turned off. The Val, still with its running lights operating, was seen by various other ships of TF-58 but was not taken under fire. Bagwell said the Val pilot was probably seeking sanctuary on the SAN JACINTO for had he been aggressive he could have fired his machine guns or dropped ordnance.

2. Sinking of "The Barbara": Both Nadeau and Bush were shown the SAN JACINTO aerial photo of a TBM sinking nose first, with a life raft containing a crew aft of the plane. Neither could identify the scene as that of June 19, 1944. Nadeau doubted there was a plane overhead when they ditched. The President did not recall "The Barbara" decending nose first. The photo, the only one in the SAN JACINTO photo file showing a ditching from the air, is not captioned as to date or occurrence.

3. USS CLARENCE K. BRONSON (DD-668) not to be confused with the USS BROWNSON (DD-518).

4. Hachiman is Japanese God of War. Equivalent to Mars in Western lore.

5. Similarity to Operation Desert Storm: President Bush's victory address to Congress, March 6, 1991 on humanitarian traits of American warriors: "I'm sure many of you saw on television the unforgettable scene of four terrified Iraqi soldiers, surrendering. They emerged from their bunker—broken, tears streaming from their eyes, fearing the worst. And there was the American soldier. Remember what he said? He said: "It's OK. You're all right now. You're all right now." That scene says a lot about America, a lot about who we are. Americans are a caring people. We are a good people, a generous people. Let us always be caring and good and generous in all we do."

6. Tarrant took pictures using illumination from the light over the triage table.

7. Guam invasion postponed because of fierce Japanese resistance on Saipan: Gailey, *Howlin Mad vs. the Army,* pg 103.

8. Inadequate aerial photos of Guam: See Gailey, Liberation of Guam, page 60-61; Photo coverage fell short of expected performance; Photographs did not reach lower echelons; Good aerial photos were lacking; See *Recapture of Guam*, US Marine Corps Monograph by Major O. R. Lodge, page 23-24. Navy photo task of Marianas only partially fullfilled; Incomplete photographic coverage: Gailey, *Howlin Mad vs. the Army*, pg 105. For Aerial photo complaints of General Shepherd: See Operations and Special Action Report, 1st Marine Provisional Brigade, dated August 19, 1944.

9. Captain's Mast in 1944 was part of the Navy's legal system of military courts. Its civilian analogy would be a minor traffic offense.

10. Photo of Mc Cain and Martin: Admiral McCain's parachute harness caught on the exit hatch of the TBM pulling him backward, according to photographer Tinsley.

Part VI

1. Intelligence photography was very much a part of the Persian Gulf War in February 1991. Questions were raised concerning ability of the United States and Coalition Forces to locate Iraq SCUD missile sites used for launching attacks on Israel and Saudia Arabia. Officials of the Coalition Forces repeatedly said aerial photgraphy was unable to locate the missile sites. "It's a problem locating the SCUDS," said Air Vice Marshall W. J. Wrollen of the Royal Air Force. Another RAF officer, Group Captain Niall Irving told a world wide TV audience the Iraquis had camouflaged the sites making discovery difficult. U.S. Marine Major General Robert B. Johnston, Chief of Staff of the Central Command, echoed the British officers, saying photography had failed to locate the SCUDS. Questioning these assessments, Jerome Pasto, the photo interpreter on the Bush photo team in 1944 wondered what had happened to stereo photography in Gulf War intelligence planning. "Stereo pairs could easily penetrate the Iraqi camouflage," said Pasto. "In addition, photography would reveal position tracks in the desert sand as the SCUD launchers moved about."

2. Geographically the Palau Islands are part of the Western Carolines, 520 miles east of the Philippines and stretching from six to eight degrees north latitude. In 1991 the islands are known as the Republic of Belau with ties to the United States through an unratified Compact of Association. The Republic became self governing in 1981. The Palau group of 200 islands extends about 77 miles in a north-northeast, south-southwest direction. The northern portion starts at Velasco Reef. At the southern end are Anguar and Peleliu, the sites of the September 1944, Marine Corps invasion. As the southern anchor of the Chichi Jima Defensive Barrier, Palau was very useful to Japan during the Pacific War, first during their conquest of the Philippines in 1941 and early 1942, and subsequently as a supply point for the New Guinea and South Pacific war fronts.

3. SOKUTEN identity: United States Naval Chronology World War II page 97 gives wrong coordinates of the sinking but corrects initial 1944 identification as a destroyer to a minelayer. Correct locale of the sinking is approximately 8' 20'N × 134' 35'E. Mistake can be attributed to the USS SAN JACINTO Action Report of Operation Snapshot which lists locale of all reported sinkings of July 25, 1944 in Malakal Harbor. In their photo report, Bush and Pasto place the SOKU-TEN location inside Velasco Reef. (See "ship damage location chart" CVL-30 Serial 0011, August 7, 1944) Station Hypo intercepted radio communications between the SOKUTEN and the Japanese Base Force Commander at Palau during May and June. The communications intelligence indicated the minelayer was engaged in mining waters throughout the Palau Islands. The SOKUTEN, using radio call sign of KO ME RI, was heard entering a Palau harbor on May 8, 1944. (See SRN #025293 at 0025 hours). Collateral communications intelligence obtained by Hypo on June 23, 1944, warned Japanese forces of mine field locations throughout the Palau island waters. (See SRN #031045, June 23, 1944, at 0851 hours). President Bush was confronted with the same type mine problem in February 1941 during Operation Desert Storm when Iraq mines damaged the United States warships, USS PRINCETON and USS TRIPOLI then operating in the Persian Gulf.

4. SAN JACINTO produced 1017 photographs: See CVL-30 Action Report Serial 0011 dated August 7, 1944, Part II. Details of the flight lines over the Umurbrogal (Bloody Nose Ridge) prepared by Jerome Pasto are included.

5. Rupertus' prediction: Issued to the 36 news correspondents and several troop commanders as the First Marine Division departed Guadacanal, the troop staging area for Peleliu. The sealed letter was authorized to be opened on D-minus 1 day (September 14, 1944). Source: Hough, The Assault on Peleliu, U.S. Marine Corps Monograph, 1950, page 35. Hough said 30 of the news correspondents did not go ashore; six did and one was killed. "News coverage of the operation was sketchy, often misleading, and, when quick conquest failed to materialize, tinged with biting criticism," wrote Hough.

6. Halsey report of 46% casualty loss: See COM THIRD FLEET Secret Serial 00174 dated December 28, 1944, page 3 item #15.

7. Coleman statement re photo coverage: See Headquarters, III Amphibious Corps Secret report dated October 1, 1944 by C-2 (Intelligence), Colonel William F. Coleman.

8. Morison concurrence: See Vol XII, page 33.

9. Intelligence available to troops: "Final plans were completed and issued by the various Task Organization Commanders concerned (in) sufficient time in advance for all subordinate commanders to study and digest them." See Secret report dated October 14, 1944, HEADQUARTERS, III AMPHIBIOUS CORPS, page 4, item #2 signed by Colonel Walter A. Wachtler, C-3 (Planning).

10. Admiral Arleigh A. Burke had a distinguished U. S. Naval career. President Dwight D. Eisenhower named him Chief of Naval Operations, the Navy's top post. Burke served two terms with Ike.

11. Bush's "Snapshot letter," self-typed to author, September 20, 1984.

Part VII

1. Testimony of Major Sueo Matoba: Tokyo War Crimes trial transcript page 15,033 et al. The testimony of Matoba was given during war crimes proceedings conducted by Commander Marianas at Guam. The Mariana command was a U.S. Navy function.

2. Suyeyoshi Tai = A Japanese army anti-aircraft unit on Chichi Jima commanded by Lieutenant Jitsuro Suyeyoshi. Source: Record of Proceeding, Board of Investigation, Commander Marianas, June 6, 1946.

3. For Operation Stalemate II, the USS SAN JACINTO

was operating as part of the Third Fleet under Admiral William F. "Bull" Halsey. All warships were the same as the Fifth Fleet of Admiral Raymond Spruance. Other than a change of admirals and staff, the principal difference was a change in numerical designation of the various carrier task groups. The fast carriers and their escorts were now called Task Force Thirty-Eight (TF-38). Admiral Marc Mitscher remained in command of air operations.

4. Eniwetok served the fast carriers briefly as an anchorage. Saipan's Tanapag Harbor and Manus Anchorage in the Admiralties were used by the carriers in September 1944. By October, Ulithi in the western Carolines, became the principal anchorage until end of the war.

5. Bush's new bomber, obtained from the replacement pool at NAS Eniwetok, carried Bureau Number of 46214. He flew this TBM1-C a total of 7.4 hours before it was shot down on September 2, 1944. Source: Bush's flight log. The fuselage number was Tare Three: source USS FINBACK 10th War Patrol Report, page 6.

6. "Fanatical defenses of modern time": see JICPOA Bulletin 2-46, page 55.

7. Grossbatteries and American carrier flight formations: See statement of Takuo Nozawa, a member of the Tokyo "Triple A" defense unit who was on Chichi Jima in JICPOA Interrogation #36, report #167, page 134.

8. "Final stronghold of Nipponese:" see statement of Major Yoshitaka Horie quoted on page 55, JICPOA Bulletin #2-46. Statements confirmed as accurate by Major Horie in letter to author, October 1990.

9. Taped interview with Colonel Thomas L. Ridge USMC (Ret) held at Officer's Club, Naval Hospital Bethesda, Maryland, February 28, 1990.

Part VIII

1. According to SAN JACINTO photo policy, the author brought a film-loaded K-20 camera to the VT-51 ready room and issued the camera with Bush's approval to John Delaney for the Mt Yoake/Asahi mission known as Strike Baker. Delaney carried the camera to "The Barbara" where it was secured on a mount in the bomb bay which had been designed to keep the K-20 safe during catapult launching and deck landings.

2. Chichi Jima Naval Radio: For tactical system see JICPOA Bulletin 2-46, figure #14, page 63; strategic system linking far outposts of the Empire see JICPOA Bulletin #64-45; Listing of strategic radio links see Station H Monthly report, page 20, dated March 17, 1942. A Nazi Germany ocean raider, the MICHEL, was using Chichi Jima as a replenishment point in early fall 1943. The MICHEL's radio transmissions with Chichi Jima were intercepted at Station Hypo with result the Nazi raider was torpedoed by the USS TARPON October 17, 1943. Source: USN Chronology page 65; also United States Strategic Bombing Survey Vol I, pg 286.

3. For opening phase of Operate Stalemate II the USS SAN JACINTO was assigned to Task Group 38.4 consisting of USS ENTERPRISE (CV-6), USS FRANKLIN (CV-13) and cruisers, USS BILOXI (CL-80), USS NEW ORLEANS (CA-32) and 12 destroyers of Destroyer Squadron Six. Commander of TG 38.4 was Rear Admiral Ralph Davison assisted by Rear Admiral H. B. Salada.

4. Specifically protecting the Emperor and movement of

Hirohito anti aircraft gunners from Tokyo: see JICPOA Interrogations #36, Report #165 page 109. The Kato radar unit commanded by Second Lieutenant Kato (no first name listed) of the Imperial Japanese Army. See JICPOA Interrogations #36, Report #165, page 110-111. Lieutenant Kato not to be confused with Colonel Takesune Kato, CO of the 308th Infantry Battalion on Chichi Jima.

5. Interspersed among the "Triple A" batteries on Chichi Jima were dummy AA guns. See JICPOA Interrogations #36, Report #167, Appendix 1.

6. Description of Chichi Jima bugle air raid alarm see JICPOA Interrogation #25, Item B-5995-2, page 2.

7. Hit on "The Barbara": In reconstructing the attack from official USN reports, statements of aviators participating in the strike and evaluating the positions of the Japanese "Triple A," military artist, Skip Rains calculated the aircraft was hit on the port side.

8. Bush parachute landing: The 16mm motion picture film footage taken by Ensign Edwards, the FINBACK's photo officer, indicates George Bush landed in the Pacific waters about 5 miles north east of Hatsune Bay. Had he landed any closer, Bush would have been in the submerged minefields planted about two miles off Chichi Jima's eastern coast by the Japanese. Disaster lurking in the undected minefield would have enveloped the FINBACK and Bush. The navigator, Dean Spratlin, told Edwards in 1991 that the sub had not been alerted to the mine danger. Other obstacles in the eastern waters off Chichi Jima were a series of rock outcroppings called Bara-bara Iwa (scattered rocks) which might have restricted the FINBACK's maneuvering.

9. Ordinance fired at Japanese boats: See Commander Torpedo Squadron 51, Secret Serial 0021 dated September 8, 1944, Report #6, Section VIII.

10. Allied airmen would be beheaded: See editorial in Japanese newspapers Mainichi and Asahi quoted in JICPOA Intrerrogation #37, Report #170.

11. Bush statement in Looking Forward: "FINBACK submerged." Not so, says Edwards. The submarine was on the surface at all times. Edwards believes Bush, riding his raft on the crest and fall of the Pacific swell, received impression the sub was submerged.

12. Still photos enlarged from Edwards 16mm motion picture film and published in various media are photo-printed backwards (flopped). The pictures show Bush port-side-to the FINBACK, when actually he came aboard starboard-side-to. Ensign Beckman's downed location was within the nine-mile range of Chichi Jima's coastal defense guns, so the FINBACK remained submerged during the rescue. Beckman clung to the periscope and was towed" to the safety of off-shore waters and brought aboard when the sub could safely surface. Beckman was later killed during the invasion of the Philippines.

13. Japanese radio facilities moved to hillside caves: See JICPOA Bulletin 2-46, page 58, et al.

Part IX

1. Bush's DFC was approved on September 13, 1946, after it had proceeded through the Navy's award process. In 1954 he was also awarded an Air Medal. The awards were originally recommended in 1944. However the split-up of Torpedo Squadron Fifty-One with Bush transferred to Squadron

VT-153, the fire at VT-51's home base Pasco Naval Station and end of war side tracked the honors.

2. New York Post copyrighted story, page 1, August 12, 1988, by Allan Wolper, Director of Journalism, Newark Campus, Rutgers University and Al Ellenberg, Special Projects Editor of the Post. The Post story quoted from VT-51 members Legare Hole and Lawrence Mueller. Neither participated in Strike Baker, September 2, 1944. A version of The Post story was distributed by Associated Press and printed in the New York Times, August 13, 1988. The Los Angeles Times originated their own story in report by Lee May on August 13, 1988. The Washington Post had its version by Dan Morgan on August 14, 1988. None of the media contacted surviving eyewitnesses Bynum, Nunnally, Foshee, Gorman or Melton.

3. Milt Moore quotes: Copyrighted 1985 by Ernest Furgurson, Bureau Chief of the Baltimore Sun, Reprinted with permission of Mr. Furgurson.

Part X

1. Sinking of HAKUUN MARU #2, HASSHO MARU, see Alden, page 132; also JANAC, page 67.

2. HI KA HE 7 was a Japanese naval coded radio call sign (Yobidashi Fugo) assigned at the time to Chichi Jima. It is a three kana-number category: "HI," "KA" and "HE" each being a separate kana. In World War II Japanese naval vessels and shore stations used a telegraphic dot-dash address system in communication with one another. The system was called "navy kana" by USN intercept operators and was identified as 48 arbitrary sounds of the Japanese language adapted for transmittal by wireless. In short it was Japanese Morse code but entirely different than the international Morse system. In addition to the 48 basic sounds, "navy kana" included numbers, nigori, and other designators. Radio call signs are familiar in United States as WNBC or KCBS. Source: CDR Fred R. Thomson USN.

Part XI

1. Bush flew a Navy R5D-1 in three flight legs: Pearl Harbor to Johnson Island (4.0 hours); Johnson to Kwajelein (8.5 hours) and Kwajelein to Guam (7.0 hours). Source: Bush aviation flight log, October 22, 1944.

2. The ZUIKAKU (25,675 tons) was sister carrier of the SHOKAKU (29,800 tons) sunk by a U.S. submarine in the Battle of Philippine Sea June 20, 1944. Both carriers were base for aircraft which hit Pearl Harbor on December 7, 1941. The ZUIHO (11,200 tons) was a light carrier converted from a tanker/oiler. Participated in the Philippine Invasion at start of hostilities, December 8, 1941 (Manila time). VT-51, Bush's squadron, received full credit for sinking the ZUIHO and shared the ZUIKAKU's sinking with other air groups of Task Force 38.

Part XII

1. Between his return home, Dec 24, 1944, and his marriage, January 6, 1945, Bush served as best man for his brother, Prescott.

RESEARCH and BIBLIOGRAPHY

Research for this book was conducted using the following books, publications, and documents consulted at locations indicated. The selection was based solely on revelance to USS SAN JACINTO and Air Group 51.

BOOKS

Alden, John D: *U. S. Submarine Attacks During World War II, published by U. S. Naval Institute Press, Annapolis, Maryland 1989.*

Brackman, Arnold C.; *The Other Nurenberg,* William Morrow & Co., New York 1987.

Bush, George; *Looking Forward,* published by Doubleday, New York, 1987.

Carter, John; *Pacific Islands Year Book,* Pacific Publications, Sydney, 1986 edition.

Cohen, Stan; *Wings to the Orient,* published by Pictorial Histories Publishing Company, Missoula, Montana, 1985.

Cohen, Stan; *Enemy on Island, Issue in Doubt, The Capture of Wake Island,* Published by Pictorial Histories Publishing Company, Missoula, Montana 1983.

Gregg, Charles T.; *Tarawa,* published by Stein and Day, 1984

Gailey, Harry A; *Howlin Mad vs. the Army,* Presidio Press, Novato, Calif, 1986

Gailey, Harry A.; *The Liberation of Guam,* published by Presidio Press, Novato, Calif, 1988.

Gailey, Harry A.; *Peleliu 1944,* published by Nautical and Aviation Publishing Company of America, Inc., Annapolis, Maryland, 1983.

Hoffman, Carl W. Major UCMC; *SAIPAN, The Beginning of The End,* published by Historical Division. U. S. Marine Corps, 1950.

Jane's Fighting Ships, 1942. Published by Macmillan, New York (edition of June 1943).

Japanese Naval and Merchant Shipping Losses, prepared by The Joint Army-Navy Assessment Committee, (JANAC) February 1947. U. S. Government Printing Office.

Kenkyusha's New Japanese-English Dictionary. Yoshitaro Takenobu, general editor. Tokyo.

Lodge, O. R. Major UCMS; *The Recapture of Guam,* published by Historical Branch, G-3 Division Headquarters U. S. Marine Corps, Washington D. C. 1954.

Malone, Mike; *Come To Micronesia,* Published by Pacific Publishing Company, Saipan, Commonwealth of Marianas, 1988.

Morison, Samuel Eliot; *History of U.S. Naval Operations in World War II,* VOL XII. Little Brown & Company 1958.

Morison, Samuel Eliot; *History of U.S. Naval Operations in World War II,* Vol VIII. Little Brown & Company 1953.

McMillan, George; *The Old Breed*, published by Infantry Journal Press, Washington, D. C. 1949.

McMillan, George; *Uncommon Valor*, Battery Press, Nashville, 1986.

Piccigallo, Philip R.; *The Japanese On Trial*, University of Texas Press, Austin, 1979.

Rochefort, Joseph J., The Reminiscences of. United States Naval Institute, Annapolis, Maryland, 1970. Special bound edition classified TOP SECRET CODEWORD.

Sledge, E.B.; *With The Old Breed at Peleliu*, Presidio Press, Novato, Calif., 1981.

Stockman, John R. Captain USMC; *The Battle For Tarawa*, published by Historical Section, Division of Public Information, Headquarters U. S. Marine Corps, Washington, D. C. 1947.

Toland, John; *The Rising Sun*, Published by Random House, 1970.

United States Naval Chronology World War II. Government Printing Office, Washington, D. C. 1955

USS SAN JACINTO, Short History of; privately published by the commanding officer, USS SAN JACINTO, San Francisco, 1945.

LIBRARY OF CONGRESS, Washington D. C. Following books located in the Jefferson Library:

Lionel Cholmondeley, Bonin Islands

Thomas James, Bonin Islands

United States Treaty, Bonin Islands.

Dale Johnson, Bonin Islands.

Matthew Perry, Bonin Islands.

Ross Gast, Bonin Islands.

Motoyoshi Inukai, Bonin Islands

Office Naval Intelligence, Geographic Monolith #60, Bonin Islands, July 3, 1942.

Commander in Chief, United States Pacific Fleet, Intelligence Bulletins by JICPOA, 1942 to 1945. (Note: also found in U.S. Navy Historical Center, Washington Navy Yard, Washington, D.C.)

NAVAL HISTORICAL CENTER, Building 57, Washington Navy Yard, Washington, D.C. I wish to acknowledge the expertise and assistance of Kathleen M. Lloyd, Head of Reference Section, Operational Archives and Michael Walker, Archives Specialist. Ms. Lloyd and Mr. Walker provided following documents:

Torpedo Squadron Fifty-One (VT-51)
- Aircraft Action Reports, May to November 1944.
- History of Squadron, September 22, 1943 to November 30, 1944.

Carrier Air Group Fifty-One (CAG-51)
- Aircraft Action Reports, May through November 1944.
- History of Fighting Squadron 51. Period September 22 1943 to December 1, 1944.

USS SAN JACINTO (CVL-30)
- Action Reports, May to November 1944.
- War Diary, December 15, 1943 to November 30, 1944.
- Activities Report, December 15, 1943 to October 14, 1944.

Listings by Operation. Following is listing of documents pertaining to Pacific Fleet operations of 1944 consulted by the author. Note: The Action Reports of the various USN warships and commands filed at the Naval Historical Center are an additional source for original combat action photographs of the Pacific War.

OPERATION FORAGER (Wake-Marcus prelude May 17-23, 1944)
- Action Report, Commander Carrier Division Three of May 25, 1944.
- See also action reports of USS SAN JACINTO (CVL-30), Air Group 51 and Torpedo Squadron 51. (Note: Greenwich Civil Time is used in the May 1944 SAN JACINTO reports of Wake-Marcus. In later 1944 reports, local time is used).

OPERATION FORAGER (Saipan, Guam, Tinian, Rota et al., June-July 1944
- Action report, Commander Carrier Division 4, Serial 00116 of July 16, 1944.
- See also Action Report, War Diary and Deck Log of USS SAN JACINTO; Aircraft Action Report of Air Group 51 both Fighter and Torpedo Squadrons, this time period.

OPERATION SNAPSHOT, July 25-27, 1944
- Carrier Division Three operation order #11-44 of July 23, 1944.
- See also listings under USS SAN JACINTO, Torpedo Squadron 51, Carrier Air Group 51.

OPERATION STALEMATE II (Raids on Chichi Jima, September 1-2, 1944)
- Action Report, USS SAN JACINTO (CVL-30) for August 4-5, 1944.
- Action Report, USS FRANKLIN (CV-13) for August 4-5, 1944.
- Report of War Patrol Number Ten of USS FINBACK (SS-230) dated October 4, 1944, Serial 030.
- Action Report Commander Carrier Division Two, Serial 00191 of September 20, 1944. Includes following reports for period August 31 to September 2, 1944:
  Action Report, USS FRANKLIN (CV-13)
  Action Report, USS ENTERPRISE (CV-6)
  Action Report, USS SAN JACINTO (CVL-30)
  Action Report, USS BILOXI (CL-80)
  Action Report, USS NEW ORLEANS (CA-32)
  Action Report, Commander, Destroyer Squadron Six.

BULLETINS OF JOINT INTELLIGENCE CENTER, PACIFIC OCEAN AREAS (JICPOA)
- Interrogations #18 to #39. A series of 22 interrogation monographs of Japanese prisoners of war, translated into English.
- Intelligence Monograph of Aguijan
  Bulletin #77A-44: Gridded target maps.
- Intelligence Monographs of Chichi Jima and Bonin Islands.
  Bulletin #15-44: Southern Nanpo Shoto.
  Bulletin #91A-44: Air target maps and photos.
  Bulletin #122-44: Information bulletin.
  Bulletin #122-A-44: Air target maps.
  Bulletin #2-46: Field survey of Japanese defenses.
- Intelligence Monographs of Guam
  Bulletin #52-44: Information Vol I & II.

Bulletin #52A-44: Air target maps and photos.
Bulletin #79A-44: Gridded air target maps.
Bulletin #79B-44: Air target maps and photos.
- Intelligence Monographs of Marcus Island
Bulletin #10-43: Air target bulletin #27.
Bulletin #75-44: Information bulletin and target survey.
Bulletin #75A-44: Air target maps and photos.
Bulletin #141-44: Target analysis.
- Intelligence Monographs of the Mariana Islands
Bulletin #7-44: Information bulletin, Marianas.
Bulletin #29-44: Weather survey for Carolines and Marianas.
Bulletin #31-44: Tide tables, Carolines and Marianas.
Bulletin #34-44: Information bulletin, Saipan, Tinian, and Rota.
Bulletin #42-44: Information bulletin, Pagan and minor Marianas.
Bulletin #42A-44: Air target maps and photos, Pagan and minor Marianas.
Bulletin #67A-44: Air target maps and photos, Pagan and minor Marianas.
Bulletin #73-44: Information bulletin for Saipan, Tinian and Rota.
Bulletin #77A-44: Gridded air target maps, Saipan Tinian and Aguijan.
Bulletin #77B-44: Air target maps and photos, Saipan, Tinian and Aguijan.
- Intelligence Monographs of Palau and Peleliu
Bulletin #33-43: Volumne I, Palau.
Bulletin #17-44: Information bulletin, Palau.
Bulletin #17A-44: Air target maps and photos.
Bulletin #17B-44: Air target maps and photos.
Bulletin #29-44: Weather survey, Carolines and Marianas.
Bulletin #31-44: Tide tables, Carolines and Marianas.
Bulletin #32-44: Potential air field site, Palau.
Bulletin #87-44: Information bulletin, Palau.
Bulletin #87A-44: Air target maps and photos, Koror.
Bulletin #87B-44: Air target maps and photos, Peleliu.
Bulletin #87T-44: Target analysis.
Bulletin #124-44: Information, southern Palau.
Bulletin #129-44: Palau gazeteer.
Bulletin #136-44: Information bulletin, northern Palau.
Bulletin #173-45: Japanese caves on Peleliu.
- Intelligence Monographs of Rota
Bulletin #34-44: Information bulletin.
Bulletin #67A-44: Air target maps and photos.
Bulletin #73-44: Information bulletin.
Bulletin #85A-44: Gridded air target maps.
Bulletin #85B-44: Air target maps and photos.
- Intelligence Monographs of Saipan
Bulletin #34-44: Information bulletin.
Bulletin #66-44: Target survey, Saipan.
Bulletin #66A-44: Air target maps and photos.
Bulletin #73-44: Information bulletin.
Bulletin #77A-44: Gridded air target maps.
Bulletin #77B-44: Air target maps and photos.
- Intelligence Monograph of Tarawa:
Bulletin #11-43: Air target bulletin #26.
- Intelligence Monographs of Tinian
Bulletin #34-44: Information bulletin.
Bulletin #67-44: Target survey.

Bulletin #67A-44: Air target maps and photos.
Bulletin #73-44: Information bulletin.
Bulletin #77A-44: Gridded air target maps.
Bulletin #77B-44: Air target maps and photos.
- Intelligence Monographs of Wake Island
Bulletin #27-43: Air target bulletin #14.
Bulletin #30-43: Enemy positions, Vol IV.
Bulletin #23A-44: Air target maps and photos.
Bulletin #23B-44: Air target maps and photos.
Bulletin #80-44: Target survey.

National Archives and Record Center. Military Reference Branch, Pennsylvania Avenue entrance, Washington, D.C. I wish to particularly ackowledge the help of John Taylor in locating the Station Hypo radio intercepts of the Japanese Fleet and to Terri Hammitt who spent weeks laboriously copying the documents for the author's files. The following records were consulted.
- Deck Log, USS SAN JACINTO (CVL-30)
- Deck Log, USS HEALY (DD-672)
- Deck Log, USS CLARENCE K. BRONSON (DD-668)
- Radio intercepts, Imperial Japanese Navy 1941-45, SRN Series. Intercepted by Station Hypo, Station Baker, Station Cast, Fleet Radio Unit, Melbourne, Australia; Fleet Radio Unit, Pearl Harbor, Hawaii.

National Archives Washington, D.C. Still Picture Division. Acknowledge the assistance, with thanks, of Dale Connelly, Jim Trimble, Fred Pernell who arranged for me to photograph the USS SAN JACINTO photo files in Record Group 80. The original negatives and prints taken and processed aboard the carrier in 1944 are well preserved in the Still Picture Division.

National Archives and Record Center, San Bruno, California. Michael Anderson located the 1941 files of the Commandant Fourteenth Naval District (Hawaii) and Twelfth Naval District (San Francisco) which are stored in San Bruno. The confidential and secret file boxes contain U.S. Naval records pertaining to communication intelligence on Japanese naval units.

UNITED STATES MARINE CORPS. Historical Center located in Washington Navy Yard, Washington D. C. Danny Crawford, Head, Reference Section, located retired Marine Corps officers involved with Chichi Jima and the Peleliu invasion. Ms. Joyce Bonnett, Head Archivist of the History and Museum Division located the operation plans of the 1944 Peleliu Invasion together with many of the photographs taken by the USS SAN JACINTO-Bush photo team and arranged for me to copy the documents in the magnificent Marine Corps Library housed in the Washington Navy Yard. Her assistant, Ms. Joyce Conyers facilitated in the photo-copy procedures.
- USMC History Box 40; Operation Stalemate II files. Includes OpPlan A501-44 with annexes comprising intelligence, comments of Admiral William F. Halsey, Peleliu beach studies, maps, photographs.

AVIATOR FLIGHT LOGS

The following pilots and aircrewmen of Air Group 51 permitted me to inspect and photo-copy their aviation flight log books. Each individual flight was recorded listing the model and bureau number of the aircraft, length of flight, pilot and crew names, category of the flight together with comments. (Note: Many of the torpedo squadron (VT-51) log books and records were destroyed in a fire at the Naval Air Station, Pasco, Washington in 1945.)

- George Bush, VT-51
- Harold Fuchs, VT-51
- Lou Grab, VT-51
- Arthur Horan, VT-51
- Sam Jackson, VF-51
- William Joyce, VT-51
- Dixie Mays, VF-51
- Milton Moore, VT-51
- Lawrence Mueller, VT-51
- Leo Nadeau, VT-51
- Harold Nunnally, VT-51
- Charles Peter, VT-51
- Joseph Smith Jr., VT-51
- Douglas West, VT-51

INTERVIEWS

I am indebted to the following persons who graciously and promptly. answered my every question . PI = Personal interview, WI = written interview and/or correspondence, TI = telephone interview.

- Adams, Nathaniel; Boise, Idaho. Fighter pilot, VF-51. (PI, WI, TI)
- Allan, Ross T. New Orleans, La. Intelligence Officer, VT-51. (WI)
- Benninghoff, H. Merrell, Ambassador, U. S. State Department. Melbourne, Florida (WI)
- Boddington, Edward;, Kansas City, Kansas. Fighter pilot, VF-51. (WI, TI)
- Brewster, Edward; Locust Valley, N. Y. Intelligence Officer, VF-51. (WI)
- Burke, Arleigh A. Admiral USN (Ret) Fairfax, Virginia. Chief of Staff, Task Force 58. (WI)
- Burns, Thomas; Crown Point, N. Y. Radioman for Louis Grab, VT-51. (PI)
- Bush, George; The White House, 1600 Pennsylvania Avenue Washington, D. C. Bomber pilot, VT-51 (WI, PI)
- Bynum, Charles; Scottsboro, Alabama. Turret gunner for Milton Moore, VT-51. (PI, WI, TI)
- Cauchois, Scott; Piedmont, Calif. U. S. Naval aviator. (PI, TI)
- Dyer, Thomas H. Captain USN, Sykesville, Maryland. Chief cryptologist, Station Hypo (WI)
- Elerding, Janet Rochefort;, Santa Ana, Calif. Daughter of Captain Joseph Rochefort USN, founder of Station Hypo. (PI, TI)
- Edwards, William, photo officer USS FINBACK. Bay St. Louis, Mississippi. (TI WI)
- Fenger, William; New Albany, Indiana. Radioman for Carl Woie, VT-51. (PI)
- Fitzwater, Marlin; Washington, D. C. Press Secretary to George Bush. (WI)
- Forshay, Jacqueline; Little Falls, N. J. Widow of VT-51 bomber pilot Douglas West. (WI, (TI)

- Foshee, Joseph; Lufkin, Texas. Turret gunner for Doug West VT-51. (PI, TI)
- Fuchs, Harold; Chatsworth, Calif. Radioman for Jack Guy, VT-51. (PI, TI)
- Gaylien, Donald; Phoenix, Ariz. Radioman for Howard Boren, VT-51. (TI)
- Gorman, Richard; Stayton, Oregon. Radioman for Milton Moore, VT-51 (TI)
- Grab, Lou, Sacramento, Calif. Bomber pilot, VT-51. (PI, WI, TI)
- Guy, Jack, Atlanta, Georgia. Bomber pilot, VT-51. (TI, WI)
- Henriksen, George; Washington, D. C. Naval Security Group Command. (PI, WI, T I)
- Hile, William; Jacksonville, Florida. VF-51 pilot (TI)
- Hole, Legare R.: Vineyard Haven, Mass. Bomber pilot of VT-51 and Executive Officer of the Squadron. (TI, WI)
- Holmes, Wilfred J. Captain USN (Ret); Honolulu, Hawaii. Station Hypo and head Navy section, JICPOA. (PI, WI, TI)
- Horan, Arthur Jr.; Bethel, Conn. Turret gunner for William McCarter, VT-51. (PI)
- Horie, Yoshitaka, Major Imperial Japanese Army, Chief of Staff toGeneral Tachibana, Chichi Jima, 1944-45. Tokyo, Japan, (WI)
- Jackson, Sam Captain USN (Ret); Boulder Creek, Calif. Fighter pilot and Divison leader, VF-51. (PI, WI, TI)
- Joyce, William; Dedham, Mass. Turret gunner for Carl Woie, VT-51, (PI)
- Kakudo, Yoshiko; San Francisco, Calif, Curator Asian Art Museum. (TI)
- Kirkup, Peter; Historian, Grumman Corp, Bethpage, Long Island. (TI, WI)
- Kisner, Homer L. Captain USN (Ret); Carlsbad, Calif. Radio Traffic Chief, Station Hypo. (PI, TI, WI)
- Kolstad, Richard O.: Bay St. Louis, Miss. Radioman for Stanley Butchart, VT-51. (PI)
- Layton, Edwin Rear Admiral; Carmel, California. Pacific Fleet intelligence officer 1940-45. (PI, WI, TI)
- Lazzarevich, Richard; Oxnard, California. VF-51 pilot. (TI, PI)
- Lenihan, Dan, Chief, Submerged Cultural Resources Unit, National Park Service, Santa Fe, New Mexico (TI, WI)
- Lewis, Grady; Eugene, Oregon. U. S. Navy Cryptographic Veterans Assn., (PI, WI, TI)
- Lotz, David, Agana, Guam. (TI, WI)
- Mays, Dixie CDR USN (Ret); Kirkland, Wash. Fighter Pilot, VF-51. (PI, TI)
- Maxwell, Albert; Myrtle Beach, South Carolina Turret Gunner for Legare Hole, VT-51. (PI, WI)
- Melvin, Arthur, Central Point, Oregon. Brother of Donald Melvin, VT-51. (WI, TI)
- Miculka, James E; Chief Ranger, War In The Pacific National Park, Agana, Guam. (WI)
- Mierzejewski, Chester; Cheshire, Conn. Turret gunner, VT-51. (WI, TI)
- Moore, Jeanne, Arlington, Texas. Widow of Milton Moore, bomber pilot VT-51. (WI, TI)
- Moore, Mahlon Jr. Orangeville, California. Brother of Milton Moore. (TI)
- Muller, Honor, Bellingham, Washington. Sister of Milton Moore, VT-51. (WI, TI)
- Myers, Fred Jr; Altus, Arkansas. Turret gunner, Donald Melvin, VT-51. (WI, TI)

- Mc Culloch, Robert J; La Porte, Indiana. USS HEALY. (WI, TI, PI)
- McLaughlin, Charles; Novato, California. Collector of USS SAN JACINTO memorabila. (TI)
- Nadeau, Leo; Ramona, Calif. Turret gunner for George Bush, VT-51. (WI, TI, PI)
- Newman, Irwin G. CDR., Naval Security Group Command, Washington, D. C. (PI, WI, TI)
- Nunnally, Harold; Santa Rosa, Calif. Radioman for Doug West, VT-51. (PI, TI)
- Pasto, Jerome; State College, Penna. Photo Interpretation Officer, USS SAN JACINTO. (WI TI)
- Peter, Charles; West Sacramento, Calif. Turret Gunner, Donald Boren, VT-51. (PI, WI, TI)
- Playstead, Richard; Burlington, Wash; Bomber pilot, VT-51. (TI, PI)
- Raquepau, John J.; Tierra Verde, Florida. Bomber pilot, VT-51. (PI)
- Rhodes, Donald; Special Assistant To The President, White House, Washington, D. C. (PI, WC, TI)
- Seno, Sadao CDR Imperial Japanese Navy (Ret), Hayama-cho, Kanagawa-ken, Japan. (WI, TI)
- Savory, Jessell, Las Vegas, Nevada. Descendent of American settlers of Chichi Jima. (TI)
- Schulz, Lester Rear Admiral; Penacook, New Hamshire White House naval aide in 1941. (WI)
- Shinomiya, Yae, Oakland, California. Head librarian, Oakland Tribune.
- Simpson, Seth. Photo librarian, Oakland, California Tribune.
- Smith, Joseph Jr; Millersville, Maryland. Turret gunner for Richard Playstead, VT-51. (PI, WI)
- Smith, Shirley; Special Assistant to The President, White House, Washington D. C. (PI, WI)
- Stromgren, Marge, Kaneohe, Hawaii. Bishop Museum. (WI, TI)
- Tarrant, John; Sun City, Florida. Pharmacist Mate, USS HEALY. (WI, TI)
- Thomson, Fred R. CDR; Silver Spring, Maryland. Radioman-in-charge, Station AE, Sitka, Alaska. (WI)
- Toland, Toshiko and John. Authors. Danbury, Conn (TI, WI)
- Van Sweringen, Bryan, Historian, Naval Security Group Command, Washington D. C. (PI, WI, TI)
- Yamada, Kiyoko; Oakland, California. Asian Library, University of California, Berkeley. (PI, TI)

ACRONYMS

In the narrative, I have attempted to avoid the military jargon that runs the Army, Navy, Marine Corps and Coast Guard. Nevertheless, a few of the abbreviations have crept into the narrative. Their translations follow:

- JICPOA = Joint Intelligence Center, Pacific Ocean Areas. Headquartered at Makalapa, Pearl Harbor.
- VT-51 = Torpedo Squadron 51. George Bush's squadron in 1943-1944.
- CAG-51 = Carrier Air Group 51. Composed of VT-51 and VF-51 aboard USS SAN JACINTO, 1944. Commanded by CDR. Charles Moore USN.
- TF-58 = Task Force 58. The fast carrier fleet composed of ESSEX and INDEPENDENCE class carriers and including fast battleships, cruisers and destroyers. Commanded by Vice Admiral Marc A. Mitscher in 1944 as part of the Fifth Fleet which was headed by Admiral Raymond Spruance.
- TF-38 = Generally same vessels as TF-58, but administratively part of the Third Fleet of Admiral William "Bull" Halsey. Admiral Mitscher was first commander, later Admiral John S. McCain.
- CTG 58.3 = Commander, Task Group Fifty eight point three. A group of warships usually composed of two ESSEX and two INDEPENDENCE class carriers. Groups as part of Task Force 58 (or 38) would be numbered one through four.
- CINCPAC = Commander-in-chief Pacific Fleet. Title held by Admiral Chester Nimitz from late December 1941 to December 1945.
- CINCPOA = Commander-in-Chief Pacific Ocean Areas. Title held by Admiral Nimitz during Pacific War.
- F6F = Grumman Hellcat fighter.
- TBF = Grumman Avenger torpedo-bomber.
- TBM = The Avenger built under license by General Motors.
- K-20 = U.S. Navy hand-held aerial camera. Manufactured by Folmer-Graflex Corporation Rochester, New York. Used 50-exposure roll film; each picture 4 × 5. Fixed focus f4.5 lens.
- F-56 = U. S. Navy Aerial Camera. Roll film, 9 wide by varied length. Lens cones from 8¼ to 40-inch telephoto lens.
- K-18 = U. S. Navy aerial camera. Exposure size 9 × 18. Used for wide angle aerial obliques in dicing proposed invasion beaches.
- FRUPAC = Fleet Radio Unit, Pacific. The Japanese code breaking unit. Successor to Station Hypo. Originally located in basement of Pearl Harbor Naval Yard administration building, Commandant 14th Naval District. Later moved to Makalapa adjacent to Pearl Harbor.
- FRUMEL = Fleet Radio Unit, Melbourne, Australia. Originally attached to the U.S. Asiatic Fleet on Corregidor Island and known as Station CAST. Was code breaking unit and processing center for intercepted Japanese naval dispatches obtained by Station Able (Shanghai) and Station Baker (Libugon, Guam). Station CAST maintained direct liaison with the Royal Navy's Far East Combined Bureau (FECB) at Singapore and with Dutch naval intelligence officers at Batavia. CAST personnel were moved by submarine to Melbourne, Australia at fall of Philippines in April 1942.
- Station "H" = Radio receiving center for intercepted Japanese naval communications located at Heeia, Hawaii on Oahu. Site now a public school. Not to be confused with Station Hypo, the processing center commanded by Joseph Rochefort.
- Station Hypo = Commanded (May 1941 to October 1942) by Joseph Rochefort, co-founder of U. S. Naval Communications Intelligence. Located in basement of the administration building, Naval Yard, Pearl Harbor from August 1941 to early 1943 when moved to Nimitz headquarters

at Makalapa and renamed FRUPAC. Hypo was the processing center for the intercepted radio communications obtained at Station H, Station K (Dutch Harbor), Station AF (Midway) and Station V (Vaitogi, Samoa). Processing included decription of the Japanese naval codes and translating to English. Space still exists and is marked with historic plaque.

- Station US = Headquarters of the U.S. Navy's crypto efforts during World War II. Located at main navy building on Constitution Avenue, Washington D. C. (now site of Viet Nam Memorial). Originally commanded by Laurence Safford. Later during war was moved to Nebraska Avenue, NW and renamed Station Negat. In 1991 known as the Naval Security Group Command. During Pacific War processed intercepts from Station S (Seattle), Station M Cheltenham, Maryland, Station W Winterhaven, Maine and intercept stations of the West Coast Communications Intelligence Network operated by the Commandants of the Eleventh (San Diego), Twelfth (San Francisco) and Thirteenth (Seattle) Naval Districts.

Rochefort Papers. A collection of documents pertaining to operations of U. S. Naval communications intelligence assembled by Captain Joseph Rochefort during his life time. Held by his daughter, Janet Rochefort Elerding who permitted the author to photo copy each record.

COPYRIGHTED MATERIAL

SPECIAL THANKS

To my wife Peggy, who edited and suggested changes in the manuscript, accompanied me on many interviews, took photographs and notes and hates war.

INDEX

About The Author

Robert Stinnett is well qualified to write this book. He was there. As a member of the Bush photo team aboard the USS SAN JACINTO (CVL-30) during World War II, he took aerial pictures from "The Barbara" piloted by Ensign George Bush. Stinnett was more than an eye witness to the Bush combat role. He participated in the anxious moments of wartime carrier operations, sharing the anxieties of combat missions with Bush and his fellow pilots and aircrewmen.

Stinnett's extensive contacts within the U. S. Naval intelligence community add depth and understanding to Bush's combat photography role during the critical Pacific battles of 1944. His comprehensive research into the intelligence records of the U. S. Navy and Marine Corps archives help explain the 1944 Bush missions. The author examined over 300,000 documents in the National Archives conducting research in depositories throughout the United States. Several documents classified TOP SECRET CODEWORD were declassified upon request of the author and form a major part of the book's narrative and graphics.

The author is an experienced news professional. He worked as staff photographer on the Oakland Tribune from 1950 to 1986. His journalistic work has been published in LIFE Magazine, Time, and Newsweek. The Associated Press News Photo Division chose a Stinnett news photograph as one of the most outstanding of the last 50 years in its publication *Moments in Time*. He is a charter member of the National Press Photographers Association and belongs to the San Francisco Bay Area Press Photographers Association, the California Press Photographers Association and Sigma Delta Chi, national journalistic honor association. He is also a member of the Explorers Club. Stinnett lives in Oakland, California with his wife Peggy. This is his first book.

The author shows President Bush his manuscript while Chief of Staff John Sununu and National Security Advisor, Brent Scowcroft look on, November 16, 1990.

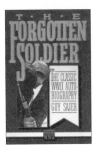